DATE			

the
CONTEMPORARY
WORLD POETS

the CONTEMPORARY WORLD POETS

Edited by

DONALD JUNKINS
University of Massachusetts, Amherst

HBJ

HARCOURT BRACE JOVANOVICH, INC.

NEW YORK CHICAGO SAN FRANCISCO ATLANTA

to
Harvey and Bette Swados,
for whom the world was,
and is,
a community

ISBN: 0-15-513817-0

Library of Congress Catalog Card Number: 75-36286

Printed in the United States of America

Cover photo by Jerome Kresch

COPYRIGHTS AND ACKNOWLEDGMENTS starting on page 400
constitute a continuation of the copyright page.

PREFACE

Poetry is good or not regardless of the age that uncovers it. Convictions on behalf of a particular age, however, usually mix critical judgment and personal taste, which is a good idea when the poems deserve the befriending. A prejudice for a good poem does credit to the art.

This is a book of contemporary poems. We've long been ready for our own language, and our best poets are giving us the world. The poems make personal claims on us. They were written during the lifetime of our immediate families. The images, ideas, experiences—even the rhythms—originate in a world we recognize as our own. We've talked over some of the events while eating; our relatives died in some of the causes. Tomas Tranströmer's "After a Death" is not about George IV, but John F. Kennedy.

Familiarity, but excellence too. We want not mere poetry, but the best poems of every age: Emily Dickinson in other anthologies, Bella Akhmadulina in this one. These poems deserve their careful typesetter, and partisan fans.

The muse says to the poet, "Seek to uncover the poem that is already there," and the poet coaxes the poem from the dark. The poet's job is to work in such a way as to seem merely to let the poem be itself; to write the poem, but to discover it in the act. Our best poets feel incidental after the fact. The illusion of ease is the price the poet pays for hard work, but it's a good price; it's also part of the illumination that separates the finished poem from the poet, and satisfies. Inevitability in art, sensibility in the artist. The sense rubs off on readers who find their way inside the rhythms and the meanings. Good readers bring the poem to life—time and time again.

What do we get from a contemporary poem? A measure of what we bring to it: ourselves, what we know, what we've done. What's a good poem doing but exploring, going into things to find itself again? Other things turn up that fit; we recognize them as our own. Openness is the reader's virtue. What's a good reader doing but feeling the way, line by line, getting used to the special light of the poem? Childlikeness is the best attitude, but any attitude works if it allows us to hear and feel and think while reading the poem.

The poets that follow are introduced by headnotes. Biographical information, provided in the first part of each headnote, gives a simple context of time and place to the poems. (All book titles have been translated into English for the reader's convenience; the books themselves are not necessarily available in English translations.) My own feelings and ideas as I moved in and around the poems—the second part of the headnotes—may encourage readers to open their own storehouses of perceptions and sensations to the poems. A reader should not merely understand a poem, but experience it. Only then can the reader meet the poet halfway. The poet makes the poem work; the reader makes the poem work.

We only go wrong sitting back on our haunches, waiting for the poem to come at us. The excitement is when we budge. We can't read in what isn't there, but we can discover what is. That discovery can buckle our knees.

Since the beginning of this project I have received the advice and practical assistance of scores of poets, editors, scholars, teachers, and friends of contemporary poetry. Without their help this book could not have been completed. For special assistance, I'm grateful to Ivar Ivask, James Tate, Richard Wilbur, Robert Bly, Frederic Will, and Robert Márquez. Also Eric Sellin, Mark Strand, Amiya Chakravarty, Robert Bagg, George Keithley, Bonnie R. Crown of the Asia Society, Makoto Ueda, Michael Benedikt, Norman Shapiro, Edith Shiffert, Sarah Lawall, A. Poulin, Jr., James Randall, Chinua Achebe, Stephen Berg, Jack Sweeney, Michael Hamburger, the staff of *Modern Poetry in Translation*, William Barker, Lee A. Jacobus, William A. Johnsen, Linda W. Wagner, William Arrowsmith, Jeremiah Allen, Willian N. Fuller, and George Cuomo.

Also Pauline P. Collins, John D. Kendall, and Yasuko Fukumi: staff members of the University of Massachusetts Library in Amherst.

And my manuscript editor, Andrea Haight; Martha Junkins, who was in every sense the co-editor; Elizabeth Mahan of the research staff of the University of Massachusetts Library, who traced down elusive information for the footnotes with skill and good cheer; and my permissions editor, Elizabeth Hock, who not only brought efficiency and good sense to certain mechanical aspects of the book, but whose enthusiasm for the content of the book continually buoyed my own hopes for the finished project.

I also owe special thanks to the poets who did new translations for this collection: Maxine Kumin, Michael S. Harper, Robert Bagg, Lucille Clifton, George Keithley, James Scully, Susanna Lang, and Henry Braun. Also to Simon Michael Bessie, former president of Atheneum Publishers, who made an exception to policy in order to allow our use of new translations of Senghor's "Black Woman" and "Congo."

DONALD JUNKINS

University of Massachusetts, Amherst
Swan's Island, Maine

CONTENTS

EDITOR'S NOTE

TRANSLATION AND TRANSLATORS

Hugh Kenner has described the idiom in Marianne Moore's translation of *Fables of La Fontaine* as sufficiently her own "to sustain an illusion that given the theme, she would have written the poem she did if La Fontaine had never existed." His praise describes the quality of translation toward which this present selection aims. Most of the poems are translations, but the book is a collection of original poems in English. Almost all the translators deserve their own space as poets in a companion anthology of contemporary American and British poetry: their translations are products of the same informed crafts, intuitions, and poetic intelligences at work in their own poems.

Excellent translations of poetry must be inventive rather than duplicative: the artistic skills and awarenesses giving rise to the original poem should be matched in the translation, not by a language expert duplicating the literal meanings of the original text, but by someone skilled in language who reinvents in a new poem the meanings and effects of the original. The poet-translator must not merely substitute the familiar poetic qualities of English for the refreshing and exciting poetic qualities of the original language, but should expand the available poetic qualities of English in the way that all first-rate original poems do. Robert Fitzgerald's translation of Homer's *Iliad*, for example, reinvents the possibilities of English in such a way that the language itself is transfused with life-giving blood. The translation is more than a translation in the old sense; it is a new and exciting English poem.

Appropriately, this anthology of world poets depends on the skills and informed enthusiasms of other contemporary poets who admire them. Almost all excellent translators of poetry are skilled poets; they translate well not only because they are practiced in the art of selection, and skilled in the use of appropriate idiom, but because they recognize what it is in a poem, even one written in another language, that makes it work, and they can do it themselves. Successful translation combines aspects of the literal with whatever-is-added to reveal the original work in its essential form and meaning; thus the translation is a creative, not a scholarly, act. "Respect the text, make it new," as Stanley Kunitz says.

MODERN VS. CONTEMPORARY

For the past century the "new" ferment of the French Symbolist poets has activated world poetry with ideas and methods. The French poets

Baudelaire (1821–1867), Verlaine (1844–1896), Rimbaud (1854–1891), and Mallarmé (1842–1898) are the first modern world poets. They believed the following: the poet is a seer who apprehends truth through intuitions and feelings; poems are symbolic visions born of sense-images, mellifluity, and associative diction; ideas in poetry can only be created by the suggestive magic of words that become symbols; "pure" poetry can be achieved through disciplined craft; poetry and music are intimately related; direct correspondences exist between the material and spiritual, and between the five senses; prose and poetry can coexist in prose poems; poems are mysteries accessible only to readers who lend themselves to the evocative overtones of the poem's words.

National poetry movements that followed the Symbolist movement as it spread to various countries, such as Acmeism and Futurism (Russia), Hermeticism (Italy), Expressionism and Realism (Germany), Modernism (Spanish America), Surrealism (Spain), Free Verse movements in Japan and Korea, and Imagism (England, United States), originated as sympathetic or unsympathetic responses to Symbolism, and constitute the ganglia-like miscellany of ideas and methods we choose to call "modern." Contemporary poetry is simply the current growing-edge of the modern poetries of many countries. Just as the early-modern movements derived their impetus directly or indirectly from the French Symbolists, much contemporary world poetry developed out of, or alongside, the Spanish poets writing immediately before, during, and after the fall of the Spanish Republic in the 1930s. In their cosmopolitan openness and anguished power, these Spanish poets personify the complexities of tones, styles, and themes of world poets for the next half-century: the simple, resonant mysticism of Machado; the intellectual clarity and stylistic purity of Jiménez; the formal elegance and disciplined intellect of Guillén; the new and unorthodox surrealism of Lorca and Alberti; the antisentimental, image-bursting realism of Hernandez. Their dead or exiled spirits became the deadened and exiled spirits of contemporary humankind, and of many contemporary poets. Because of the Spanish poets, and despite the fact that they themselves are transitional (between the Modernism of Rubén Darío and later Modernists in Spain), the Spanish Civil War serves, not as a dividing line between modern and contemporary poetry, but as a transitional moment in world poetry between various national modern movements whose poets continued to write, many of them, into the following decades, and the contemporary world poets of the years 1930–1975.

Early-modern poets of the twentieth century wrote within a literary climate still feeling the effects of Darwin's scientific theories of natural selection and the origin of the species (Naturalism), Freud's psychological theories of psychoanalytic technique and human sexuality (Psychological Realism), and Marx's economic and political theories of the Industrial Revolution and world capitalism (Realism, Futurism, Expressionism). The contemporary poets write in a different world, one shaken by the bomb-physics of the 1940s, sedated by the tranquilizer-chemistry of the 1950s, and politicized by, among other things, the United States/Vietnam war of the 1960s. The contemporary world is a technological world of factory-polluted waters and computer-controlled interplanetary journeys, a social-political world not only pocked by genocidal acts at Dachau, Babi Yar, My Lai, and Cyprus, but also made smaller by the world anticolonialist movement, the black-freedom movement, the Third-World movement, and the women's liberation movement.

No contemporary poet can fully reflect all the social-political-scientific forces of the years 1930–1975. In the work of most contemporary poets, however, can be found one or more of the revived emphases in world poetry since the 1930s, an incomplete list of which includes: a new version of gothic surrealism, a renewed idealization of nature, a new articulation of the ancient myths, a renewed celebration of the clarities and rhythms of ordinary speech, a new distrust of science, a renewed embracing of socio-political reform movements, another psychological orientation of the imagination, and a renewed exploration of poetic forms. Contemporary world poetry, because of these affinities with the Romantic poetry movement of the nineteenth century, can best be described as both a neoromantic and a neosymbolist poetry. Unlike earlier romanticisms, however, which celebrated human perfectibility and emphasized the goodness of natural humankind, contemporary world poetry tends to idealize human acceptability, in spite of imperfection, within the human community. The themes of contemporary world poetry are the eternal themes: human love, human suffering, human freedom.

ON THE SELECTIONS

One of the many replies from American poets in answer to queries about this project contained the following from Mark Strand: "That international style which strikes one as a strange amalgam of pseudo-narrative, journalese, surrealism and nervous meditation is not in his work . . . but he's a beautiful poet." The poet is Jorge Guillén, and the comment, which reflects one of the criteria for selecting the poets, describes many of them.

The guiding principle of the selective process was excellence: the best translations of the best poems of the best world poets, 1930–1975. Mediocre translations were rejected outright; excellent translations of good poems were chosen in preference to fair translations of excellent poems. Where excellent translations were unavailable, as in the cases of, for instance, the Dutch poet Lucebert, the Estonian Maria Under, the Indonesian W. S. Rendra, and the Puerto Rican Luis Palés Matos, the poets were excluded. Good poets (as opposed to excellent poets) who might have been included for the sake of national or linguistic representation were also excluded.

The question arose early whether to include poets whose first language is English. To leave out Derek Walcott, Christopher Okigbo, Hugh MacDiarmid, and Sylvia Plath, however, simply because they write in English, would imply that translated poems ought not to be read in the same aesthetic vicinity as first-language poems, and would undermine the worldwide scope of this collection. They were included.

The most difficult choices related to poets whose work appeared both before and after the Spanish Civil War. Every anthologist's page quota is tight, but especially so when the choices must reflect the prevailing mood, tone, feeling, and style of a poet's work weighed against the time span of the poet's life. Akhmatova is a great poet, but is she modern or contemporary, or both? If she is both, what then of Mayakovsky, who died young but whose work was a generative force in Russian literature long after his death; and what of Pasternak, Blok, Mandelstam? The same question could be asked of Ezra Pound, Georg Trakl, Carlos Drummond de Andrade. The major consideration in each of these cases, as well as many others, was whether the poet seemed to have more affinities with the prevailing poetic spirit before or after the 1930s. In some cases it was almost an impossible distinction either to make or to defend. In the case of Akhmatova, although her poems could be read with equal poignancy in the same collection with Neruda, Senghor, and Alfonsina Storni, it seemed clear that her life's work was closer to the literary age that gave rise to Vincente Huidobro, Rabindranath Tagore, Robert Frost, and her countrymen Pasternak and Mayakovsky. And so also with Pound, Trakl, Carlos Drummond, and Attila József, who were not included but who are, indisputably, excellent modern poets.

ALGERIA

MOHAMMED DIB

1920–

Mohammed Dib was a rugmaker, journalist, and schoolteacher before he became a poet and fiction writer. He studied in Oujda, Morocco, and in Tlemcen, Algeria, where he was born. Jean Cayrol and Albert Camus encouraged him as a young writer, and the haunting, evanescent landscapes of his poems are reminiscent of Camus's novel *The Plague.* Dib considers his own inner sources to be a refined lyricism and a taste for the fantastic; and he maintains "a certain spatial vision of the world." Dib won the Prix de l'Unanimité for his complete works, and the Prix René Laport for his volume of poems *Guardian Shadow* (1961). An earlier book of poems, *At the Cafe,* appeared in 1955.

The poems of Mohammed Dib reveal the essential quietness of elemental things and bring invisible realities into focus, like photographic images appearing in the developing fluid. A world just below the surface of awakened feelings casts light into the world of dreams. Dib's gauze-like, synesthetic lines both veil and unveil unexpected feelings and things. Soft forebodings rise up and die down. Images are signals from another place, another life. Dib's poems are graphic omens of the spirit.

MERIDIAN

In broad daylight—suddenly
It appears to be night.
I dream that a shadow embraces me
And life becomes cheerful.

Then—suddenly—I awake.
But there is only a bee with dazzling wings
Buzzing around me.

It slowly describes circles
Above a mass of jonquils
And the light makes the silence grow.

ELEMENT (NO. 2)

The strong silence of legs
The silence of green thorns
And arms around the neck,

My wife, against the hunger
Which one cannot erase,
Her eyes closed, sings.

It is snowing again. The star
Which kills the daylight on her body
Is in ashes, completely in ashes

And cries out near me, a slight
Mouth, neither pale nor red,
A sleeping Lorelei of blood.

ELEMENT (NO. 4)

A very pale rain
Burns all the gardens
Sleeping peacock is it time?

An immense rosette
Drinks up our bodies to the bone
Our hands are pursued by wolves.

Is it time, open mouth?
Black water seeks a heart
Without ever losing its breath

Having heard
The foliage of blood
On a high hill.

ELEMENT (NO. 2)
Lorelei: the name of a rock in the Rhine River that gives a remarkable echo. In German legend the Lorelei is a maiden who threw herself into the Rhine in despair over a faithless lover, and became a siren who lured fishermen to destruction.

MAD HOUR

The mad hour stalks about. It is black,
And you shall know it
By its surfeit of black hate,
Its cries and its excessive wind.

Born of ancient limestone
And the flames of the sea,
In death's behalf its ring-doves
Shine forth strangely.

You shall know it when you meet it:
It is the hour of mourning, the hour
Of tawny blood on the vines,
The mad hour of light.

CONTRE-JOUR

The birds appear,
A flame is lit
And there is the woman

With no name nor relatives nor veil
Wandering about with eyes closed,
The woman covered with the freshness of the sea.

But suddenly the birds reappear
And the flame lengthens
More than just a glimpse at the end of the room

And there is the sea,
The sea whose slumbering arms hold the sun,
Neither East nor North, neither obstacle nor sandbar,
        the sea,

CONTRE-JOUR

contre-jour: light that illuminates an object from behind (i.e., the object is between the viewer and the source of light); backlighting. Literally, *contre:* against; *jour:* day, light, dawn. Used figuratively in the expression *à contre-jour:* "in a false light."

Nothing but the tenebrous sweet sea
Fallen from the stars, bearing witness to the
    mutilations of the sky,
Solitude, whispers, omens,

Nothing but the sea,
With dead eyes,
With no waves nor wind nor sails,

Suddenly the birds reappear,
And there is the woman
Neither star, nor dream, nor geyser, nor wheel, the
    woman

The birds return
And there is nothing but the sea.

Translations by **Eric Sellin**

ARGENTINA

ALFONSINA STORNI

1892–1938

Alfonsina Storni was born in Switzerland but was taken to live in Argentina when she was four years old, and later became a citizen. Independent and lonely, and finding it difficult to earn a steady living, she worked at various times as a teacher, milliner, and advertising-copy writer, and also traveled with a theatrical company. In her life and poems Alfonsina fought for the social and psychological emancipation of Spanish American women. Incurably ill of cancer, she drowned herself in the sea at Mar del Plata the day after she wrote and mailed to a publisher "I Am Going to Sleep." She wrote eight books of poems, including *Inquietude of Roses* (1916), *Lassitude* (1920), *Ocre* (1925), and the *World of Seven Wells* (1934).

The poems of Alfonsina Storni reach out to embrace cities, mountain ranges, people—then reach back in to touch her own inner wounds. Passionate, rebellious, uncompromising, Storni combines the intimacies of diary entries with the openness of public declarations, and her images color her bleak landscapes like drops of blood on pavement. Sexual metaphors burst within the poems with elegant, outrageous, and childlike clarity. Anticonventional, antipatriarchal, Alfonsina Storni's poems affirm women's freedoms in life and art.

YOU WOULD HAVE ME WHITE

You would have me white,
You want me to be foam,
You want me to be pearl.
To be a lily chaste
Above all others.
With subdued perfume.
Closed corolla.

corolla: the delicate leaves that form the inner and most conspicuous part of a flower.

Nor should a moonbeam
Have filtered in to me.
Nor may a daisy
Call herself my sister.
You want me spotless,
You want me pure,
You want me snow white.

You who have held all
Goblets in your hand,
Your lips stained purple
With fruits and honey.
You who at the banquet,
Covered with vine leaves,
Neglected the meat
In feasting to Bacchus.
You who dressed in red
Sped to Ruin
In the black
Gardens of Envy.

MEN IN THE CITY

The woods of the horizon
are on fire;
eluding flames,
the swift blue bucks
of twilight
cross.

Little golden goats
migrate toward
the vault
and recline
on the blue moss.

Below,
the city
rises up,
a cement rose,

motionless on its stem
of dark cellars.

Its black pistils—
towers, cupolas—
emerge,
waiting for lunar
pollen.

Suffocated
by the flames of the fire
and lost
among the petals of the rose,
almost invisible,
crossing back and forth
the men . . .

THE WHITE TALON

In this splendor of clean sky
I immerse my eyes, and immersing them I weep.
Golden tears cover the sky,
the clean sky.

Ah, it seems to me that a white talon
must swoop down suddenly
and carry me through the curving sky,
a white talon.

SIERRA

An invisible hand
silently caresses
the sad pulp
of the rolling worlds.

Someone, I don't know who,
has steeped my heart
in sweetness.

In the August snow
the blossom of the peach tree—
early flowering—
opens to the sun.

Stretched out on the sierra's
ochre ridge,
a frozen
woman of granite;
the wind howls
the grief of her lonely bosom.

Butterflies
of moon
sip
her frozen
breasts
by night.

And on my eyelids,
a tear swells
older than my body.

ONE

He travels on the train I travel on.
Perhaps he's coming from the beach?
His firm flesh
has the cast
of ancient heroes, and the vermillion current
in his mouth, as in a narrow, dark canal,
is stifling him.

His skin,
the color of honey,
denounces the water that bathed it.
(A moment ago, perhaps, were his cheeks,
his broad shoulders, the heroic upstroke
of his swimmer's arms
not cleaving the sheaves of blue water?
Was it not a stoic
flower—

the whole of his elastic, elegant,
swimmer's body,
flung forward
in victorious effort?)

The train window copies his rock-hard torso
lurking under the white line of his shirtfront.
(In another life did he used to sail up the Corsican
sea with the first moon,
sweet adventure his lure?)
Now he displays a handkerchief
of fine silk over his heart,
and his trousers fall upon an elegant stocking.

From my seat, I watch expressionless,
without looking almost, his copper profile.
Does he sense it perhaps? Does he know
my desire is upon his taut neck—
this desire of mine to slide my hand smoothly
over his powerful shoulder?

I AM GOING TO SLEEP

Teeth of flowers, coif of dew,
hands of grass, come, fine nurse,
make ready for me the earthen sheets
and the quilt of weeded moss.

I am going to sleep, nurse, put me to bed.
Set a lamp at the head of my couch;
a constellation; whichever you like;
they are all nice; turn it down a little.

Leave me now: you can hear the buds breaking . . .
a celestial foot rocks your cradle from above,
and a bird fashions compasses for you

so that you can forget . . . Thank you. Oh, one request:
if he telephones again
tell him not to keep trying, that I have left . . .

Translations by **Rachel Benson**

AUSTRIA

INGEBORG BACHMANN

1926–1973

Ingeborg Bachmann was born in Klagenfurt and grew up in a valley town in Carinthia. Her first poems were published in 1951 in Viennese newspapers, while she was working for a broadcasting station. Bachmann studied philosophy in Vienna, traveled widely, and lived in Paris, Munich, Frankfurt, Rome, and Zurich. After completing her doctoral dissertation on Heidegger she wrote stories, radio-plays, and librettos. She was visiting professor of poetry at the University of Frankfurt in 1959–60, received the Büchner Prize in 1964, and read her poems at the 1967 Poetry International. Two volumes of her poetry are *Time on Loan* (1953) and *The Supplication to the Great Bear* (1956).

Ingeborg Bachmann achieves startling effects in her poems with unexpected observations juxtaposed against archetypal images of wind, caves, fish, fog, and meadows. Minor chords echo from a vast twilight where the meanings of things begin with simple statements that gradually glow toward prophecy. Bachmann's imaginative images are the raw material of a sinewy, psychological lyricism, and her personal voice moves easily among wide-ranging metaphors from the plant and animal kingdoms.

WOOD AND SHAVINGS

Of hornets I'll say nothing,
since they're easy to recognise.
Nor are the current revolutions
any danger.
Death has at all times been the conclusion
that followed a hubbub.

But of mayflies and women
take heed, of Sunday huntsmen,
cosmeticians, the undecided, the well-meaning,
whom contempt has never reached.

From the woods we carried brushwood and trunks,
and for long the sun didn't rise on us.
Intoxicated by the paper on the moving belt
I no longer recognise the branches,
nor the moss, fermented in darker inks,
nor the word, true and presuming,
carved in the bark.

Consumption of pages, banners,
black placards . . . by day and by night,
beneath these and other stars, vibrates
the machine of belief. But on the wood,
so long as it's still green, and with gall,
so long as it's still bitter, I'm ready
to write what was in the beginning.

See that you stay awake!

The hornet swarm follows the trail
of the shavings that flew, and at the well
against the lure
that once weakened us
our hair bristles.

MY BIRD

Whatever happens, the ravaged world
sinks back into twilight,
the woods have its sleeping-draught ready,
and from the tower that the watchman has left
the eyes of the owl look calmly and steadily down.

Whatever happens, you know your time,
my bird, you take your veil
and fly to me through the mist.

We gaze out into a world the crowd inhabits.
You come when I beckon, swoop out,
whirring plumage and down—
My ice-grey shoulder-companion, my weapon,
stuck with that feather, my pen, my only weapon.
My only adornment, a veil and feather from you.

And when in the needle dance beneath the tree
my skin burns
and the hip-high bush
tempts me with fragrant leaves,
when my hair dangles,
sways and aches for moisture,
the stars' debris tumbles
right onto my head.

When helmeted by smoke
I once more know what's happening,
my bird, my night's stand-by,
when I'm set on fire in the night,
it crackles in the dark wood,
and I beat the spark out of me.

If I remain on fire as I am,
loved by the fire,
till the resin runs out of the trunks,
trickles on the wounds and tangles
the earth in a warm web,
(and even if you rob my heart in the night,
my bird in faith and my bird in trust)
there moves into the light
the watch-tower that you,
at peace, fly to
in a wonderful calm—
whatever happens.

FOG LAND

In winter my beloved one
is among the beasts of the forest.
The vixen knows that I
must return before morning, and laughs.
How the clouds tremble!

FOG LAND
vixen: a female fox; also, a shrewish, ill-tempered woman.

And on my snow-collar falls
a coat of brittle ice.

In winter my beloved one
is a tree among trees and invites
the luck-deserted crows
to her beautiful boughs. She knows
that at dawn the wind will lift
her stiff and frost-trimmed evening-
dress and chase me home.

In winter my beloved one
is among the fish and dumb.
A slave to the waters stirred
by the stroke of her fins within,
I stand on the shore and watch,
till the ice-floes drive me away,
how she plunges, swirls and twists.

And struck again by the hunting-cry
of the bird that stiffens its wings
above me, I fall down flat
on the open field: she plucks
the hens, and the white collar-bone
she throws me I hang round my neck
and go off through the bitter down.

Unfaithful is my beloved one,
I know, she sometimes glides
on high heels to the town,
in the bars with a straw she kisses
the glasses deep in the mouth,
and has words for everyone.
But this language I don't understand.

Fog land have I seen.
Fog heart have I eaten.

SONGS IN FLIGHT

Dura legge d'Amor! ma, ben che obliqua,
Servar convensi; pero ch'ella aggiunge
Di cielo in terra, universale, antiqua.
Petrarch, *I Trionfi*

I

The palm branch breaks in the snow,
the staircase crashes down,
the town lies stiff and glitters
in the strange winter-shine.

The children shout and straggle
up the mountain of hunger,
white flour they eat
and worship heaven.

The rich winter tinsel,
the gold of the mandarins,
are snatched in the wild squalls,
the blood orange rolls.

III

The Sporades, the islands,
the beautiful patchwork in the sea,
swum around by cold currents,
still bow down their fruit.

The white saviors, the ships
—O lonely sail-hand!—
point, before they vanish,
back towards the land.

Dura legge . . . : Harsh is the law of love! Although it is tortuous, it ought to be obeyed; because it comes to earth from heaven, ancient and universal.

mandarins: small, spiny, Chinese orange trees; or their reddish-yellow fruit.

Sporades: all Greek islands of the Aegean outside the Cyclades (which cluster in a circle around Delos).

V

Away with the snow from the spiced town!
The fruit air must go through the streets.
Strew the currents,
bring the figs, the capers!
Revive summer anew,
renew the cycle,
birth, blood, faeces and phlegm,
death—hook into the weals,
inflict with lines
the faces
suspicious, lazy and old,
outlined in chalk and soaked in oil,
sly from haggling,
familiar with danger,
the lava-god's anger,
the angel smoke
and the infernal blaze.

IX

The black cat,
the spilt oil,
the evil eye:

ill luck!

Touch the coral-horn,
hang the horns outside the house,
dark, no light!

XI

You want the summer lightning, throw the knives,
and tear the warm veins open to the air;

blinding you, the last fireworks soar,
soundlessly springing from the open pulses;

madness, contempt, then the revenge,
and already the remorse and disavowal.

weals: ridges raised on the flesh by the blows of a rod, or lashes.

You still notice how your blades get blunt,
and at long last you feel how love ends:

with honest thunderstorms and pure breath.
And in the dream dungeon it shuts you up.

Where its golden hair hangs down
you reach for it, the ladder into nothingness.

A thousand and one nights high are the rungs.
The step off into emptiness is the last step.

And where you rebound are the old places,
And every place you give three drops of blood.

Out of your mind, you hold rootless locks.
The bell rings, and it is enough.

XIV

Wait for my death then listen to me again,
the snow-basket tilts and the water sings,
all sounds flow into the Toledo, it thaws,
a harmony melts the ice.
O great thawing!

You can expect much!

Syllables in the oleander,
a word in the acacia's green,
cascades from the walls.

Clear and tremulous
it fills the brooks,
music.

Translations by **Daniel Huws**

BANGLADESH

JIBANANANDA DAS

1899–1954

Jibanananda Das was born in Barisal, East Bengal. Because his father opposed early formal schooling, Jibanananda was first educated at home by his mother. Later he graduated from the University of Calcutta, in West Bengal, with a master's degree in English literature. Das taught both at Calcutta City College and at Barisal, but the language of his poems has the flavor of Bangladesh (East Bengal) dialect, slightly different from the common speech of West Bengal. His home was in a small riverside town. In 1954 he was fatally injured in a streetcar accident in Calcutta. The Indian National Academy of Letters, the Sahitya Akademi, gave its highest award posthumously to his *Selected Poems.* Other books include *Fallen Feathers* (1928), *Gray Manuscript* (1936), *The Great Earth* (1944), and *Darkness of the Seven Stars* (1948).

The mellifluous and dreamlike poems of Jibanananda Das celebrate the senses, yet they express a biting, ironic view of the world. Jibanananda's sounds are liquid, his landscapes reverie-like, and his vision detached; it is as if we are reading the poems through softly lighted glass. The lives of nonhuman things are humanized, and the *kash*-grass and the *sirish*-grove become the grass and trees of our own landscapes.

GRASS

This dawning fills the earth
    With soft green light like tender lemon leaves;
Grass as green as the unripe pomelo—such a fragrance—
    The does tear it with their teeth!
I, too, crave this grass-fragrance like green wine;
    I drink glass after glass.

pomelo: largest known citrus fruit; pear-shaped with coarse, dry flesh.

I stroke the body of the grass—I smooth it eye to eye;
    My feathers on the wings of the grass
I am born as grass amid grass from some deep mother-grass,
    I descend from the sweet darkness of her body.

TWENTY YEARS LATER

If I meet her again twenty years from now!
Again in twenty years—
Beside a sheaf of grain, perhaps,
In the month of *Kartik*—
When the evening crow goes home—the yellow river
Flows softened through reeds, *kash*-grass into the fields!

Perhaps no grain is left in the field;
There is no need for haste.
Straw from the nest of the goose,
Straw from the nest of the bird
Is scattered—night, winter, dew at Mania's house.

Our life has traversed decades—
If suddenly I meet you again on a country road!
Perhaps the midnight moon emerged from behind massed leaves,
Slim dark branches across its face,
Sirish or plum
Casuarina, mango;
Then after twenty years I think of you no more!

TWENTY YEARS LATER

month of Kartik: a fall month overlapping September and October. In the ancient and exact Bengali calendar, the dates of the month change according to lunar calculations.

kash: long stemmed grass that in the fall bears beautiful white flowers which throw a cloud-like sheen along the river banks and the edges of rice-fields in Bengal.

sirish: a Bengal tree that blazes with massive red flowers in the spring and summer months.

casuarina: a species of tree whose long whiplike branches, longitudinally grooved, bear small leaves at the joints of the stems. The clustering flowers and the shadow of the leaves give an eerie beauty to the Bengal landscape.

Our life has traversed decades—
If we suddenly meet again on a country road!
Then, perhaps, the owl ventures down to the field
    In the darkness of the acacia lane,
    In gaps of the peepul windows—
    Where does it hide itself?
Descending as quietly as eyelids, where do the kite's wings rest—

Golden, golden kite—the dew has hunted down the kite—
Twenty years from now, if suddenly I meet you in that mist!

Translations by **Mary Lago** *and* **Tarun Gupta**

IMMEMORIAL FOXES

Immemorial foxes who enter the mountain-forest in quest of kill,
At the close of famous daylight, silently, and chance upon
A sudden clearing where all around they see
Mounds of snow in the moonlight;—could they like human souls
    declare themselves,
Then in their hearts a piercing wonder would dawn—
As, in my quivering nerves
Shoots a dark design, when you appear
Suddenly, on the edge of life.

THE CORPSE

Here, where the silver moon lies wet among the reeds,
And mosquitoes have hopefully built their homes;

Where, wrapped in themselves, and silent in desire,
The golden fish devour the blue mosquitoes;

Where, in this far corner of the world, the river lies
Deep and alone, tinged with the color of the silent fish;

TWENTY YEARS LATER
peepul: Indian species of fig tree.
kite: bird of the hawk family noted for graceful and sustained flight.

And lying next to the field, in the midst of tall grass,
Endlessly at the pale red cloud the river stares;

Or in the darkness of the starlit sky
Stirs the head of a woman with towering dark-blue hair:—

The world has other rivers, but this river is
The red cloud, the yellow moonlight carved in patches;

Ended all other lights and darkness, here remain
Only the cloud, and the fishes red and blue;

Here forever floats the corpse of Mrinalini Ghoshal,
Red and blue, silvery and silent.

Translations by **Chidananda Das Gupta**

Mrinalini Ghoshal: the name of a Bengali woman, though Das is not referring to a particular woman. "Mrinalini" literally means a lotus.

BRAZIL

JOÃO CABRAL DE MELO NETO

1920–

João Cabral was born in Recife, Brazil, and attended school there in the northeast province of Pernambuco. As a child he studied with the Marist Brothers, Catholic missionary-teachers. João Cabral served as a member of the Brazilian diplomatic corps in Spain, England, France, and Switzerland, and as consul general he lived in Barcelona for many years. His early poetry was influenced by the surrealism of Murilo Mendes, and he published his first book of poems, *Stone of the Sleep,* in 1942. In 1969 João Cabral was elected to the Brazilian Academy of Letters. Later poetry includes: *The Engineer* (1945), *Dog Without Feathers* (1950), and *Last Education of a Stone* (1966).

The poems of João Cabral are musical, foreboding, as though someone is keeping time to inner music by shaking beads in a gourd, and the rattlers arrive. Simply, directly, João Cabral elucidates the bitter facts about the human-animal creature. His cryptic eloquence is steeped in an earthy pastoralism; his images are born from clarities honed by the tight lip and the backward glance across the empty field. Information is still coming in, and João Cabral passes on the straight-talk of the already dead.

WEAVING THE MORNING

One rooster does not weave a morning,
he will always need the other roosters,
one to pick up the shout that he
and toss it to another, another rooster
to pick up the shout that a rooster before him
and toss it to another, and other roosters
with many other roosters to criss-cross
the sun-threads of their rooster-shouts
so that the morning, starting from a frail cobweb,
may go on being woven, among all the roosters.

2

And growing larger, becoming cloth,
pitching itself a tent where they all may enter,
inter-unfurling itself for them all, in the tent
(the morning) which soars free of ties and ropes—
the morning, tent of a weave so light
that, woven, it lifts itself through itself: balloon light.

THE EMPTINESS OF MAN

The emptiness of man is not like
any other: not like an empty coat
or empty sack (things which do not stand up
when empty, such as an empty man),
the emptiness of man is more like fullness
in swollen things which keep on swelling,
the way a sack must feel
that is being filled, or any sack at all.
The emptiness of man, this full emptiness,
is not like a sack of bricks' emptiness
or a sack of rivets', it does not have the pulse
that beats in a seed bag or bag of eggs.

2

The emptiness of man, though it resembles
fullness, and seems all of a piece, actually
is made of nothings, bits of emptiness,
like the sponge, empty when filled,
swollen like the sponge, with air, with empty air;
it has copied its very structure from the sponge,
it is made up in clusters, of bubbles, of non-grapes.
Man's empty fullness is like a sack
filled with sponges, is filled with emptiness:
man's emptiness, or swollen emptiness,
or the emptiness that swells by being empty.

Translations by **Galway Kinnell**

WINDOWS

Here is a man dreaming
along the beach. Another
who never remembers dates.
Here is a man running away
from a tree; here is another
who's lost his boat, or his hat.
Here is a man who is a soldier;
another being an airplane;
another going, forgetting
his hour, his mystery
his fear of the word "veil";
and in the shape of a ship,
still another who slept.

Translated by **Jean Valentine**

THE DRAFTED VULTURE

When the droughts hit the backland they make
the vulture into a civil servant—free no more.
He doesn't try to escape. He's known for a long time
that they'd put his technique and his touch to use.
He says nothing of services rendered, of diplomas
which entitle him to better pay.
He serves the drought-dealers like an altar-boy,
with a green-horn zeal, veteran though he is,
mercifully dispatching some who may not be dead,
when in private life he cares only for bona fide corpses.

2

Though the vulture's a conscript, you can soon tell
from his demeanor that he's a real professional:
his self-conscious air, hunched and advisory,
his umbrella-completeness, the clerical smoothness
with which he acts, even in a minor capacity—
an unquestioning liberal professional.

THE MAN FROM UP-COUNTRY TALKING

The man from up-country disguises his talk:
the words come out of him like wrapped-up candy
(candy words, pills) in the icing
of a smooth intonation, sweetened.
While under the talk the core of stone
keeps hardening, the stone almond
from the rocky tree back where he comes from:
it can express itself only in stone.

2

That's why the man from up-country says little:
the stone words ulcerate the mouth
and it hurts to speak in the stone language;
those to whom it's native speak by main force.
Furthermore, that's why he speaks slowly:
he has to take up the words carefully,
he has to sweeten them with his tongue, candy them;
well, all this work takes time.

Translations by **W. S. Merwin**

CEMETERY IN PERNAMBUCO

(Our Lady of Light)

Nobody lies in this earth
because no river is at rest
in any other river, nor is the sea
a potter's field of rivers.

None of these dead men here
comes dressed in a coffin.
Therefore they are not buried
but spilled out on the ground.

CEMETERY IN PERNAMBUCO
potter's field: public burial place for paupers, unknown persons, and criminals.

Wrapped in the hammocks they slept in,
naked to sun and rain,
they come bringing their own flies.
The ground fits them like a glove.

Dead, they lived in the open air.
Today they inhabit open earth,
so much the earth's that the earth
does not feel their intrusion.

Translated by **Jane Cooper**

CANADA

ANNE HÉBERT

1916–

Anne Hébert was born and raised in a village twenty miles west of Quebec. A childhood sickness made her an invalid for many years, and she was educated at home by her parents. The "classical purism" of her critic father (Maurice) influenced her writing, but she is more accurately characterized by her own imaginative use of symbolist and surrealist techniques, and her poems have influenced contemporary Quebecois poetry. Her most common subject is a feminine spirit tormented by repression. She has been a scriptwriter for the National Film Board of Canada, and since the mid-fifties has lived frequently in France. Three volumes of poetry, *Dreams in Suspension* (1942), *The Tomb of Kings* (1953), and *Poems* (1960), have won her such awards as the Molson Prize (1967) and a Governor General's Award (1961).

The poems of Anne Hébert bring us to our own senses: rare touchings, colors, smells, pain. Domestic visions enshroud great things, and a thin voice breaks the silence like a snapping whip. Anne Hébert chooses subjects like an archeologist familiar with old terrain, and her poems lay delicate fingers on the extraordinary. Inert things come alive, and we are summoned closer to the fragmented parts of our unfamiliar selves.

THE THIN GIRL

I am a thin girl
And I have lovely bones.

I take care of them
And pity them strangely.

I polish them endlessly
Like old metals.

Jewels and flowers
Are out of season.

One day I'll seize my lover
And make myself a silver reliquary out of him.

I'll hang myself
In his absent heart's place.

Who is this
Cold and unexpected guest in you, filled space?

You walk
You stir,
Every gesture
A frightful ornament in a bezel of death.

I receive your trembling
Like a gift.

And sometimes
In your breast, fixed,
I open
My watery eyes

Bizarre and childish dreams
Are stirring
Like green water.

THE ALCHEMY OF DAY

Let no girl wait on you on that day when you bind your wild wounds, bloody beast, to the black pine's low branches.

Don't tell the girls around the rusty fire, don't warn the girls with violet hearts.

All seven of them will appear in your room carrying blue pities in quiet amphorae hoisted on their hair.

THE THIN GIRL

bezel: the setting that holds a gem in place; also, a sloping edge or face, especially on a cutting tool.

THE ALCHEMY OF DAY

amphora: an ancient Greek jar or vase with a large oval or egg-shaped body, a narrow neck, and two handles rising almost to the mouth.

They'll slide the long thread of their mauve shadows like the back of underwater flames in a quiet processional freize along the four winds of your walls.

Don't warn the girls with green felt feet cut out of antique rugs reserved for the slow unrolling of sacred sorrows, soft meadow mowed by the sun, silent and thick grass without the cry's stark space,

Nor the hidden strong vibration of an underground love like the excessive passion of the sea when its song starts to sail.

The first girl alerted will gather her sisters one by one and tell them softly about the wounded love moored in the leaves of your open veins.

The darkest of those dear sisters will bring you balsam just blossomed out of bitter hearts, old desecrated cellars, flower beds of medicine and midnight diagnoses,

While the slowest will remake her face with burnt tears like a lovely stone brought to light by patient and precise excavations.

There she is, delegating a girl of salt to bring you gorgeous baskets of her bright harvest. On the way she weighs your tears like dew plucked off a sinking garden with the tips of fingernails.

See, the one called Veronica folds large clean sheets and dreams of trapping a tortured face in her veils unrolled like bright mirrors of water.

The feverish girl stuck with brass thorns hurries now that night, risen to its full height, stirs its ripe palms like black sunflowers.

Soon she'll place her hands tightly over your eyes like a living oyster where death meditates, centuries of perfect dreams, the white blood of a hard pearl.

Oh you trembling in the wind, the beauty of your face hoisted on the masts of the four seasons,

Veronica: The legendary Veronica wiped the bleeding face of Jesus on the way to Calvary; the image of His face is supposed to have appeared on the veil or handkerchief she used.

You grating with sand, annointed with pure oils, naked in certain miracles of agile color and powerful water,

Beware of the silent coming of chalk compassions with faces of mixed clays.

Poise the green against the blue, and, possessor of power, don't be afraid of ochre and purple, let the word rush out bound to the world like an arrow to its arc,

Let the given gift ripen its strange alchemy in impetuous traffic,

Utter wild things in the sun, name everything facing the tumult of the great crumbling and irritated corpses.

The walls of broken blue glass break like circles of water in the sea,

And the heart's sharp pain designs its own supple fence.

Called for a second time, day rises in words like huge poppies exploding on their stems.

OUR HANDS IN THE GARDEN

We got this idea
To plant our hands in the garden.

Branches of ten fingers
Saplings of bones
Cherished rock garden.

All day long
We waited for the red bird
And the fresh leaves
Of our polished nails.

No bird
Nor spring
Was trapped in the lair of our severed hands.

For just one flower
One small star of color
The swoop of calm wings

Just one pure note
Repeated three times

We'll need another season
And our hands must melt like water.

Translations by **A. Poulin, Jr.**

BREAD IS BORN

How do you make bread talk, this old treasure all wrapped up in its strictures like a winter tree, anchored so that its nakedness is set off against the see-through day?

If I lock myself up in the darkroom of my mind's eye with this everlasting name stamped there, and if I importune the old flat syllable to yield its shifting images

what I hear are a thousand blind and bitter animals thumping against the door, a servile pack of hounds, slack and submissive in their mangy pelts, who've been chomping on words like grass since the dawn of time.

But a clean sweep of space stretches out for the poet, an open field of wilderness and want, while on the far side of the horizon time breaks open and the taste of bread, salt, water sprouts like flat blue stones under the sea. It's always like this, the age-old hunger.

Suddenly the hunger flows forth, it kneels on the ground, it plants its round heart there in the shape of a deep sleep.

O that long first night, face pressed against the cracked earth, listening, taking the blood's pulse, all dream banished, all movement arrested, all attention swelling to love's tip.

The raw stubble pokes out of the land. An underground source tells its green head of hair to break through. The earth's belly bares its flowers and fruits in the great noon sun.

The sky dusts itself blue; our stained hands flush with the fields are like great fresh poppies.

All the shapes and colors that are called up from the earth rise on the upbeat like a visible exhaled breath.

The land throbs and bleats. Its wool grows white under the summer's jarring glare, the sour cicada song.

The millstones with their porous rough grains have the muffled ardor of huge looking glasses condemned to reflect nothing.

All they can do is serve in the shadows, be heavy and dark, hard and grating so as to shatter the heart of the harvest, grind it to dust, to a stifling dry downpour.

It makes living flowers of these odd, pointy beach shells. The seafaring sun crystallizes them in a bright spray. The kernels open at once for us, singing, giving up their true, well-crafted forms.

After that, we will sleek the milky dough, make it lie out in its flat torpor, becalmed, still lacking breath where it sleeps like a little pond.

And what if by chance the wind should rise? What if our souls should give themselves up entirely? What if their nights were clotted with roots, what if great holes were bored in their days?

Even so, this bitter teaspoonful will outlast us, will outlast all those who come after us. Crushed like October leaves to release their musky smell, it will thrive in the guise of yeast.

In the reek of roasted flesh, on the blackened stone, in the midst of all this disorderly feasting, see how a pure ancient act shines forth in the primal night. See how that slow ripening of crust and dough heart begins while Patience sits on the rim of the fire.

And nothing may touch its silence until morning.

Under the ashes which unmake themselves like a bed, watch the round loaves and the square loaves puff up. Feel their deep animal heat and the elusive heart perfectly centered like a captive bird.

Oh, we live again! Day begins again at the skyline! God can be born in His turn, a pale child to be put on the cross in His season. Our work has already risen brown and pungent with good smell.

We offer Him some bread for his hunger.

And in time we will sleep, heavy creatures, witness to the festival and the drunkenness that morning catches us in. And daylight straddles the world.

Translated by **Maxine Kumin**

CHILE

PABLO NERUDA

(NEFTALÍ RICARDO REYES)

1904–1973

Pablo Neruda was born in a frontier town in southern Chile. His father, who worked on the railroads, was killed when Neruda was a boy. When Neruda was sixteen he moved to Santiago to attend high school; he went on to the University of Chile and at twenty published his first book of poems, *Twenty Poems of Love and One Ode of Desperation.* He became a Chilean consul in the Far East at twenty-three, and was later a consul in Argentina and Mexico. In 1944 Neruda won a senate seat from the nitrate mining district but was hounded by the secret police for openly attacking the dictator González Videla; in 1948 he escaped to Paris, where he remained until Videla's government fell. He lived from 1953 on Isla Negra, a small island off the coast near Santiago, until he died shortly after the right-wing coup d'état in 1973. Neruda won the Nobel Prize for Literature in 1971. His books of poetry include *Residence on the Earth* (1931, 1937),*The Heights of Macchu Picchu* (1966), and *We Are Many* (1967).

In his poems Pablo Neruda is amphibian, at ease in the land of human destinies and in the waters of the unconscious. He loves "waves, rocks, wasps, with an oceanic and drunken happiness." He makes no bargains with generals, and he names politicians and political systems that exploit the common man for what they are. Neruda's poems are lyric and symphonic at the same time. Images of passion, soaring birds, abandoned things, are orchestrated in such a way that they illuminate each other's separateness as they gather together in discords and harmonies resonant with human life.

SEXUAL WATER

Rolling down in big and distinct drops,
in drops like teeth,
in heavy drops like marmalade and blood,
rolling down in big drops, the water
is falling,

like a sword made of drops,
like a river of glass that tears things,
it is falling, biting,
beating on the axle of symmetry, knocking on the seams of the
soul,
breaking abandoned things, soaking the darkness.

It is nothing but a breath, more full of moisture than
crying,
a liquid, a sweat, an oil that has no name,
a sharp motion,
taking shape, making itself thick,
the water is falling
in slow drops
toward the sea, toward its dry ocean,
toward its wave without water.

I look at the wide summer, and a loud noise coming from a barn,
wineshops, cicadas,
towns, excitements,
houses, girls
sleeping with hands over their hearts,
dreaming of pirates, of conflagrations,
I look at ships,
I look at trees of bone marrow
bristling like mad cats,
I look at blood, daggers and women's stockings,
and men's hair,
I look at beds, I look at corridors where a virgin is sobbing,
I look at blankets and organs and hotels.

I look at secretive dreams,
I let the straggling days come in,
and the beginnings also, and memories also,
like an eyelid held open hideously
I am watching.

And then this sound comes:
a red noise of bones,
a sticking together of flesh
and legs yellow as wheatheads meeting.

I am listening among the explosion of the kisses,
I am listening, shaken among breathings and sobs.

I am here, watching, listening,
with half of my soul at sea and half of my soul on land,
and with both halves of my soul I watch the world.

And even if I close my eyes and cover my heart over entirely,
I see the monotonous water falling
in big monotonous drops.
It is like a hurricane of gelatin,
like a waterfall of sperm and sea anemones.
I see a clouded rainbow hurrying.
I see its water moving over my bones.

Translated by **James Wright** *and* **Robert Bly**

LETTER TO MIGUEL OTERO SILVA, IN CARACAS (1948)

Nicolas Guillen brought me your letter, written
invisibly, on his clothes, in his eyes.
How happy you are, Miguel, both of us are!
In a world that festering plaster almost covers
there is no one left aimlessly happy but us.
I see the crow go by; there's nothing he can do to harm me.
You watch the scorpion, and polish your guitar.
Writing poetry, we live among the wild beasts, and when we
touch
a man, the stuff of someone in whom we believed,
and he goes to pieces like a rotten pie,
you in the Venezuela you inherited gather together

LETTER TO MIGUEL OTERO SILVA, IN CARACAS
Miguel Otera Silva: Venezuelan poet, essayist, and novelist whose revolutionary views resulted in his incarceration and exile from Spain.
Nicholas Guillen: Cuban poet; see p. 62.

whatever can be salvaged, while I cup my hands
around the live coal of life.
What happiness, Miguel!
Are you going to ask where I am? I'll tell you—
giving only details useful to the State—
that on this coast scattered with wild rocks
the sea and the fields come together, the waves and the pines,
petrels and eagles, meadows and foam.
Have you ever spent a whole day close to sea birds,
watching how they fly? They seem
to be carrying the letters of the world to their destinations.
The pelicans go by like ships of the wind,
other birds go by like arrows, carrying
messages from dead kings, viceroys,
buried with strands of turquoise on the Andean coasts,
and seagulls, so magnificently white,
they are constantly forgetting what their messages are.
Life is like the sky, Miguel, when we put
loving and fighting in it, words that are bread and wine,
words they have not been able to degrade even now,
because we walk out in the street with poems and guns.
They don't know what to do with us, Miguel.
What can they do but kill us; and even that
wouldn't be a good bargain—nothing they can do
but rent a room across the street, and tail us
so they can learn to laugh and cry like us.
When I was writing my love poems, which sprouted out from me
on all sides, and I was dying of depression,
nomadic, abandoned, gnawing on the alphabet,
they said to me: "What a great man you are, Theocritus!"
I am not Theocritus: I took life,
and I faced her and kissed her,
and then went through the tunnels of the mines
to see how other men live.
And when I came out, my hands stained with garbage and
sadness,

Theocritus: Greek poet from Syracuse who wrote during the third century B.C.; the inventor of bucolic (pastoral) poetry.

I held my hands up and showed them to the generals,
and said: "I am not a part of this crime."
They started to cough, showed disgust, left off saying hello,
gave up calling me Theocritus, and ended by insulting me
and assigning the entire police force to arrest me
because I didn't continue to be occupied exclusively with
metaphysical subjects.
But I had brought joy over to my side.
From then on I started getting up to read the letters
the sea birds bring from so far away,
letters that arrive moist, messages I translate
phrase by phrase, slowly and confidently: I am punctilious
as an engineer in this strange duty.
All at once I go to the window. It is a square
of pure light, there is a clear horizon
of grasses and crags, and I go on working here
among the things I love: waves, rocks, wasps,
with an oceanic and drunken happiness.
But no one likes our being happy, and they cast you
in a genial role: "Now don't exaggerate, don't worry,"
and they wanted to lock me in a cricket cage, where there would
be tears,
and I would drown, and they could deliver elegies over my grave.

I remember one day in the sandy acres
of the nitrate flats; there were five hundred men
on strike. It was a scorching afternoon
in Tarapaca. And after the faces had absorbed
all the sand and the bloodless dry sun of the desert,
I saw coming into me, like a cup that I hate,
my old depression. At this time of crisis,
in the desolation of the salt flats, in that weak moment
of the fight, when we could have been beaten,
a little pale girl who had come from the mines
spoke a poem of yours in a brave voice that had glass in it and
steel,
an old poem of yours that wanders among the wrinkled eyes
of all the workers of my country, of America.

Tarapaca: northernmost province of Chile, rich in mineral deposits.

And that small piece of your poetry blazed suddenly
like a purple blossom in my mouth,
and went down to my blood, filling it once more
with a luxuriant joy born from your poem.
I thought of you, but also of your bitter Venezuela.
Years ago I saw a student who had marks on his ankles
from chains ordered on him by a general,
and he told me of the chain gangs that work on the roads
and the jails where people disappeared forever. Because that is
what our America has been:
long stretches with destructive rivers and constellations
of butterflies (in some places the emeralds are heavy as apples).
But along the whole length of the night and the rivers
there are always bleeding ankles, at one time near the oil wells,
now near the nitrate, in Pisagua, where a rotten leader
has put the best men of my country under the earth to die, so he
can sell their bones.
That is why you write your songs, so that someday the disgraced
and wounded America
can let its butterflies tremble and collect its emeralds
without the terrifying blood of beatings, coagulated
on the hands of the executioners and the businessmen.
I guessed how full of joy you would be, by the Orinoco, singing
probably, or perhaps buying wine for your house,
taking your part in the fight and the exaltation,
with broad shoulders, like the poets of our age—
with light clothes and walking shoes.
Ever since that time, I have been thinking of writing to you,
and when Guillen arrived, running over with stories of you,
which were coming loose everywhere out of his clothes
—they poured out under the chestnuts of my house—
I said to myself: "Now!" and even then I didn't start a letter to
you.
But today has been too much for me: not only one sea bird,
but thousands have gone past my window,
and I have picked up the letters no one reads, letters they take
along

Pisagua: little town near the northern Chilean border.
Orinoco: the most important Venezuelan river, the third longest in South America.

to all the shores of the world until they lose them.
Then in each of those letters I read words of yours,
and they resembled the words I write, and dream of, and put in
poems,
and so I decided to send this letter to you, which I end here,
so I can watch through the window the world that is ours.

ENIGMAS

You've asked me what the lobster is weaving there with his golden
feet?
I reply, the ocean knows this.
You say, what is the ascidia waiting for in its transparent bell?
What is it waiting for?
I tell you it is waiting for time, like you.
You ask me whom the Macrocystis alga hugs in its arms?
Study, study it, at a certain hour, in a certain sea I know.
You question me about the wicked tusk of the narwhal, and I
reply by describing
how the sea unicorn with the harpoon in it dies.
You enquire about the kingfisher's feathers,
which tremble in the pure springs of the southern tides?
Or you've found in the cards a new question touching on the
crystal architecture
of the sea anemone, and you'll deal that to me now?
You want to understand the electric nature of the ocean spines?
The armored stalactite that breaks as it walks?
The hook of the angler fish, the music stretched out
in the deep places like a thread in the water?

I want to tell you the ocean knows this, that life in its jewel boxes
is endless as the sand, impossible to count, pure,
and among the blood-colored grapes time has made the petal
hard and shiny, made the jellyfish full of light
and untied its knot, letting its musical threads fall
from a horn of plenty made of infinite mother-of-pearl.

ENIGMAS
ascidia: a small invertebrate water animal.
Macrocystis alga: giant kelp.
narwhal: an arctic whale valued commercially for its oil and its ivory tusk.

I am nothing but the empty net which has gone on ahead
of human eyes, dead in those darknesses,
of fingers accustomed to the triangle, longitudes
on the timid globe of an orange.

I walked around as you do, investigating
the endless star,
and in my net, during the night, I woke up naked,
the only thing caught, a fish trapped inside the wind.

Translations by **Robert Bly**

NICANOR PARRA

1914–

Nicanor Parra was born in Chillán, a provincial capital in southern Chile. His father was a schoolteacher. In 1933 Parra entered the University of Chile; four years later he published his first book of poems, *Songbook Without a Title.* After having taught in secondary schools in Chile, and having studied at Brown University in the United States, he became Professor of Mathematics and Physics at the University of Chile. Parra has read his poems in England, France, Russia, Mexico, Cuba, and the United States, and is currently Professor of Theoretical Physics at the Instituto Pedagogico of the University of Chile in Santiago. His books of poems include *Poems and Anti-Poems* (1967) and *Emergency Poems* (1972).

In his poems Nicanor Parra walks around convention, steps over tradition, and says remarkable things that both delight us and caricature our insipidities, foolishnesses, iconoclasms, trespasses. The voice in the poems is chatterbox, and the effect excoriative. Parra is a master of the varied persona, a quick-change artist: Lear's fool, shrimp, chicken thief, hangman. Like Charlie Chaplin he takes on The Champ. The poems hit like sniper bullets. He is the contemporary poet's contemporary poet.

THE BORDERS OF CHILE

It's not true that Chile is bordered by the Andes,
by the Saltpeter Desert, by the Pacific Ocean, by
the meeting of two oceans: it's just the opposite.
It's the Andes that are bordered by Chile, it's the

Pacific that reaches the rim of Aconcagua.
It's the 2 oceans that break the monotony of the south country
into a thousand pieces. The Valdivia River
is the longest lake in Chile. Chile is bordered on the
North by the Fire Brigade, on the South by the Education
Department, on the East by the Nahuelbuta Range, and
on the West by the emptiness that makes the waves
of the Ocean named above, on the South by González
Videla. In the middle is a great cowpile
surrounded by soldiers, priests and education
majors who souken it up through copper water pipes.

I, SINNER

I, imperfect gentleman
I Nijinsky at the edge of the abyss,

I, obscene sexton
Child prodigy of the garbage pile,

I, nephew—I, grandchild
I, totally untrustworthy schemer,

I, Lord of the Flies
I, mangler of swallows,

I, fútbol player
I, swimmer of the Estero las Toscas,

THE BORDERS OF CHILE

Aconcagua: the largest volcano in Chile.

Valdivia River: also called the Cale-Calle River; its wide estuary extends eleven miles to the Pacific at Corral Bay.

Nahuelbuta: pre-Andean mountain range extending 90 miles in south-central Chile, rising to 4,725 feet.

González Videla: an ex-president of Chile. Videla forced many reformist leaders into exile, including Pablo Neruda.

souken: suck.

I, SINNER

Nijinsky: Vaslav (1890–1950), Russian ballet dancer and choreographer, widely regarded as one of the greatest male dancers in history.

Estero las Toscas: a small dirty river in Chillán.

I, violator of Tombs
I, Satan, afflicted with goiter,

I, draft dodger
I, citizen with the right to vote,

I, shepherd of Hell
I, boxer beaten by his own shadow,

I, illustrious drinker
I, priest of the laden table,

I, champion of the cueca
I, undisputed champion of the tango
The huarache, the rhumba, the waltz,

I, protestant preacher
I, shrimp, I head of the family,

I, petit bourgeois
I, professor of occult sciences,

I, communist, I conservative
I, collector of old icons,

(I, V.I.P. tourist)

I, chicken thief
I, Nijinsky, hovering,

I, hangman with no hood
I, Egyptian demigod with a bird's head,

I, standing on a cardboard rock:
Let there be darkness
Let there be chaos,
                let there be clouds,

I, congenital delinquent
Caught in the act
Stealing flowers by moonlight,
Beg you, Cowboys and Indians alike,
To forgive me
But I do not plead guilty.

cueca: a flirtatious dance.

EVERYTHING SEEMED FINE BEFORE

now everything seems awful

an old crank telephone
used to be all it took
to make me the happiest person in the world
or a wooden bench—anything—

sunday mornings
I used to go to the thieves' market
and come back with a wall clock
—that is to say the frame that held the clock—
and all the spider webs that came with it
or a brokendown Victrola
to my little hut in la Reina
where my Chamaco waited for me
with his mother of that time

those were happy days
the nights at least were painless

HOW MANY TIMES DO I HAVE TO TELL YOU

Get some insecticide
Get the spider web off the ceiling
Wash the windows
They're covered with fly specks.
Dust the furniture
And most important of all:
get rid of these pigeons:
They're all the time messing on my car!

Where the devil did you leave the matches!

EVERYTHING SEEMED FINE BEFORE
la Reina: a country residential community on the outskirts of Santiago, in the foothills of the Andes.
chamaco: (Spanish) boy or lad.

AS I WAS SAYING

number one in everything
there has not been is not will not be
a man of greater sexual prowess than I
once I got a baby-sitter
to come seventeen consecutive times.

I am the discoverer of Gabriela Mistral
before me nobody knew what poetry was all about
I'm an athlete: I run the hundred meters
in the blink of an eye

as everyone knows I brought talking pictures to Chile
in a certain sense you could say
I'm the first bishop of this country
the first manufacturer of hats
the first person to see the possibility
of space travel

I told Che Guevara "Bolivia, No"
I laid it out for him in full detail
I warned him his life would be in danger

if he had listened to me
what happened to him would not have happened
remember what happened to Che Guevara
in Bolivia?
they used to call me an imbecile in college
but I was the best student in the class
I was just as you see me now
young—good looking—intelligent
a genius I would say
irresistible
with a dong long as a donkey's
schoolgirls can sense the size a block away
in spite of the fact I do my best to disguise it.

Gabriela Mistral: pseudonym of Chilean poet Lucile Godoy y Alcayaga (1899–1957), winner of the Nobel Prize for Literature in 1945.

Che Guevara: (1928–67), Argentine revolutionary, medical doctor, and expert in guerilla warfare who fought for reform movements in Guatemala, Cuba, the Congo, and Bolivia, where he was shot to death by the army.

SEVEN

the basic themes of lyric poetry are seven
the first one is the pubis of a maiden
then the full moon the pubis of the sky
a small stand of trees bowed down with birds
a sunset like a picture post card
the musical instrument they call a violin
and the absolute marvel of a bunch of grapes.

WARNINGS

No praying allowed, no sneezing.
No spitting, eulogizing, kneeling
Worshipping, howling, expectorating.

No sleeping permitted in this precinct
No inoculating, talking, excommunicating
Harmonizing, escaping, catching.

Running is absolutely forbidden.

No smoking. No fucking.

Translations by **Miller Williams**

PEOPLE'S REPUBLIC OF CHINA

AI CH'ING

(CHIANG HAI-CH'ENG)

1910–

Ai Ch'ing was born in Chekiang province, where his family owned a general store. Encouraged by his father, he studied Western languages and poetry, and went to Paris in the twenties to study painting. There he became interested in the poetry of Rimbaud and Apollinaire, and when he was arrested in China in 1932 for "harboring dangerous thoughts," he wrote poetry in prison. *Big Dike River,* his first book, appeared in 1936. He joined the Communist Party in 1941, in Yenan, and taught at the Lu Hsun Academy of Arts from 1941 to 1945. Two volumes of poetry, *Selected Works* and *Selected Poems,* appeared in 1951 and 1955. In 1953 he was elected to the committee of the All-China Federation of Literary and Arts Circles. After the war he worked for land reform movements within the Party but gradually fell from favor and was ousted from the Party for "bourgeois individualism" in 1957, although he was cleared of the charges in 1961.

The poems of Ai Ch'ing range across the great land of China: odes to farmers ravaged by the hungry earth, hymns to peasants brutalized by marauding soldiers, songs in praise of the revolution. With directness and simplicity, he speaks for the Chinese people. When he celebrates the revolution it is as if one is flying low on a carpet across the expanse of China, waving to the rock-splitters, the people outside the small huts in the cooperatives, young people in lorries, the people in black-wood boats. The poems are unrestrained, glowing. China!

SNOW FALLS ON CHINA

Snow falls on the Chinese land;
Cold blockades China. . . .

The wind like an old woman with many grievances
Closely follows behind
And stretches out her claws,

Tugs at clothes.
Her words are as old as the earth,
Complaining, never ceasing.

From the forests
Driving their carts
Come the farmers of China,
Wearing their fur caps—
Where do they want to go?

I tell you, I too
Am a descendant of farmers;
Like you, my face
Is etched with pain,
So deeply do I know
Those months, those years of labor,
Knowing how people live in the plains,
Passing hard days.
No, I am not happier than you.
—Lying in the river of time,
Often the tides of distress
Have entirely overwhelmed me.
In exile and in prison cells
I spent my most precious youth.
My life
Like yours
Is haggard.

Snow falls on the Chinese land;
Cold blockades China. . . .

Along the rivers of a snowy night
A small oil flame drifts slowly
In a ragged boat with a black sail.
Facing the lamp and hanging her head,
Who sits there?

O you
Snot-haired and dirty-faced young woman,
Is this your warm house,
A warm and happy nest and cave,
Burned out by the invader?

On such a night as this
You lost your husband's protection.
In terror of death you were teased
Utterly
By the enemy's bayonets.

Aiee, on so cold a night
Numerous old mothers
Crouch in homes not theirs,
Like strangers
Not knowing
Where tomorrow's wheels will take them.
The roads of China
Are as rugged as theirs.

Snow falls on the Chinese land;
Cold blockades China. . . .

Throughout the snowy pasture in the long night
Are lands bitten by the beacons of war.
Numerous men of tillage
Live in the village of Absolute Despair.
The cattle they fed are robbed,
The fat rice fields plundered.
Over the hungry earth,
Facing the dark sky,
They hold out shivering hands
Asking for succor.

Oh, pain and distress of China,
Endless like the snowy night.

Snow falls on the Chinese land;
Cold blockades China. . . .

O China
On this lampless night,
Can my weak lines
Give you a little warmth?

THE HIGHWAY

From this small humble village hidden in a valley,
From the powerful mountains have I come,
From the dim smoky tile-roofed house,
With a farmer's candor and with a farmer's troubles I come;
I run up the slopes of the mountain—
Now let wild air and sunlight
And the ocean-like wilderness stretching out from the foot of the mountain
Utterly destroy my troubles,
And let the endless area of blue skies,
So wide, so wide,
Loosen my heartstrings.
Let us walk in this enclosure of air,
And when we grow tired,
Let us rest among the roots of old trees,
Listening to the little streams among rock cliffs,
Watching the eagles, looking on rock doves.
And the mule trains carrying coal sacks,
And the men in rags,
And the weak whips and the weary voices
As they turn
Into a strange, dark ravine.
And we follow them,
Thinking of the ravine and the old temple,
And the row of small huts and co-operatives.

Then the lorries pass!
Oh, roar of thunder!
Everywhere merchandise flowing,
Young people in lorries waving their hands at me,
Their presence
Making my heart beat wildly.
And the sedan chairs passing,
The gleam of wet metal,
White wings of the sunlight,
Blood on the mountain veins,
And myself watching them

Intoxicated,
Racing after them with my heart's blood.

Oh, my soul reaches to freedom,
My lungs expand in the freshness of air,
My eyes penetrate all distance,
My legs stumble because I am happy.

Strong hands, strong hammers split the rock:
Explosions of dynamite,
There where the ten-thousand-foot precipice cuts across the road:
Stones, earth, cement,
Perspiration of a thousand workmen,
Sun shining above them,
Oceans of amusing blue;
And down below lies the broad river
Full of black-wood boats and ragged sailcloth
Motionlessly floating on the surface.
Oh, from here
They are like little pepper grains!
O pitiable heart, O simple heart,
Seeing again the broad white plains,
You awaken
Into deep pride of life.

Even though I were an ant or grasshopper
Crawling or flying along this highway
I would be happy,
Wearing a pair of sandals
And a summer hat made of wheat stalks,
Walking the new highway,
Pursuing freedom
In love and gaiety.
O road laid before me, how broad you are!
How even you are!
How unrestrained your progress!
How freely
You reach into far places!
We can follow the road you travel
As snakelike you climb to heaven,
Or as a string tying up the earth—
Looking around me I see

Rivers, mountains, roads, villages,
Clusters of beautiful forest,
Harmony everywhere,
And it seems to me now
That I stand on the heights of the world!

Translations by **Robert Payne**

MAO TSE-TUNG

1893–

Mao Tse-tung was born in the village of Shao Shan in Hunan province, where he attended primary school, worked on the family farm, and cultivated not only an early love for the classics and great Chinese novels but a hatred for Confucianism. At fourteen, hoping to become a teacher, Mao went to school in Hsiang-hsiang where he became interested in reform movements aimed at the Manchu government. At nineteen he enrolled in junior college in Changsha, where he wrote political articles, served six months in the republican army, and also attended Teachers' Training College. At twenty-five he studied briefly at the National University in Peking, but could get only a small job in the newspaper room of the library; unable to support himself in Peking, he returned in 1919 to Changsha, where he became editor of the Hsiang River Review. In the early summer of 1921 he was one of twelve members who attended the First Congress of the Chinese Communist Party in Shanghai. In 1934, surrounded by Chiang Kai-shek and the Kuomintang with a million men, Mao and his army of 85,000 broke out of the encirclement and began the Long March, not only from Yatu to Shenshi (6000 miles), but to Peking, fifteen years later, where Mao officially assumed the leadership of the new People's Republic on October 1, 1949. Mao's poems have been rarely published in China: an early collection, *Wind Sand Poems,* was given to only a few friends; eighteen poems were printed as a group in the Chinese journal *Poetry,* in 1957.

The poems of Mao Tse-tung are presentational, restrained, understated: small tapestries of greenblue landscapes, blood, and war. Mao is contemporary and fresh in his use of images, although his forms are classical. With one stroke of his watercolor brush he captures the lyrical beauty of the Chinese landscape and the miseries of the revolutionary army, as in "Loushan Pass"; yet the feeling is immense, as in ancient Chinese tapestries where valleys, mountains, lakes take up the whole scene except for the person fishing in the lower corner, and our eyes turn to the title : "Person Fishing." In the sixty-word "Loushan Pass" only

three words, "bugle," "iron," and "blood," tell us that it is a war poem. Mao says: "We pointed our finger at China." Mao asks, "Who is master of nature?"

CHANGSHA

I stand alone in cold autumn.
The River Hsiang goes north
around the promontory of Orange Island.
I see the thousand mountains gone red
and rows of stained forests.
The great river is glassy jade
swarming with one hundred boats.
Eagles flash over clouds
and fish float near the clear bottom.
In the freezing air a million creatures compete for freedom.
In this immensity
I ask the huge greenblue earth,
who is master of nature?

I came here with many friends
and remember those fabled months and years of study.
We were young,
sharp as flower wind, ripe,
candid with a scholar's bright blade
    and unafraid.
We pointed our finger at China
and praised or damned through the papers we wrote.
The warlords of the past were cowdung.

Do you remember
how in the middle of the river
we hit the water, splashed, and how our waves slowed down
    the swift junks?

Changsha: the capital of Hunan, Mao's home province, on the east bank of the Hsiang River, which flows north into the Yangtze. Mao studied there, 1913–18.

Orange Island: in the Hsiang River, where Mao often went with school friends.

fabled: also "turbulent" and "exciting."

papers we wrote: In September 1915 Mao published a pamphlet opposing the restoration of the monarchy.

TOWER OF THE YELLOW CRANE

China is vague and immense where the nine rivers pour.
The horizon is a deep line threading north and south.
Blue haze and rain.
Hills like a snake or tortoise guard the river.

The yellow crane is gone.
    Where?
Now this tower and region are for the wanderer.
I drink wine to the bubbling water—the heroes are gone.
Like a tidal wave a wonder rises in my heart.

TO KUO MO-JO

On our small planet
a few houseflies bang on the walls.
They buzz, moan, moon,
and ants climb the locust tree and brag about
    their vast dominion.
It is easy for a flea to say
it topples a huge tree.
In Changan leaves spill in the west wind,
the arrowhead groans in the air.
We had much to do
and quickly.
The sky-earth spins
and time is short.

TOWER OF THE YELLOW CRANE

Tower of the Yellow Crane: a tower on a cliff west of Wuchang, a pilgrimage site for scholars and poets.

nine rivers: tributaries of the Yangtze.

deep line: probably the Peking-Hankow railroad.

snake or tortoise: the Snake Hill and Tortoise Hill face each other on either bank of the Yangtze at Hankow.

TO KUO MO-JO

Kuo Mo-Jo: The full title is "Reply to Kuo Mo-Jo." Kuo had written a poem dealing with the Monkey King and his fight with the skeleton spirit, a subject of Wu Cheng-en's classical book *Journey to the West.*

Changan: a commercial town in Chekiang province, on the railroad to Shanghai, 20 miles NE of Hangchow.

Ten thousand years is long
and so a morning and an evening count.
The four oceans boil and clouds fume with rain.
The five continents shake in the wind of lightning.
We wash away insects
and are strong.

LOUSHAN PASS

A hard west wind,
in the vast frozen air wild geese shriek to the morning moon,
frozen morning moon.
Horse hoofs shatter the air
and the bugle sobs.

The grim pass is like iron
yet today we will cross the summit in one step,
cross the summit.
Before us greenblue mountains are like the sea,
the dying sun like blood.

POEM FOR LIU YA-TZU

I cannot forget how in Canton we drank tea
and in Chungking went over our poems
    when leaves were yellowing.
Thirty-one years ago and now we come back
    at last to the ancient capital
    Peking.

LOUSHAN PASS

Loushan Pass: the Lou Mountain Pass in Kweichow province that dominates the highest peak of the Loushan range. The Red Army took the pass twice in 1935.

POEM FOR LIU YA-TZU

Liu Ya-tzu: a Chinese poet and statesman, close literary friend of Mao.

Canton, Chungking: in 1925–26 Mao lectured in Canton on the agrarian movement, and he visited Liu. In 1945 the two poets met again in Chungking where Mao had come to negotiate with Chiang Kai-shek, and Mao gave Liu the text of "Snow."

Thirty-one years ago: Mao first came to Peking in 1918.

In this season of falling flowers I read
    your beautiful poems.
Be careful not to be torn inside.
Open your vision to the world.
Don't say that waters of Kumming Lake are too shallow.
We can watch fish better here than in the Fuchun
    River in the south.

THE GODS

On the death of his wife Yang Kai-hui

I lost my proud poplar and you your willow.
As poplar and willow they soar straight up into the ninth heaven
and ask the prisoner of the moon, Wu Kang, what is there.
He offers them wine from the cassia tree.

The lonely lady on the moon, Chang O, spreads her vast sleeves
and dances for these good souls in the unending sky.
Down on earth a sudden report of the tiger's defeat.
Tears fly down from a great upturned bowl of rain.

POEM FOR LIU YA-TZU

Kumming Lake: the lake at the Summer Palace in Peking.

Fuchun River: in the later Han dynasty, the poet Yen Kuang preferred not to live at court and retired to the country to become a fisherman on the Fuchun River in the south.

THE GODS

Yang Kai-hui: Mao's wife, executed by Kuomintang general Ho Chien in 1928. "Yang" means "poplar." The poem is also addressed to Li Shu-yi, a teacher at Changsha whose husband Liu Chi-shun was killed in 1933. Liu means "willow."

Wu Kang: In Chinese legend, Wu Kang was punished by having to cut down a cassia tree 5000 feet high. Between each ax blow it would heal itself.

wine from the cassia tree: wine of the gods.

Chang O: In Chinese legend, Chang O stole the elixir of immortality from the Western Mother Goddess and fled to the moon to become its goddess.

the tiger: Chiang Kai-shek.

SNOW

The scene is the north lands.
Thousands of li sealed in ice,
ten thousand li in blowing snow.
From the Long Wall I gaze inside and beyond
and see only vast tundra.
Up and down the Yellow River
the gurgling water is frozen.
Mountains dance like silver snakes,
hills gallop like wax bright elephants
trying to climb over the sky.
On days of sunlight
the planet teases us in her white dress and rouge.
Rivers and mountains are beautiful
and made heroes bow and compete to catch the girl—lovely
earth.
Yet the emperors Shih Wang Ti and Wu Ti
were barely able to write.
The first emperors of the Tang and Sung dynasties were crude.
Genghis Khan, man of his epoch
and favored by heaven,
knew only how to hunt the great eagle.
They are all gone.

Only today are we men of feeling.

CLIMBING LUSHAN

The mountain looms firmly over the Great River.
I climb four hundred bends to its green lush peak.
With cool eyes I stare at the rim of mankind
and the sea beyond.

SNOW
li: a Chinese unit of distance.
Shih Wang Ti: first emperor of the Chin dynasty, 247–210 B.C.
Wu Ti: emperor of the Han dynasty, 140–87 B.C.
Genghis Khan: Mongol conqueror; ruled A.D. 1206–27.

CLIMBING LUSHAN
Lushan: Lu Mountain, a summer resort in Kiangsi province.
Great River: the Yangtze.

Hot wind blows rain in the sky and down
to the river.
Clouds over the nine tributaries and the floating yellow
crane,
where waves ripple toward the Three Wu. White mist
flies up.
Who knows where Tao, the ancient poet, has gone?
Is he farming in the Land of the Peach Blossoms?

TO A FRIEND

White clouds hang over the Mountain of Nine Questions.
The daughters of the emperor rode the wind
down to a jade meadow
where a thousand tears fell and dappled the bamboo.
Now their dresses are a hundred folds of silk,
a million sunclouds of red blossoms.

In Tungting Lake snow waves rise to heaven
and people of the Orange Island sing and make the earth vibrate.
I want to dream of the immense
land of the hibiscus shiny with young morning sun.

Translations by **Willis Barnstone,** *with* **Ko Ching-Po**

CLIMBING LUSHAN

Three Wu: The ancient state of Wu is now Kiangsi province. "Three" may refer to the Yangtze, Hwai, and Yellow rivers, whose sediments over the centuries have formed the flat alluvial lowlands behind the coast.

Tao: poet, a magistrate in Kiangsi province.

TO A FRIEND

Mountain of Nine Questions: Chiuyi Mountain; in mythology each summit represented a question.

daughters of the emperor: Emperor Yao's daughters mourned his death by weeping so hard that a nearby bamboo grove was dappled by their tears. Spotted bamboo now grows in Hunan and Kiangsi provinces.

Tungting Lake: a large lake in Hunan.

Orange Island: see note on page 52.

land of the hibiscus: Hunan.

PEOPLE'S REPUBLIC OF THE CONGO

TCHICAYA U TAM'SI

1931–

Tchicaya U Tam'si was born in Mpili, Middle Congo. His father was First Deputy to the French National Assembly, and U Tam'si went to France when he was fifteen. He studied at the Orleans Lycée and the Lycée Janson de Sailly in Paris, and later produced African folklore programs on French radio. In 1960 he returned to the then Belgian Congo and directed Lumumba's party newspaper, *Congo,* in Léopoldville. U Tam'si now lives in Paris, where he works for the Department of Education of UNESCO. His first of five books of poems, *Bad Blood,* appeared in 1955, followed by *Brushfire* (1957), *Epitome* (1962), which was awarded the Grand Prize at the Dakar Festival of 1966, and *The Belly* (1964).

The poems of Tchicaya U Tam'si cast dark and colorful dream shadows across the sometimes desolate, sometimes verdant landscapes of the Congo. Images of the body dominate scenes of human misery, often etched by U Tam'si's black humor, that carry his meanings in a personal grammar relying more on oral speech than written logic. U Tam'si calls it his "logic of reverberation." The poems derive much of their intensity from the dance, music, and sculpture of the Congo, but it is U Tam'si's own passionate vision that transforms such grotesqueries as floating dead bodies and deformed babies into a poetry of imagist prophecy.

THE FLIGHT OF THE VAMPIRES

in the morning we found the brush was scorched
and the sun smoked over
as usual we ate
boiled squash
then went to see
the swallower of fire
to help along the difficult digestion
in that dog-day heat

over fish-remains were straying
cockroaches, ants
and buffaloes black and hornless
hyenas whimpered behind our beds

the ochre moon
was split in two
by cries of woman giving birth

and look a mother had her child
one with two heads
the mother herself had two round breasts
banded about by cactus-root

the baby had a single leg

the trees in the fire-scorched brush
took hold of the woman and her child
she scratched at the ground

the winds had teeth sharp as a dog's

and now the winds
those selfsame winds have brought
new leaves to the trees
feathered the parrots
scented the jackals
waiting
until some mother later
gives birth
to a child
with three heads
and maybe no legs at all
spreading more devastation
over the grassy plain

here are the vampires
the sky is still blue
the soul is losing
all of its fragrant water
pissed out drop by drop

Translated by **Norman Shapiro**

from THE DEAD

Live: Wash off your guilt
They are dead.

They are dead
so that no evil grass may spring
so that no essence of teak or okoumé
will leave its ashes
in flames of this fire lit for no household gods
so that the sea ovulating upon each cape too sharply formed
or phallus at the quick of her flesh of seminal water
so the sea ovulating
to set free the seagulls oh sea oh sea
so that these lips of my inborn forgetfulness
recite the immemorial credo
twice they died
shameful because the sun was a demon to them
they are dead
the river gives them justice and mixes with salt
their bodies their souls
I see in the deep, red within black,
the shapes of their mummies stinking the putrid water
and I facing the saltmaker, am I their shadow?
I think only
that my head is rounded
from rolling only
on your body
on your body
on your body
at the whim of my torments
oh sea!
not feeling the graze of any tree's bark
on these dirty sores at my temples
they are dead
by what signs shall I know when their destiny is dawning
the free river which will carry their absence to the sea?

THE DEAD
okoumé: mahagony gaboon, a high grade ebony, pink to pinkish brown.

THE BELLY REMAINS

Certainly the belly remains chaste
beneath a treasury of white bones
then open to a soldier's song
losing body and joys
in the flames of his passion
As at Mont Ségur
As elsewhere when
a festival of the fallow corpse
devises its torments

Before the poster announcing the spectacle
he hears the bells quarrelling
from song to song
under his own sky
when he no longer knows
which night has swallowed
the bodies and goods of a crown
stretched on its back and its spine.

Certainly, the belly remains.
Is it more soiled than chaste?
Because of its heartbreaks?
But love for love
is surely more desolating than the rest.
But love for life
he who was dropped from the belly
is taken by the earth
God be thanked the prophets fall
most often on their backs
most often with arms opened wide
most often
their bellies to the sky!

Translations by **Gerald Moore**

THE BELLY REMAINS

Mont Ségur: Montségur, an Albigensian fortress in southern France destroyed by Simon de Montfort in 1244. The Albigenses believed in only two forces, good and evil, and regarded all matter as evil.

CUBA

NICOLÁS GUILLÉN

1902–

Nicholás Guillén was born in Camagüey, Cuba. His father, who edited a newspaper, was killed by government troops in 1917. A one-time law student, typesetter, clerk, journalist, editor, lecturer, and radio speaker, Guillén published his first book of poems, *Motifs of Sound,* in 1930. He fought in the Spanish Civil War for the Republicans, both in person and with his antifascist poems. In 1939 he ran for mayor of Camagüey and was narrowly defeated. Guillén has represented Cuba as a cultural diplomat to Vietnam, China, the Soviet Union, and the republics of Eastern Europe, and in 1953 he received the Stalin Prize in Moscow. He became president of the Union of Cuban Writers and Artists in 1961 and now edits its cultural periodical, *La Gaceta de Cuba.* Later books include *West Indies, Ltd* (1934), *The Dove of Popular Flight* (1958), and *The Great Zoo* (1967).

The poems of Nicholás Guillén reflect the life of twentieth-century Cuba: caramel women dancing, black blood on the canefields, revolutionary feet in the rich brown earth. Although Guillén's poetic vision ranges from carousing good humor in his early work to political dead-seriousness in his recent books, the poems always grow out of an atmosphere of suffering, and are always enlivened with the rhythms and totems of Africa transplanted into Cuba. Guillén sings and accuses. He writes the mulatto poem.

MY LITTLE WOMAN

Black as she is,
I wouldn't trade
the woman I got
for no other woman.

She wash, iron, sew,
and, man,
can that woman cook!

If they want her
to go dancing

or go eat,
she got to take me,
she got to bring me back.

She say: "Daddy,
you can't leave me 't all,
come get me,
come get me,
come get me,
let's have a ball."

OVENSTONE

The abandoned evening
moans, undone by rain.
Memories fall from the sky
and slip through my window.
Heavy, broken sighs,
chimeras burned to ashes.
Slowly, slowly, you appear:
hands in their
cane-liquor orbit,
tireless, dance-burned feet,
your thighs, tongs for spasm,
and your mouth, an edible
fruit, and your waist
of generous caramel.

Then, golden arms, bloodthirsty teeth,
and suddenly your betrayed eyes;
next your washed skin, prepared
for the siesta;
a sudden jungle-smell, your throat
calling (I don't know, I imagine), moaning
(I don't know, I think), complaining (I don't know, I
suppose, I believe)
. . . your deep throat
twisting out forbidden words.

A river of promises
falls from your hair,
lingers at your breasts,

then thickens in a pool of molasses on your belly
and violates the firm flesh of nocturnal secrets.

Burning coals and ovenstones
on this cold evening of rain and silence.

SMALL ODE TO A BLACK CUBAN BOXER

Your gloves
cocked before a squirrel-quick body
and the punch in your smile!

Boxer, the North is hard and cruel.
The very Broadway
that like a vein bleeds out
to scream beside the ring
wherein you bound, a brand new rubber monkey,
without resorting to the ropes
or the cushions of a clinch . . .
the very Broadway
that oils its melon-mouth with fear
before your fists of dynamite
and stylish patent leather shoes . . .
is the same Broadway
that stretches out its snout, its moist enormous tongue,
to lick and glut upon
our canefields' vital blood!

It's clear
you're not aware of certain things down here,
nor of certain things up there;
for training is tough, muscle a traitor,
and one must gain—you say with joy
—a bull-like strength, to make the punch hurt more.
Your English,
only a bit more shaky than your feeble Spanish,
is good enough inside the ring
for you to understand that filthy slang
spit from the jaws of those you waste
jab by jab.
In truth, perhaps that's all you need.

And, as you certainly will think,
you've got it made.

For after all, it's great
to find a punching bag,
work off some fat beneath the sun—
to leap,
to sweat,
to swim—
and from shadow-boxing to a fight,
from the shower to the table,
come out polished, fine, and strong,
like a newly-crafted cane
with the aggressiveness of a black jack.

So now that Europe strips itself
to brown its hide beneath the sun
and seeks in Harlem and Havana
jazz and *son:*
the Negro reigns while boulevards applaud!
Let the envy of the whites
know proud, authentic black!

Translations by **Robert Márquez** *and* **David Arthur McMurray**

CAN YOU?

for Lumir Civrny, in Prague

Can you sell me the air that passes through your fingers
and hits your face and undoes your hair?
Maybe you could sell me five dollars' worth of wind,
or more, perhaps sell me a cyclone?
Maybe you would sell me
the thin air, the air
(not all of it) that sweeps
into your garden blossom on blossom

SMALL ODE TO A BLACK CUBAN BOXER
son: a Cuban dance: "a cross between the blues and the bugaloo."
CAN YOU?
Lumir Civrny: Czechoslovakian poet, a friend of Guillén's.

into your garden for the birds,
ten dollars of pure air.

The air it turns and passes
with butterfly-like spins.
No one owns it, no one.

Can you sell me some sky,
the sky that's blue at times,
or gray again at times,
a small part of your sky,
the one you bought—you think—with all the trees
of your orchard, as one who buys the ceiling with the house?
Can you sell me a dollar's worth
of sky, two miles
of sky, a fragment of your sky,
whatever piece you can?

The sky is in the clouds.
The clouds are high, they pass.
No one owns them, no one.

Can you sell me some rain, the water
that has given you your tears and wets your tongue?
Can you sell me a dollar's worth of water
from the spring, a pregnant cloud,
as soft and graceful as a lamb,
or even water fallen on the mountain,
or water gathered in the ponds
abandoned to the dogs,
or one league of the sea, a lake perhaps,
a hundred dollars' worth of lake?

The water falls, it runs.
The water runs, it passes.
No one holds it, no one.

Can you sell me some land, the deep night
of the roots, the teeth of
dinosaurs and the scattered lime
of distant skeletons?
Can you sell me long since buried jungles, birds now extinct,
fish fossilized, the sulphur
of volcanoes, a thousand million years

rising in spiral? Can you
sell me some land, can you
sell me some land, can you?

The land that's yours is mine.
The feet of all walk on it.
No one owns it, no one.

PROBLEMS OF UNDERDEVELOPMENT

Monsieur Dupont calls you uncultured
because you cannot say who was
Victor Hugo's favorite grandson.

Herr Müller has started to scream
because you do not know (exactly)
the day that Bismarck died.

Mr. Smith,
an Englishman or Yankee, I cannot tell,
explodes when you write *Shell.*
(It seems that you eliminate an *l*
and, what is more, pronounce it *chel.*)

Well, so what?
When your turn comes,
tell them to say Huancavelica,
and where the Aconcagua's found,
and who was Sucre,
and in what spot on the planet
Martí died.
(Please:
have them always speak to you in Spanish.)

Translations by **Robert Márquez**

PROBLEMS OF UNDERDEVELOPMENT
Huancavelica: a town in the Peruvian Andes.
Aconcagua: see note on page 41.
Sucre: Antonio José de Sucre (1793–1830) was a Venezuelan general, one of the liberators of South America and first president of Bolivia.
Martí: José (1853–1895), poet-patriot who organized the movement that led to Cuban independence from Spain.

CZECHOSLOVAKIA

MIROSLAV HOLUB

1923–

The son of a railway worker and a language teacher, Miroslav Holub did not begin to write poems until he was thirty, when he also began his clinical research as an immunologist. Holub has attended scientific congresses in many countries East and West, and in addition to his poetry writes travel books and scientific articles. Eight books of poems include *Day Service* (1958), *Achilles and the Tortoise* (1960), and *Where the Blood Flows* (1963).

The poems of Miroslav Holub magnify the edges of death: haunting poems about things that once were intimate; sardonic poems that detail both the absurd and the human in ordinary daily rituals. Images of animals recall the abandoned past. Images of domestic clutter become keys to another way of seeing. Holub takes us to the forgotten or unknown, and familiarizes it—like someone turning over sofa cushions to reveal the lost coins.

DEATH IN THE EVENING

High, high.

Her last words wandered across the ceiling
like clouds.
The sideboard wept.
The apron shivered
as if covering an abyss.

The end. The young ones had gone to bed.

But towards midnight
the dead woman got up,
put out the candles (a pity to waste them),
quickly mended the last stocking,
found her fifty nickels
in the cinnamon tin

and put them on the table,
found the scissors fallen behind the cupboard,
found a glove
they had lost a year ago,
tried all the door knobs,
tightened the tap,
finished her coffee,
and fell back again.

In the morning they took her away.
She was cremated.
The ashes were coarse
as coal.

SILENCE

Garlands of fatted words are strung through the city
  from mouth to mouth,
Since spring the voices have blared from pillar to post
  and now pitch on the shoulders of autumn,
The youths babble their birdshit in the official ear,
  nothing venture nothing win,
And eight Hail Marys have coaxed a calf
  out of a barren cow.

The ton-heavy drone of voices climbs
  to the first heaven.
But despite the cock-a-doodle-doo, despite
  the bogeymen of the woods and lip-smacking devourers
  of dried butterflies,
In the beginning and the end silence
  endures like a knife,
The silence drawn from the sheath at the moment
  when we have our backs
  to the last wall,
When we lean upon
  nothing but the green breath of the sea,
When we lean upon
  the sheer weight of the earth,

When we lean upon
  ourselves alone,
Screened by our sweat from words.

It is the silence we learn
  the whole of a lifetime,
The silence in which you hear
  a small boy
  ask deep within,
What do you think, mum?

THE VILLAGE GREEN

The memorial of our heroes
has crumbled into stone:
the last casualty of the last war.

The sky over that spot
is healing the scar,
the goose fanfare
calls the wounded sward back to life.

But under the ground a mouse
says to another,
about to give birth:
Not here, come a bit farther!

A DOG IN THE QUARRY

The day was so bright
  that even birdcages flew open.
The breasts of lawns
  heaved with joy
and the cars on the highway
  sang the great song of asphalt.
At Lobzy a dog fell in the quarry
  and howled.

A DOG IN THE QUARRY
Lobzy: a small town in western Bohemia.

Mothers pushed their prams out of the park opposite
because babies cannot sleep
   when a dog howls,
and a fat old pensioner was cursing the Municipality:
they let the dog fall in the quarry and then leave him there,
and this, if you please, has been going on since morning.
Towards evening even the trees
   stopped blossoming
and the water at the bottom of the quarry
   grew green with death.
But still the dog howled.

Then along came some boys
and made a raft out of two logs
and two planks.
And a man left on the bank
a briefcase, in which bread is planted
   in the morning
so that by noon
   crumbs may sprout in it
(the kind of briefcase in which documents
   and deeds
   would die of cramp),
he laid aside his briefcase
and sailed with them.

Their way led across a green puddle
to the island where the dog waited.
It was a voyage like
   the discovery of America,
a voyage like
   the quest of Theseus.
The dog fell silent,
   the boys stood like statues

Theseus: According to Greek legend, Theseus, before he became King of Athens, sailed to Crete to rescue Athenian boys and girls condemned to be sacrificed to the Minotaur; he killed the monster and freed Athens from the yearly tribute of lives that had been exacted by Minos, King of Crete.

and one of them punted with a stick,
the waves shimmered nervously,
tadpoles swiftly
   flickered out of the wake,
the heavens
   stood still,
and the man stretched out his hand.

It was a hand
   reaching out across the ages,
it was a hand
   linking
   one world with another,
   life with death,
it was a hand
   joining everything together,
it caught the dog by the scruff of its neck

and then they sailed back
to the music of
an immense fanfare
of the dog's yapping.

It was not a question of that one dog.

It was not a question of that park.

Somehow it was a question
of our whole childhood,
   all of whose mischiefs
   will eventually out,
of all our loves,
of all the places we loved in
   and parted never to meet again,
of every prospect
   happy as grass,
unhappy as bone,
of every path up or down,
of every raft and all the other machines
we search for at our lathes
   and drawing-boards,

of everything we are reaching out for
round the corner of the landscape.

It was not an answer.

There are days when no answer is needed.

Translations by **George Theiner** *and* **Ian Milner**

ECUADOR

JORGE CARRERA ANDRADE

1903–

Jorge Carrera was born in Quito, Ecuador, and edited the magazine *La Idea* when he was still a teenager. He studied philosophy and literature in France and Spain, and his first book of poems, *The Ineffable Reservoir,* was published in 1922. He was Secretary General of the Socialist Party, 1927–28, and in the thirties edited for a publishing house in Paris. Jorge Carrera has been an Ecuadorian consul in China and Japan, has worked with UNESCO, and since 1940 has been the consul general in San Francisco.

The poems of Jorge Carrera are formal, pastoral, equatorial. He is a poet of soft vowels, of thresholds, and his colorful images deepen the sense of landscape and human residence in the poems. Rural scenes magnify into focus in a way that refreshes our sense of the earth's abundance. His effects are corn-like, hushed, as he identifies a vast yearning in all living things.

WINDY WEATHER

I have a professor of classical literature
who has taught me to hate the written word:
He is the country wind, the sweet old man
whom farmers call Don Ventura.

Don Ventura's a maniac. He goes out at dawn,
searching through the limp damp grass
for the yardstick of integrity in knowledge.
He roams the forest, croaking to himself.

Kneeling foliage give him their blessings.
The mill pond roars and the waters tremble.

WINDY WEATHER
ventura: (Spanish) happiness, luck.

Later, in the quiet of a tree, Don Ventura
is a sage priest dictating his lessons.

He reads the forecast of rain in clouds,
and calls at every door to leave his warnings.
Neighbors with an ear to the ground
begin shouting: *Here comes Don Ventura!*

LIFE OF THE CRICKET

An invalid since time began,
he goes on little green crutches,
stitching the countryside.

Incessantly from five o'clock
the stars stream through
his pizzicato voice.

Hard worker, his antennae,
dragging like fish-lines,
troll the high floods of air.

At night a cynic,
he lies inert in his grass house,
songs folded and hung up.

Furled like a leaf,
his folio preserves
the records of the world.

Translations by **John Malcolm Brinnin**

SIERRA

Corn hangs from the rafters
by its canary wings.

Little guinea-pigs
bewilder the illiterate silence
with sparrow twitter and dove coo.

There is a mute race through the hut
when the wind pushes against the door.

The angry mountain
raises its dark umbrella of cloud
lightning-ribbed.

Francisco, Martín, Juan
working in the farm on the hill
must have been caught by the storm.

A downpour of birds
falls chirping on the sown fields.

THE GUEST

Against the huge black door of the night
twelve knocks resound.

Men sit up in their beds:
fear glides over them with icy scales.

Who can it be? Through the houses
fear slips unsandalled.

Men see the flame of their lamps
blown out by the clamorous knocking:

the unknown guest is calling,
and a thin blue flame runs along their eyelids.

Translations by **Muna Lee de Muñoz Marín**

BIOGRAPHY FOR THE USE OF THE BIRDS

I was born in the century of the death of the rose
when the motor had already driven out the angels.
Quito watched the last stagecoach roll,
and at its passing the trees ran by in good order,
and the hedges and houses of the new parishes,
on the threshold of the country
where slow cows were ruminating the silence
and the wind spurred its swift horses.

My mother, clothed in the setting sun,
put away her youth in a deep guitar,
and only on certain evenings would she show it to her children,
sheathed in music, light, and words.
I loved the water-writing of the rain,
the yellow gnats from the apple tree,
and the toads that would sound from time to time
their bulging wooden bells.

The great sail of the air maneuvered endlessly.
The mountain range was a shoreline of the sky.
The storm would come, and at the roll of its drum
its drenched regiments would charge;
but then the sun with its golden patrols
would bring back translucent peace to the fields.

I would watch men clasp the barley,
horsemen sink into the sky,
and the wagons filled with lowing oxen
go down to the coast fragrant with mangoes.

The valley was there with its farms
where dawn touched off its trickle of roosters,
and westward was the land where the sugarcane
rippled its peaceful banner, and the cacao
held close in a coffer its secret fortune,
and the pineapple girded on its fragrant cuirasse,
the naked banana its tunic of silk.

All has gone now, in sequent waves,
like the futile cyphers of the foam.
The years go leisurely entangling their lichens,
and memory is scarcely a water-lily
showing on the surface timidly
its drowned face.
The guitar is only a coffin for songs,
and the head-wounded cock laments.
All the angels of the earth have emigrated,
even the dark angel of the cacao tree.

Translated by **Donald Devenish Walsh**

cuirasse: a piece of closefitting armor for breast and back.

ENGLAND

TED HUGHES

1930–

Ted Hughes was born in Mytholmroyd, Yorkshire, and played as a child on the moors and farms in the valley country. He moved to Mexborough when he was seven, studied poetry at grammar school, and was writing his own poems when he was fifteen. Hughes served two years in the National Service as a ground wireless mechanic in the RAF, and graduated from Cambridge in 1954 after switching from English to anthropology and archaeology. He has worked as a rose gardner, night-watchman, zoo attendant, and school teacher. Hughes married Sylvia Plath in 1956. His first book, *The Hawk in the Rain,* appeared in 1957, followed by *Lupercal* (1960), *Wodwo* (1967), and *Crow* (1971).

The poems of Ted Hughes are contemporary bestiaries with a double edge: animal and human kingdoms cross over. Like the bull Moses, the poems are deliberate in their leisure. The mood is ominous, the posture concentrated, the voice relaxed. Past ages lurk in the bottom-water of every poem, and images work their way through the humanizing slime. Darkness is formal: the path of mankind is as the crow flies.

THE THOUGHT-FOX

I imagine this midnight moment's forest:
Something else is alive
Beside the clock's loneliness
And this blank page where my fingers move.

Through the window I see no star:
Something more near
Though deeper within darkness
Is entering the loneliness:

Cold, delicately as the dark snow,
A fox's nose touches twig, leaf;

Two eyes serve a movement, that now
And again now, and now, and now

Sets neat prints into the snow
Between trees, and warily a lame
Shadow lags by stump and in hollow
Of a body that is bold to come

Across clearings, an eye,
A widening deepening greenness,
Brilliantly, concentratedly,
Coming about its own business

Till, with a sudden sharp hot stink of fox
It enters the dark hole of the head.
The window is starless still; the clock ticks,
The page is printed.

SONG

O lady, when the tipped cup of the moon blessed you
You became soft fire with a cloud's grace;
The difficult stars swam for eyes in your face;
You stood, and your shadow was my place:
You turned, your shadow turned to ice
        O my lady.

O lady, when the sea caressed you
You were a marble of foam, but dumb.
When will the stone open its tomb?
When will the waves give over their foam?
You will not die, nor come home,
        O my lady.

O lady, when the wind kissed you
You made him music for you were a shaped shell.
I follow the waters and the wind still
Since my heart heard it and all to pieces fell
Which your lovers stole, meaning ill,
        O my lady.

O lady, consider when I shall have lost you
The moon's full hands, scattering waste,
The sea's hands, dark from the world's breast,
The world's decay where the wind's hands have passed,
And my head, worn out with love, at rest
In my hands, and my hands full of dust,
        O my lady.

A VEGETARIAN

Fearful of the hare with the manners of a lady,
Of the sow's loaded side and the boar's brown fang,

Fearful of the bull's tongue snaring and rending,
And of the sheep's jaw moving without mercy,

Tripped on Eternity's stone threshold.

                                        Staring into the emptiness,
Unable to move, he hears the hounds of the grass.

TO PAINT A WATER LILY

A green level of lily leaves
Roofs the pond's chamber and paves

The flies' furious arena: study
These, the two minds of this lady.

First observe the air's dragonfly
That eats meat, that bullets by

Or stands in space to take aim;
Others as dangerous comb the hum

Under the trees. There are battle-shouts
And death-cries everywhere hereabouts

But inaudible, so the eyes praise
To see the colours of these flies

Rainbow their arcs, spark, or settle
Cooling like beads of molten metal

Through the spectrum. Think what worse
Is the pond-bed's matter of course;

Prehistoric bedragoned times
Crawl that darkness with Latin names,

Have evolved no improvements there,
Jaws for heads, the set stare,

Ignorant of age as of hour—
Now paint the long-necked lily-flower

Which, deep in both worlds, can be still
As a painting, trembling hardly at all

Though the dragonfly alight,
Whatever horror nudge her root.

THE BULL MOSES

A hoist up and I could lean over
The upper edge of the high half-door,
My left foot ledged on the hinge, and look in at the byre's
Blaze of darkness: a sudden shut-eyed look
Backward into the head.
                                        Blackness is depth
Beyond star. But the warm weight of his breathing,
The ammoniac reek of his litter, the hotly-tongued
Mash of his cud, steamed against me.
Then, slowly, as onto the mind's eye—
The brow like masonry, the deep-keeled neck:
Something come up there onto the brink of the gulf,
Hadn't heard of the world, too deep in itself to be called to,
Stood in sleep. He would swing his muzzle at a fly
But the square of sky where I hung, shouting, waving,
Was nothing to him; nothing of our light

THE BULL MOSES
byre: a cow house.

Found any reflection in him.
                                        Each dusk the farmer led him
Down to the pond to drink and smell the air,
And he took no pace but the farmer
Led him to take it, as if he knew nothing
Of the ages and continents of his fathers,
Shut, while he wombed, to a dark shed
And steps between his door and the duckpond;
The weight of the sun and the moon and the world hammered
To a ring of brass through his nostrils.
                                        He would raise
His streaming muzzle and look out over the meadows,
But the grasses whispered nothing awake, the fetch
Of the distance drew nothing to momentum
In the locked black of his powers. He came strolling gently
    back,
Paused neither toward the pig-pens on his right,
Nor toward the cow-byres on his left: something
Deliberate in his leisure, some beheld future
Founding in his quiet.
                                        I kept the door wide,
Closed it after him and pushed the bolt.

WITCHES

Once was every woman the witch
To ride a weed the ragwort road;
Devil to do whatever she would:
Each rosebud, every old bitch.

Did they bargain their bodies or no?
Proprietary the devil that
Went horsing on their every thought
When they scowled the strong and lucky low.

Dancing in Ireland nightly, gone
To Norway (the ploughboy bridled),

WITCHES
ragwort: the tansy ragwort, a common European weed.

Nightlong under the blackamoor spraddled,
Back beside their spouse by dawn

As if they had dreamed all. Did they dream it?
Oh, our science says they did.
It was all wishfully dreamed in bed.
Small psychology would unseam it.

Bitches still sulk, rosebuds blow,
And we are devilled. And though these weep
Over our harms, who's to know
Where their feet dance while their heads sleep?

THRUSHES

Terrifying are the attent sleek thrushes on the lawn,
More coiled steel than living—a poised
Dark deadly eye, those delicate legs
Triggered to stirrings beyond sense—with a start, a bounce, a
stab
Overtake the instant and drag out some writhing thing.
No indolent procrastinations and no yawning stares,
No sighs or head-scratchings. Nothing but bounce and stab
And a ravening second.

Is it their single-mind-sized skulls, or a trained
Body, or genius, or a nestful of brats
Gives their days this bullet and automatic
Purpose? Mozart's brain had it, and the shark's mouth
That hungers down the blood-smell even to a leak of its own
Side and devouring of itself: efficiency which
Strikes too streamlined for any doubt to pluck at it
Or obstruction deflect.

With a man it is otherwise. Heroisms on horseback,
Outstripping his desk-diary at a broad desk,
Carving at a tiny ivory ornament
For years: his act worships itself—while for him,

WITCHES
blackamoor: an African black.

Though he bends to be blent in the prayer, how loud and
    above what
Furious spaces of fire do the distracting devils
Orgy and hosannah, under what wilderness
Of black silent waters weep.

CROW'S UNDERSONG

She cannot come all the way

She comes as far as water no further

She comes with the birth push
Into eyelashes into nipples the fingertips
She comes as far as blood and to the tips of hair
She comes to the fringe of voice
She stays
Even after life even among the bones

She comes singing she cannot manage an instrument
She comes too cold afraid of clothes
And too slow with eyes wincing frightened
When she looks into wheels

She comes sluttish she cannot keep house
She can just keep clean
She cannot count she cannot last

She comes dumb she cannot manage words
She brings petals in their nectar fruits in their plush
She brings a cloak of feathers an animal rainbow
She brings her favorite furs and these are her speeches

She has come amorous it is all she has come for

If there had been no hope she would not have come

And there would have been no crying in the city

(There would have been no city)

PHILIP LARKIN

1922–

Philip Larkin was born in Coventry, where his father was city treasurer for twenty-two years. At the local King Henry VIII grammar school Larkin wrote stories and poems for the school magazine; he published his first poem soon after enrolling in St. John's College, Oxford. At graduation he went to work in the public library of Wellington, a small town in Shropshire, and has since been a librarian at University College, Leicester; Queen's University, Belfast; and the University of Hull. In addition to two novels and a collection of jazz reviews, Larkin has published five books of poems, including *The North Ship* (1945), *The Less Deceived* (1955), *The Whitsun Weddings* (1964), and *High Windows* (1974). He received the Queen's Gold Medal for Poetry in 1965, and has been the subject of a BBC Monitor film. Larkin edited the *Oxford Book of Twentieth Century English Verse.*

The poems of Philip Larkin are characterized by their worldly skepticism, their colloquial diction, and their disciplined craft. Larkin's subjects are the ordinary experiences of ordinary people, and his tones are in the minor key. His ironic view overlooks the precious and the pompous in the "tradition" of English poetry, and concentrates on commonplace occurrences that he distinguishes, not by their dramatic intensities, but by his personal interest in them as a poet. Larkin's forthright elegance and antisocial insights provide windows along the routine corridors of human life.

AFTERNOONS

Summer is fading:
The leaves fall in ones and twos
From trees bordering
The new recreation ground.
In the hollows of afternoons
Young mothers assemble
At swing and sandpit
Setting free their children.

Behind them, at intervals,
Stand husbands in skilled trades,
An estateful of washing,
And the albums, lettered

Our Wedding, lying
Near the television:
Before them, the wind
Is ruining their courting-places

That are still courting-places
(But the lovers are all in school),
And their children, so intent on
Finding more unripe acorns,
Expect to be taken home.
Their beauty has thickened.
Something is pushing them
To the side of their own lives.

NEXT, PLEASE

Always too eager for the future, we
Pick up bad habits of expectancy.
Something is always approaching; every day
Till then we say,

Watching from a bluff the tiny, clear,
Sparkling armada of promises draw near.
How slow they are! And how much time they waste,
Refusing to make haste!

Yet still they leave us holding wretched stalks
Of disappointment, for, though nothing balks
Each big approach, leaning with brasswork prinked,
Each rope distinct,

Flagged, and the figurehead with golden tits
Arching our way, it never anchors; it's
No sooner present than it turns to past.
Right to the last

We think each one will heave to and unload
All good into our lives, all we are owed
For waiting so devoutly and so long.
But we are wrong:

NEXT, PLEASE
prinked: dressed up for show.

Only one ship is seeking us, a black-
Sailed unfamiliar, towing at her back
A huge and birdless silence. In her wake
No waters breed or break.

HIGH WINDOWS

When I see a couple of kids
And guess he's fucking her and she's
Taking pills or wearing a diaphragm,
I know this is paradise

Everyone old has dreamed of all their lives—
Bonds and gestures pushed to one side
Like an outdated combine harvester,
And everyone young going down the long slide

To happiness, endlessly. I wonder if
Anyone looked at me, forty years back,
And thought, *That'll be the life;*
No God any more, or sweating in the dark

About hell and that, or having to hide
What you think of the priest. He
And his lot will all go down the long slide
Like free bloody birds. And immediately

Rather than words comes the thought of high windows:
The sun-comprehending glass,
And beyond it, the deep blue air, that shows
Nothing, and is nowhere, and is endless.

CUT GRASS

Cut grass lies frail:
Brief is the breath
Mown stalks exhale.
Long, long the death

It dies in the white hours
Of young-leafed June

With chestnut flowers,
With hedges snowlike strewn,

White lilac bowed,
Lost lanes of Queen Anne's lace,
And that high-builded cloud
Moving at summer's pace.

THE EXPLOSION

On the day of the explosion
Shadows pointed towards the pithead:
In the sun the slagheap slept.

Down the lane came men in pitboots
Coughing oath-edged talk and pipe-smoke,
Shouldering off the freshened silence.

One chased after rabbits; lost them;
Came back with a nest of lark's eggs;
Showed them; lodged them in the grasses.

So they passed in beards and moleskins,
Fathers, brothers, nicknames, laughter,
Through the tall gates standing open.

At noon, there came a tremor; cows
Stopped chewing for a second; sun,
Scarfed as in a heat-haze, dimmed.

The dead go on before us, they
Are sitting in God's house in comfort,
We shall see them face to face—

Plain as lettering in the chapels
It was said, and for a second
Wives saw men of the explosion

Larger than in life they managed—
Gold as on a coin, or walking
Somehow from the sun towards them,

One showing the eggs unbroken.

FINLAND

PAAVO HAAVIKKO

1931–

Paavo Haavikko was born in Helsinki. To fulfill part of his military obligation he worked in a hospital. Haavikko was married to novelist Marja-Liisa before her death in 1966, and has two children by her. He writes novels, short stories, and plays, and is currently an executive of Otava, a Helsinki publishing house. Haavikko has published seven books of poetry and has been translated into French and Swedish. His first book of poems, *The Ways to Far Away* (1951), was followed by *The Bowmen* (1955), *Leaves, News* (1958), and *Winter Palace* (1959).

The poems of Paavo Haavikko are reverie-like meditations that interweave legend, history, and personal vision. Connections grow between man's deepest intuitions and his everyday routines. The reader gets the feeling of a high-speed camera in slow motion: places on vast journeys remind us of things inside ourselves. These airy poems are mock-solemn, wry, and their dream landscapes re-create our fascination with the transiency of human affairs.

from THE WINTER PALACE

THE SECOND POEM

And I asked him,
The bird
Who is identical with myself,
I asked him for the road, and he said:
It is best to leave early,
As soon as the morning papers
Burst forth from the night, like leaves . . .

When the paper came, I folded it up,
Not caring to read it,
Started out
Across the square.
Of course, I tend to exaggerate;

But then, in my mind,
Fingernails come as big as
Tortoises . . .
And I proceeded

Towards this person whose name is Fear,
His manners CD,
His memory O, or less.

I was matchstick-size, and I lit the paper
To be able to see through the rain.
It rained and rained,
There I was, cowering,
Striking the match, and again, at last it caught fire
And the smoke flew—

Such terrible coughing!
As if someone was breathing
Live birds

And a tinkle,
A bottle a-tinkle

And in that bottle,
Presumably, an exalted being—
I almost cried,
In a bottle!
The being I wanted to meet,
In the bottle.

It was Fear,
It cried out and it burned,
If it had a beard, that burned,
If it had archives, they burned,
It was a terrible fire,
Spreading from line to line.

And the bottle was wrapped in papers
Like an apple-tree in autumn.
And it crept out of the bottle.
That was a crazy journey.

CD: Corps Diplomatique, as abbreviated on the license plates of foreign embassy motor vehicles in Finland.

And it was she, she jumped from stone to stone,
Line to line,
It's all on fire, up to fifteen lines
From here,
There she was, bounding along, and I asked her:

O being, exalted, flying fox, I ask you, tell me:
Where is the region that is no place?

And she replied,
It is no place.
I am a rose,
I grew big, the world burst out of me,
And the shame of it
Makes me cry!
I want to be empty again!
I! Abort myself!
Oh, that I left my world,
Here no one knows me!

And those were all
The words we had.

That was the journey along the rocks
By the sky's shore.

from THE BIRTHPLACE

THE WOOD OF THE PINE-TREE

The wood of the pine-tree, used with great care,
All the way from the Balkan forests to these woodlands, here
With care, the dampers are closed before dusk, to keep the heat
in the stove,
How immutable this world is, terrifying, it is here, always here,
Only we move,
And I have to make up my mind what to do, what to begin
Waiting for the letter that will not come,

Bring me the dead man's letter, gilt-edged, through the forest
It is a great forest, its greatness reaches from the Balkan to this
wood,

It is the inheritance of generations, the poets, also, rest there,
Oh, at last I can say it, they rest there,
Dug down, squeezed down with great effort under the sod,
It is true: they are resting,
I envy them this great forest, the wind makes me bend forward
And take up my staff in the endless storm,
The wind blowing across their graves,

But the dawn, the dawn, most important of all: weak glimmer
above the treetops,
While we, ourselves, move across the frozen lake, going where?
to a flowering.

from THE BOWMEN

IN THE DREAM

In the dream
A golden vessel
In the dream
An open sky

The vessels were gold

The King's men tied us
Ankles to treetops
Bent the trees down

The trees' green
Bursts into rage
We rage
Against life everlasting
And it is torn

The green
Greening inside us

We fly
Against the door-jamb
Of the air

The air
Weeps for us

We were the King's bowmen
We are leaves on the trees

The leaves
Touch air

Not heavy
Like the King's treasure

We go
Trees
Into the reddening glow.

Translations by **Anselm Hollo**

FRANCE

YVES BONNEFOY

1923–

Yves Bonnefoy was born in Tours. He studied philosophy at the University of Paris and mathematics at the University of Poitiers. His first book of poems, *On the Motion and Motionlessness of Douve,* was published in 1954, followed by *Yesterday's Reigning Desert* (1958). He has also translated Shakespeare and written a collection of critical essays, *The Improbable* (1959). Bonnefoy has taught literature and lectured in the United States and other countries; he now lives in Paris and edits *L'Ephémère,* a review of art and literature.

In Yves Bonnefoy's poems anguish and joy are inseparable from sexual passion. His marbled landscapes are ruinous, reptilian. With exquisitely restrained language Bonnefoy explores archetypal features. For him the real world is both ethereal and immediate, chaste and desiring, tormenting and lovely. In the *Douve* sequence—where Douve is at times a woman, a river, a landscape—the journey is from light to dark, from life to death, from motion to motionlessness.

from THEATER

I

I saw you running on the terraces,
I saw you fight against the wind,
The coldness bled on your lips.

And I have seen you break and rejoice at being dead—O more beautiful
Than the lightning, when it stains the white windowpanes of your blood.

II

The dying summer had chapped you with listless pleasure, we felt only scorn for the marred joys of living.

"Rather ivy," you would say, "the way it clings to the stones of its night: presence without exit, face without roots.

"Last radiant windowpane ripped by the sun's claw, rather in the mountains this village to die in.

"Rather this wind . . ."

III

It was a wind stronger than our memories,
Stupor of clothing and cry of rocks—and you moved in front of
  those flames,
Head graphlined, hands split open, all
Bent on death on the exulting drums of your gestures.

It was day of your breasts:
And you reigned at last absent from my head.

from THE SALAMANDER

I

And now you are Douve in the last room of summer.

A salamander darts on the wall. Its gentle human head gives off the summer's death. "I want to be engulfed in you, narrow life," cries Douve. "Empty lightning, run on my lips, pierce me!

"I love blinding myself, surrendering myself to the earth. I love no longer knowing what cold teeth possess me."

II

All one night I dreamed you fibrous, Douve, the better to offer you to flame. And green statue wed by bark, the better to rejoice in your glittering head.

THE SALAMANDER

salamander: In mythology, salamanders are imbued with the power to withstand fire; also used figuratively to refer to a spirit who can withstand fire, a woman who lives chastely in the midst of temptations, a soldier who exposes himself to fire in battle.

Feeling beneath my fingers the dispute of lips and the embers: I could see you smiling at me. And this broad day in you of the coals, blinding me.

III

"Look at me, look at me, I ran!"

I am near you, Douve, I light your way. Nothing between us but this stony lamp, this stilled shadow, our hands the shadow takes. Startled salamander, you do not move.

Having lived that instant when the nearest flesh turns knowledge.

IV

Thus we stayed awake, high in the night of being. A thicket gave.

Secret break, by what bird of blood did you pulse through our darkness?

To which room were you returning, where the horror of dawn deepened on the panes?

When the salamander reappeared, the sun
Was already very low on every land,
The flagstones took on beauty from this radiant body.

And already he had cut that last
Bond which is the heart reached in darkness.

Thus, rocky landscape, his wound opened
A ravine to die in, under a motionless sky.
Still turned toward the windows, his face
Lighted with those old trees where he could die.

from THE ORANGERY

SO WE WILL WALK ON THE RUINS

So we will walk on the ruins of a vast sky,
The far-off landscape will bloom
Like a destiny in the vivid light.

The long-sought most beautiful country
Will lie before us land of salamanders.

Look, you will say, at this stone:
Death shines from it.
Secret lamp it is this that burns under our steps,
Thus we walk lighted.

THE PLACE OF THE SALAMANDER

The startled salamander freezes
And feigns death.
This is the first step of consciousness among the stones,
The purest myth,
A great fire passed through, which is spirit.

The salamander was halfway up
The wall, in the light from our windows.
Its gaze was merely a stone,
But I saw its heart beat eternal.

O my accomplice and my thought, allegory
Of all that is pure,
How I love that which clasps to its silence thus
The single force of joy.

How I love that which gives itself to the stars by the inert
Mass of its whole body,
How I love that which awaits the hour of its victory
And holds its breath and clings to the ground.

Translations by **Galway Kinnell**

RENÉ CHAR

1907–

René Char was born at l'Isle-sur-Sorgue, a town of water wheels in the Vaucluse, in southern France. He was a leader in the French Resistance during World War II. An art critic as well as a poet, he resides mainly in Provence. His first book of poems, *The Arsenal,* was published in 1929, followed by such collections as *The Hammer Without a Master* (1934), *The Early Risers* (1950), and *Common Presence,* his selected poems (1964).

In the poems of René Char, terror and a fateful, muted joy surround routine experience. In an atmosphere of yearning, Char re-creates mankind's primordial anticipations of the seemingly awesome events that burst upon human life: things as unexpected as visitors, and as ordinary as death. The submergence of rational horror in irrational resignation creates a sense of calm, of postponed apocalypse. His animal-kingdom poems are also human-animal poems in which Char delivers messages from the unconscious. Things happen under cover.

THE DISCOVERERS

They came, the woodsmen from across the mountain,
Unknown to us, rebels against our ways,
Many of them came.
A herd of them appeared along the crest between the cedars,
Then in the fields, amongst the crops, always kept green and
irrigated.
They were hot from their long walk.
Their caps hid their eyes, their feet stumbled aimlessly.
They saw us and they stopped.
Visibly they had never expected to find us here,
Our soil ready, our furrows neat,
Oblivious to their stares.
We nodded to them and encouraged them.

The most outspoken came forward, then after them the others,
uprooted and slow.
"We have come," they said, "to help you get ready for the
oncoming
Hurricane, your merciless enemy.
We don't know any more about it than you do—

Just the stories and secrets of our ancestors.
But why are we incomprehensibly happy with you and suddenly
like children?"

We thanked them and sent them back.
But first we gave them a drink, and their hands trembled and
their eyes laughed at the corners.
Men of trees and axes, able to keep their heads under any terror,
But not very clever at conducting water, at aligning bricks, or at
fixing things up with pretty colors.
They know nothing about winter gardens, cold frames, or the
housekeeping of joy.
Maybe we should have convinced them and overcome them,
For the agony of the hurricane is very disturbing.
Yes, the hurricane will be coming pretty soon,
But is that any reason for getting wrought up and anticipating
the future?
As we are now there is nothing urgent to be afraid of.

Translated by **Kenneth Rexroth**

FOUR POEMS ON THE CAVE PAINTINGS AT LASCAUX

BIRD MAN DEAD AND BISON DYING

Long body which had the enthusiasm which it is difficult to hold,
At the moment perpendicular to the Beast that's wounded.

Yes, without entrails, and killed!
Killed by the female Beast, who was everything, and who,
appeased, now dies;
And the Birdman, dancer over the chasm, spirit, always ready to
be born,
Bird and bad fruit of black magic saved through cruelty.

FOUR POEMS ON THE CAVE PAINTINGS AT LASCAUX

Lascaux: site of a prehistoric cave in France, discovered in 1940 by four boys searching for a dog; the walls are decorated with remarkable paintings of animals. To avert deterioration, the cave was closed in 1963.

BLACK STAG

The waters were talking to the ear of heaven.
Stags, you have achieved the crossing of a thousand years of space,
From the darkness of rock to the gentle touch of air.

The hunter who is pushing you, the genius who is watching you,
How I love their passion, from my wide shore!
And what if I had their eyes, in this instant full of hope?

THE BEAST IT IS IMPOSSIBLE TO NAME

The Beast it is impossible to name brings up the rear of the graceful herd, like a buffoonish cyclops.
Eight odd puns are her ornamentation, dividing her madness into parts.
The Beast belches piously in the agricultural air.
Her sides crammed and hanging are full of pain, ready to be free of their burden.
From her hoof to her futile weapons, she is wrapped in a strong odor.

So I saw, in the frieze at Lascaux, our mother, fantastically disguised,
Wisdom, with her eyes full of tears.

YOUNG HORSE WITH MISTY MANE

How beautiful you are, spring, horse,
Combing the skies with your mane,
Covering the roses with foam!
Love of all kinds huddles in your great breast:
From the white Lady of Africa
To the Magdalene in the mirror:
The statue that goes to war, the mercy which meditates.

Translated by **Robert Bly**

cyclops: in ancient Greek mythology, a one-eyed giant.

ALBERTO GIACOMETTI

Laundry spread out, clothing and house-linens held by clothespins, hung on a washline. Its indifferent owner let it spend the night outside. A fine colorless dew was displayed on the stones and grass. Despite the promise of heat, the fields still didn't dare to chatter. Among the deserted farms, the beauty of the morning was total, for the farmers hadn't opened their doors, with large locks and big keys, to wake up buckets and implements. The poultry yard complained. A couple of Giacometti, leaving the nearby path, appeared in the area. Naked or not. Slender and transparent, like the windows of burned out churches, graceful, just as ruins having suffered much in losing their former weight and blood. Yet proud with determination in the manner of those who are engaged untremblingly under the irreducible light of the undergrowth and of disasters. Those passionately fond of oleander stopped before the farmer's bush and inhaled its fragrance for a long time. The laundry on the line was frightened. A stupid dog ran off without barking. The man touched the womb of the woman, who tenderly thanked him with a gaze. But only the water of the deep well, under its little granite roof, rejoiced in that gesture, because it perceived its remote meaning. Inside the house, in the simple guest room, the great Giacometti was sleeping.

Translated by **Charles Guenther**

from FOUR FASCINATORS

I

THE BULL

It's never night when you die,
Ringed by shouting shadows,
Sun with two similar horns.

Wild beast of love, verity in the blade,
Couple which stab one another unique among all.

ALBERTO GIACOMETTI

Giacometti: Alberto (1901–66), Swiss painter and sculptor best known for thin, elongated bronze figures that seem to embody the modern human condition of isolation and alienation.

II

THE TROUT

Banks which crumble bejeweled
In order to fill the whole mirror,
Gravel where stammers the boat
Which the current hurries and turns up,
Grass, grass, always stretched,
Grass, grass, never at ease,
What becomes of your creature
In the transparent storms
Where her heart plunged her?

Translated by **Richard Stern**

FRANCIS PONGE

1899–

Francis Ponge was born in Montpellier but lived as a child in Avignon. He studied in Paris, where his father was a professor of English at the Lycée Condorcet. Ponge was a soldier, an insurance man, and a Resistance organizer of journalists, and he has also worked in publishing houses and lectured in many countries of Europe. He was a member of the Communist Party from 1936 to 1946. Since 1952 he has been a professor at the Alliance Française of Paris. Books of poems include *Twelve Small Writings* (1926), *Prejudiced in Favor of Things* (1942), *The Rage of Expression* (1952), and *Soap* (1967).

The poems of Francis Ponge are relentlessly inspective, laboratory-like. Ponge describes, describes again; the physical surface analogizes the essence. The metaphor is the thing itself; the object is the subject. Ponge's poems reflect the shadowless light of logic, but it is a logic humanized by the play of syllables and Ponge's own wit: he says, "Wouldn't it be this, poetry: a sort of *syl-lab-logism?"*

THE FROG

When the rain in short slivers bounces in the saturated fields, a dwarf amphibia, a one-armed Ophelia, hardly as big as a fist, leaps at times under the poet's steps and plunges into the next pool.

Let the nervous creature go. It has lovely legs. Its whole body is gloved with impermeable skin. Meagre meat its long muscles are of an elegance neither fleshly nor fishly. But to leave the fingers the quality of fluid is allied with it to the efforts of living. Goiterous it pants. . . . And this heart that beats big, these wrinkled eyelids, this haggard mouth move me to pity to let it go.

Translated by **Cid Corman**

THE OYSTER

The size of a handy pebble, the oyster is coarser looking and, though of a less clear-cut coloring, brilliantly chalkish. It is a stubborn, closed world. Still, it can be opened: you have to put it in the fold of a rag, start in on it with a rugged and slightly crooked blade, keep at it for several tries. The prying fingers get sliced, the fingernails are snapped off: it is a rough kind of work. The pounding you have to give it stamps its casing with white rings, a sort of halo.

Once there on the inside you find a whole world, food and drink: under a *firmament* (literally speaking) of mother-of-pearl the sky above sags over the sky below, forming no more than a small pond, a viscous greenish bag, that rises and ebbs in sights, in smells, fringed with a blackish lace along the edges.

On rare occasions, within the nacreous throat, a little form becomes a pearl, with which to adorn yourself at once.

Translated by **Tod Perry**

RULE

One's had enough of
the snow so dear
to postal cards.

Better the frost,
the frost and the wind
with no cloud in the sky,

the serum, the acid,
and fresh air in the face
for your glassy eyes,

for your delicate fingers,
and for the discreet
snail of sex.

Translated by **Donald Justice**

THE NUPTIAL HABITS OF DOGS

The nuptial habits of dogs are really something! In a village in Bresse, in 1946 . . . (I want to be precise because, considering this famous evolution of species, if it were to hasten . . . or if there were to be an unexpected mutation: one never knows) . . .

What a strange ballet! What tension!

This motion engendered by the specific passion is beautiful. Dramatic! And how lovely those curves! With critical moments, paroxystic, and drawn-out patience, perseverance of a maniacal immobility, circumlocutions in very slow revolutions, circumvolutions, pursuits, strolling in a special way.

Oh! And that music! What a variety!

All those individuals like spermatozoa, who come together after unbelievable, ridiculous detours.

But what music!

That hunted female; cruelly importuned; and those male hunters, grumblers, musicians.

This lasts a good week . . . (more perhaps: I'll correct it at the end).

What maniacs those dogs. What stubbornness. What heavy brutes. What chumps! Sad. Narrow-minded. What pains in the ass.

Ridiculously stubborn. Plaintive. Ears cocked, on the scent. Busy. Scenting. Raising and knitting their brows, sadly, comi-

THE NUPTIAL HABITS OF DOGS
Bresse: region of eastern France that was formerly an ancient lake bottom.

cally. Everything strained: ears, backs, legs. Growling. Plaintive. Blind and dumb to everything else but their specific determination.

(Compare this to the grace and the violence of cats. To the grace of horses also.)

But it wasn't my bitch. It belonged to my neighbor, Féaux the postman: I was unable to look at it close enough, observe the organs of the lady, her smell, her movements, her losses of seed.

I was unable to determine if she had begun by being provocative, or if it had only come to her (her condition, her discharges, her smell, then the males and their attention, so long, so importunate), if it had only been a painful surprise for her, only a timid groan, with calculated and consenting movements.

What a sad story! How life, revealed to her at that moment, must have appeared harassing, bothersome, absurd!

And there she is, wounded for life,—morally also! But she will have her pretty little puppies . . . Alone to herself, for a little while . . . Then those males will leave her alone, and what joy with her little ones, even what fun, what fullness,—despite an occasional rough house between her paws and under her belly, and a lot of fatigue.

The fact is, we did not sleep much for a week . . . But that's of no importance: you can't always have everything,—sleep and something like a series of nocturnal performances at the Classic Theater.

The moon there above (above the passions) also seemed to me to have played an important part.

Translated by **Serge Gavronsky**

GERMAN DEMOCRATIC REPUBLIC

JOHANNES BOBROWSKI

1917–1965

Johannes Bobrowski was born in Tilsit, East Prussia. His father worked on the railroads. Bobrowski went to school in Rastenburg, Königsberg, and Berlin, where he studied the history of art. From 1941 to 1949 he was a prisoner of war in the Soviet Union. After his release, he made his living reading manuscripts for a publishing house in East Germany. His first book of poems, *Sarmatian Days,* was published in West Germany in 1961, and he won the 1962 Pris der Gruppe 47. Bobrowski committed suicide in 1965, in East Berlin. Other books: *Shadowland Streams* (1962) and *Storm Signal* (1967).

Softly deliberate, reportorial, personal, the poems of Johannes Bobrowski describe village life in Eastern Europe against the backdrop of the serenity of nature. The footsteps of the dead, imprinted on streets, floors, and meadow grass, tread through the poems like heavy weights. Soldiers rape; slavemasters murder. The poems give us sunken eyes looking in a mirror, the weariness of an endless road. They say: remember, bear witness.

CALAMUS

The water-wind, a howl,
flies around
with sails of rain.
A blue dove
has spread its wings
across the wood.
Lovely in the broken iron
of the fern
the light moves
with the head of a pheasant.

Breath,
I send you out,

calamus: an aromatic marsh plant with sword-shaped leaves, called by some English herbalists Sweet Flag or Sweet Rush.

find a roof,
enter through a window, regard
yourself in the white mirror,
turn without sound,
a green sword.

THE LATVIAN AUTUMN

The thicket of deadly nightshade
is open, he steps
into the clearing, the dance
of the hens around the birch stumps is forgotten, he walks
past the tree round which the herons flew, he has sung
in the meadows.

Oh that the swath of hay,
where he lay in the bright night,
might fly scattered by winds
on the banks—
when the river is no longer awake,
the clouds above it, voices
of birds, calls:
We shall come no more.

Then I light your light,
which I cannot see, I placed
my hands above it, close
round the flame, it stood still,
reddish in nothing but night
(like the castle which fell
in ruins over the slope,
like the little winged snake
of light through the river, like the hair
of the Jewish child)
and did not burn me.

LATVIAN SONGS

My father the hawk.
Grandfather the wolf.
And my forefather the rapacious fish in the sea.

I, unbearded, a fool,
lurching against the fences,
my black hands strangling a lamb
in the early light. I,

who beat the animals
instead of the white
master, I follow the rattling caravans
on washed-out roads,

I pass through the glances
of the gipsy-women. Then
on the Baltic shore I meet Uexküll, the master.
He walks beneath the moon.

Behind him, the darkness speaks.

REPORT

Bajla Gelblung,
escaped in Warsaw
from a transport from the Ghetto,
the girl took to the woods,
armed, was picked up
as partisan
in Brest-Litovsk,
wore a military coat (Polish),
was interrogated by German
officers, there is
a photo, the officers are young
chaps faultlessly uniformed,
with faultless faces,
their bearing
is unexceptionable.

LATVIAN SONGS
Uexküll: A Herr von Uexküll appeared before the city council in Riga in the seventeenth century, charged with murdering one of his servants.

KAUNAS 1941

Town,
branches over the river,
copper-colored, like branching candles.
The banks call from the deep.
Then the lame girl
walked before dusk,
her skirt of darkest red.

And I know the steps,
the slope, this house. There is no
fire. Under this roof
lives the Jewess, lives whispering
in the Jews' silence
—the faces of the daughters
a white water. Noisily
the murderers pass the gate. We walk
softly, in musty air, in the track of wolves.

At evening we looked out
over a stony valley. The hawk
swept round the broad dome.
We saw the old town, house after house
running down to the river.

Will you walk over
the hill? The grey processions
—old men and sometimes boys—
die there. They walk
up the slope ahead of the slavering wolves.

Did my eyes avoid yours
brother? Sleep struck us
at the bloody wall. So we went on
blind to everything. We looked
like gipsies at the villages
in the oakwood, the summer
snow on the roofs.

Kaunas: city of south-central Lithuania, pop. 150,000. From 1918 to 1940 the provisional capital; occupied 1941–44 by German forces who virtually annihilated the Jews of Kaunas. When the Russians approached, the Germans destroyed most of the city.

I shall walk on the stone banks
under the rainy bushes,
listen in the haze of the plains.
There were swallows upstream
and the woodpigeon called
in the green night:
My dark is already come.

VILLAGE

Still the strange land
like drums, distant.
I come down the road.
Under the field-birch
the shepherd, in the rustle of leaves, in the rain-sound
of a cloud. Towards evening
a song of measured tones,
low cries
by the bushes.

Village between marsh and river,
bleak in your early winter's
crow-light—the road around the alders
overgrown, the huts soft with the stain
of rain and peatsmoke—you
my unending light,
my lacklustre light,
written on the edges
of my life, you old light.

Image of the hunter, conjuration,
animal-headed,
painted in the icy
cave, in the rock.

Translated by **Ruth** *and* **Matthew Mead**

GERMAN FEDERAL REPUBLIC

PAUL CELAN

(PAUL ANTSCHEL)

1920–1970

Paul Celan was born in Rumanian Bukovina, a town occupied by the Soviet army in 1940 and by the Nazis in 1942. His parents were executed in a concentration camp, but he survived a labor camp and lived in Paris until his death by suicide in 1970. Celan translated Rimbaud, Valéry, Char, Blok, Essenin, and Mandelstam. He wrote eight books of poetry, the first, *Sand from the Urns,* appearing in 1948; others include *Poppy and Memory* (1952), *Speech-grille* (1955), and *Rose Without an Owner* (1963).

Paul Celan's poems are darkly declarative, cryptic, like messages taken from the pockets of dead sentries. The voice is solitary, removed; the present is indistinguishable from the barren past. The act of love foreshadows the fact of death. That which is alive is slowly hardening; the inanimate sprouts living things. Celan's landscapes are bleak; his images recall our most disturbing dreams.

CORONA

Autumn eats its leaf out of my hand: we are friends.
From the nuts we shell time and we teach it to walk:
then time returns to the shell.

In the mirror it's Sunday,
in dream there is room for sleeping,
our mouths speak the truth.

My eye moves down to the sex of my loved one:
we look at each other,
we exchange dark words,

corona: a small circle or disk of light appearing around the sun or moon, or any crown of light; also a crownlike or cuplike part of a flower, between the corolla and the stamens.

we love each other like poppy and recollection,
we sleep like wine in the conches,
like the sea in the moon's blood ray.

We stand by the window embracing, and people look
up from the street:
it is time they knew!
It is time the stone made an effort to flower,
time unrest had a beating heart.
It is time it were time.

It is time.

HOMECOMING

Snowfall, denser and denser,
dove-colored as yesterday,
snowfall, as if even now you were sleeping.

White, stacked into distance.
Above it, endless,
the sleigh track of the lost.

Below, hidden,
presses up
what so hurts the eyes,
hill upon hill,
invisible.

On each,
fetched home into its today,
an I slipped away into dumbness:
wooden, a post.

There: a feeling,
blown across by the ice wind
attaching its dove- its snow-
colored cloth as a flag.

CORONA
conches: large spiral-shaped shells.

BELOW

Led home into oblivion
the sociable talk of
our slow eyes.

Led home, syllable after syllable, shared
out among the dayblind dice, for which
the playing hand reaches out, large,
awakening.

And the too much of my speaking:
heaped up round the little
crystal dressed in the style of your silence.

TO MY RIGHT

To my right—who? The deathwoman.
And you, to my left, you?

The travelling-sickles at the extra-
celestial place
mime themselves whitish-grey
into moon swallows,
into star swifts,

I dip to that place
and pour an urnful
down you,
into you.

I HEAR THAT THE AXE HAS FLOWERED

I hear that the axe has flowered,
I hear that the place can't be named,

I hear that the bread which looks at him
heals the hanged man,
the bread baked for him by his wife,

I hear that they call life
our only refuge.

MEMORY OF FRANCE

Together with me recall: the sky of Paris, that giant autumn
crocus . . .
We went shopping for hearts at the flower girl's booth:
they were blue and they opened up in the water.
It began to rain in our room,
and our neighbour came in, Monsieur Le Songe, a lean little
man.
We played cards, I lost the irises of my eyes;
you lent me your hair, I lost it, he struck us down.
He left by the door, the rain followed him out.
We were dead and were able to breathe.

LARGO

You of the same mind, moor-wandering near one:

more-than-
death-
sized we lie
together, the time-
less one teems
under our breathing eyelids,

the pair of blackbirds hangs
beside us, under
our whitely drifting
companions up there, our

meta-
stases.

Translations by **Michael Hamburger**

MEMORY OF FRANCE

Le Songe: In French, "le songe" means "the dream," or "dreaming"; sometimes, in idiomatic expressions, "thinking."

LARGO

metastases: transformations; from Greek, *meta* (after) and *histanai* (to place).

GREECE

ODYSSEUS ELYTIS

(ODYSSEUS ALEPOUDHELIS)

1911–

Odysseus Elytis was born in Iraklion, Crete, where he began his education, and summered as a young boy on islands in the Aegean. He later studied law at the University of Athens (1930–35) and literature at the Sorbonne (1948–51), and has been an art critic, translator, painter, director for the National Broadcasting System in Athens, and president of the Governing Board of Greek Ballet. In the Greek-Italian conflict of World War II he fought on the Albanian front as a second lieutenant in the Greek army. Elytis is currently a businessman. Books of poems include *Orientations* (1940), *Axion Esti* (1959, First State Prize), and *The Sovereign Sun* (1971).

The poems of Odysseus Elytis are votive, expansive, annointive: they spread out and touch the Greek islands, bodies of men and women, sunken ships, flowers, ruined temples, trees, moons, goats, herbs, goddesses. . . . Elytis's words touch us like the words of ancient creeds, and his poems move inside us like psalms.

AXION ESTI

PART III, THE GLORIA

PRAISED BE the wooden table
the blond wine spotted by the sun
the water doodling across the ceiling
the philodendron on duty in the corner

The walls hand in hand with the waves
a foot that gathered wisdom in the sand
a cicada that convinced a thousand others
conscience radiant like a summer

PRAISED BE the hatching heat
the beautiful boulders under the bridge
the shit of children with its green flies
a sea boiling and no end to it

Axion Esti: from the Orthodox Greek liturgy; lit. "It is worthy."

The sixteen deckhands hauling the net
the restless seagull slowly cruising
stray voices out of the wilderness
the crossing of a shadow through the wall

THE ISLANDS with all their minium and lampblack
the islands with the vertebra of some Zeus
the islands with their boatyards so deserted
the islands with their drinkable blue volcanoes

Facing the *meltemi* with jib close-hauled
Riding the south-wester on a reach
the full length of them covered with foam
with dark blue pebbles and heliotropes

Sifnos, Amorgos, Alonnisos
Thasos, Ithaka, Santorini
Kos, Ios, Sikinos

PRAISED BE the scarab-shaped knocker
the brash tooth in icy sunshine
April sensing that it was changing sex
the fountain's bud just as it opens

The wheelbarrow tilting on its side
the goldbug that set fire to the future
the water's invisible aorta throbbing
to make the gardenia stay alive

THE FLOWERS home-fed by Nostalgia
the trembling flowers, infants of rain
the small and four-legged ones on the footpath
those high among suns, and the dream-walking

minium: red lead; red oxide used in making paint and in glassmaking.
meltemi: the north wind in the early part of August.
jib: a triangular sail set forward of the mainsail.
close-hauled: pulled in tightly for sailing as directly into the wind as possible.
on a reach: sailing with the boat approximately at right angles to the wind, usually with the sails let out part way.
heliotrope: a garden herb with reddish-blue blossoms.
scarab: a broad-backed beetle, especially the black dung beetle held sacred by the ancient Egyptians, or its image cut from a stone or gem.

The modest with red engagement rings
the haughty riding across the meadows
those fashioned of pure sky
the thoughtful, and those inlaid by Fancy

Lily, Rose, Jasmine
Violet, Lilac, Hyacinth
Carnation, Narcissus, Aster

THE GIRLS, blue grass of utopia
the girls, those Pleiades led astray
the girls, those Vessels of the Mysteries
full to the brim and bottomless

Stringent in darkness yet delicious
carved out in light yet all darkness
turning on themselves like a lighthouse
those sun-devouring ones, the moon-walking

Ersi, Myrtó, Marina
Eleni, Roxani, Fotini
Anna, Alexandra, Cynthia

The hatching whispers among sea-shells
one lost like a dream: Arignóta
a distant light that says: sleep
bewildered kisses like a crowd of stars

The bit of blouse that the wind eats
the mossy peach-fuzz on the shin
the cunt's violet-scented salt
and the cold water of the full moon

Pleiades: in Greek mythology, the seven daughters of Atlas and the nymph Pleione; transformed (astronomy) into a group of six stars, the invisible seventh "lost" (Merope, who concealed herself out of shame for having loved a mortal).

Arignóta: a girl who left the island of Lesbos for Sardis on the mainland. Sappho wrote about her: "she who walks among the Lydian women, outshining even the stars."

PRAISED BE the oil-lamp's motion
black with shadows and full of ruins
the page written under the soil
the song Liyerí sang in Hades

The carved monsters on the icon screen
the ancient poplars, bearers of fish
the lovable Korae of the stone arm
Helen's neck so like a shore line

THE TREES starry with good will
the musical notation of another world
the ancient belief that there always exists
the very obvious yet still unseen

The shadow that bends them against the earth
something yellow in their remembering
their ancient dancing over graves
their wisdom with no price to it

Olive, Pomegranate, Peach
Pine, Poplar, Plane Tree
Oak, Beach, Cypress

Translated by **Edmund Keeley** *and* **George Savidis**

HEROIC AND ELEGIAC SONG FOR THE LOST SECOND LIEUTENANT OF ALBANIA

7

The trees are of coal which the night does not kindle.
The wind runs wild beating its breast, the wind still beating its breast

AXION ESTI

Liyerí: probably a reference to the folksong known as "Liyerí ston Adhi" (the slender girl in Hades). The girl in question begs to be raised to the upper world in order to see how her kin are grieving for her, only to learn that her kin are in fact not mourning for her but enjoying life as usual.

Korae: the richly colored statues of maidens on the Acropolis.

Nothing happens. Forced to their knees the mountains roost
Beneath the frost. And roaring out of the ravines,
Out of the heads of the corpses rises the abyss . . .
Not even Sorrow weeps any longer. Like the mad orphan girl
She roams about, wearing on her breast a small cross of twigs
But does not weep. Surrounded only by pitch-black Acroceraunia
She climbs to the peak and sets the moon's disk there
Perhaps the planets will turn and see their shadows
And hide their rays
And stand poised
Breathless with amazement at the chaos . . .

The wind runs wild beating its breast, the wind still beating its
breast
The wilderness is muffled in its black shawl
Crouching behind months of cloud it listens
What is there to listen for, so many cloud-months away?
With a tangle of hair on her shoulders—ah, leave her alone—
Half a candle half a flame a mother weeps—leave her alone—
In the empty frozen rooms where she roams leave her alone!
For fate is never a widow
And mothers are here to weep, husbands to fight
Orchards for the breasts of girls to blossom
Blood to be spent, waves to break into foam
And freedom to be born always in the lightning flash!

13

In the distance crystal bells are ringing—

They speak of him who was burnt by life
Like the bee in the fountain of wild thyme;
Of the dawn strangled between the breasts of the mountains
Just as it was announcing a radiant day;
Of the snowflake which flashed across the mind and was lost
When the whistle of the bullet was heard far away
And the Albanian partridge flew high in the air wailing!

Translated by **Paul Merchant**

Acroceraunia: in Albania, the NW prong of the Ceraunian mountains plus the Karabunum peninsula and Cape Linguetta.

SEVEN DAYS TO THE NEVERNESS

SUNDAY.—Morning in the Temple of the Calfbearer. I say:
Let beautiful Myrto become as true as a tree, and
allow her little lamb gazing straight through the eyes of my
assassin, in that instant, to punish the bitterest future.

MONDAY.—The feel of newborn grass and water about my
feet. Therefore I am. Before or after the look which will
grind me to stone, the right hand upraises a gigantic blue
ear of corn. To grow into the New Zodiac.

TUESDAY.—Departure of numbers. The 1 wrestles with the
9 on a desolate beach, swarming with black pebbles, piles
of seaweed, wild skeletons among the rocks. My two
favorite old horses are neighing, rearing above the steam
which rises from the sulphur of the sea.

WEDNESDAY.—From the other side of the Lightning. The
burnt hand will flower again. To straighten the seven folds
of the world.

THURSDAY.—A door opens: stone steps, geranium flowers
and a little further, translucent roofs, kites, and fragments
of seashells in the sun. A goat slowly munches the centuries,
the smoke rising with intense peace inside his horns.
The hour when the gardener's daughter is kissed secretly,
in extreme pleasure a flower pot falls and bursts. This sound,
could I save it?

FRIDAY.—(Feast of the Ascension) of the women I have
loved hopelessly. Echo: Mar-in-nna. Hel-le-nni. With
every toll of the bell the Easter flower enters my arms.
Later a strange light, and two quite different pigeons carry
me upwards in an ivy covered house.

Calfbearer: famous Greek sculpture of a man bearing a calf.
Myrto: in mythology, a maenad whose wounded hand Dionysus healed with myrtle.

SATURDAY.—Grim and silent men slaughter the cypress tree
of my lineage; for the feast of Engagement or Death.
They dig the surrounding earth and sprinkle clove water. I
have already pronounced the words which flatten the magnet
of infinity.

Translated by **Stuart Montgomery**

YANNIS RITSOS

1909–

Yannis Ritsos was born in Monemvasia, South Peloponnese. He studied in Yithion and Athens before falling ill with tuberculosis, spent years in sanitariums in Athens and Crete, and has also spent considerable time in prison for antifascist activities. At the time of the regime of Metaxas in 1936, one of his long poems, "Epitaphios," was burned in Athens. Ritsos was put under house arrest by the Greek government in 1967, his books were banned, and he was interned on the island of Yioura. Forty volumes of poetry include *Tractors* (1934), *Moonlight Sonata* (1956, First State Prize), *The Prison Tree and the Women* (1963), and *Helen* (1972).

The poems of Yannis Ritsos humanize the Greek myths at the expense of political bullies, and restate the principles of classical justice in behalf of contemporary Greeks. For Ritsos, poems are creeds of freedom. When legendary Greek figures rise within the poems, cast in new light and old shadows, the effect is libational. Ritsos summons us to behold the ways of humankind, and we become quiet, as we do when nearby olive trees and beehives deepen the silence of evening.

AND RELATING THEM . . .

The way we, words, ideas have declined, we can't be bothered
with old or recent glories, with Aristeides' biographies—and when
one of us

AND RELATING THEM . . .
Aristeides: an Athenian, surnamed "the Just," who fought at the battle of Marathon in 490 B.C. and in 489 was archon.

sometimes starts reminiscing about the 300 or the 200, at once
the others cut him short with scorn, or at least sceptically. But
sometimes, as now,
when the weather clears up—on a Sunday, sitting under a
eucalyptus,
in this inexorable light, a secret longing comes over one
for the old glories—no matter that we call them cheap—when the
procession started at dawn,
in front the trumpeter, behind the chariots heavy with branches of
myrtle and wreaths,
then the black bull and young men carrying wine and milk
pitchers
for the liberations and beautiful oil and perfume bottles—
but what was most dazzling, at the end of the procession, dressed
entirely in purple,
the Archon of Plataea who the rest of the year was not permitted
to touch iron and had to dress entirely in white, now dressed
in purple,
carrying a long sword, crossing the town majestically,
towards the heroes' graves, holding a pitcher from the state
utensils, and
after the grave stones had been washed, after the rich sacrifices,
he'd raise
the cup of wine and pouring it over the tombs recite:
"I am offering this cup to the bravest men who fell
for the freedom of the Greeks,"—and a shiver would pass through
the nearby laurel woods,
a shiver which still flutters through the leaves of these eucalyptuses
and on these patched clothes all different colors hung in the sun
to dry.

the 300: refers to the Spartans (the Lacedaimonians) who fought under Leonidas at Thermopylae (480 B.C.).

the 200: refers to the 200 hostages held in a concentration camp at Haidari, near Athens, during the German occupation of Greece in World War II. The hostages were executed (probably at Kesariani, near Athens, on May Day 1944) as a reprisal for the killing of several Germans in a train that came under the attack of partisan (guerilla) forces representing the Greek resistance.

Archon of Plataea: archon is the general term for office holder in a state; Plataea is a city in southern Boeotia between Cithaeron and the river Asopos. The Plataeans joined the Athenian army at Marathon, and Athens' fleet in 480 B.C., when the town, like Athens, was sacked.

THE DECLINE OF ARGO

Tonight talking of how things pass, age, become cheap—
beautiful women, exploits, poems—we remembered
the legendary ship when it was brought to Corinth one spring
night,
eaten by woodworm, fading, its tholepins torn off,
full of patches, holes, memories. The long procession through the
woods,
with torches, wreaths, flutes, contests of youths. The old Argo was
a magnificent offering to Poseidon's temple. Beautiful night; the
chanting of the priests;
an owl hooting from the temple's pediment; the dancers would
jump lightly
on the ship imitating rough action with improper grace, the
motion
of non-existent oars, sweat, blood. Then an old sailor
spat at their feet and walked away to the small woods to piss.

A PLOUGH, BY ITSELF

Everything was decreed, safe, logical,
even human. The municipal temples played their part;
Athena protected justice; always present, although invisible,
she presided over the meetings of the Areios Pagos. When the
jury
was split, the balance of justice
would always favor the accused.
Those were good days—
they almost don't sound true now. Did they ever exist?

THE DECLINE OF ARGO

Argo: A generation before the Trojan War, according to Greek legend, Jason sailed to Colchis in the ship Argo to recover the golden fleece.

tholepins: pins that hold oars in place.

Poseidon: Greek god of the sea.

A PLOUGH, BY ITSELF

Areios Pagos: the Areopagus, ancient Athenian court. See Aeschylus' *Eumenides*, where Athena casts the deciding vote in favor of Orestes.

Were they a dream? Maybe their frequent recollection in rainy
autumn sunsets falsifies.
When we celebrated the ploughing
of the fields,
the priest, bending over the ground to trace the first groove, at the
foot of the Acropolis,
would recite: "Never refuse fire and water to anyone.
Never mislead anyone who asks for the way. Never leave
a corpse disinterred. Don't kill the bull that pulls the plough."
Beautiful words, really;—just words, then, like now,
fire was for burning your neighbor's fields, water to flood them,
the bull, red ribbons round its neck, is boiling in the thief's pot.
Only the plough, by itself (maybe driven by an invisible hand)
still ploughs the barren fields now overgrown with mallows and
wild lilies.

MIDNIGHT

Every night, on the twelfth stroke of the clock, the old woman
pushes her hair back from her eyes with a strange motion
as if catching a thief by the jacket jumping from the window.
Then
she wakes completely. She puts on her slippers. She approaches
the mirror. She looks at herself in it;
she looks at the space between her eyes looking back at her from
behind the mirror, at the spiderwebs, at the drops of damp.
She hears, just then, the fine leaves of gold falling in the paved
yard,
the snail crawling up the big store-room padlock,
the worms that stir in the flower pots and the old coffins. The
dead, she says,
don't wear out shoes—they walk softly, on soft things. The dead
walk inside us or sometimes, to economise, even wear our shoes.

UNACCEPTABLE

He stands before the marble table. He persists.
He chips a block of ice with a small hammer.
Bits fly loose, melt. The cold
numbs his fingers, his body. He persists.

A statue, he says, of warmth—the absent warmth,
the desired, he says. The ice melts. The statue melts.
The water runs on the marble. The roaring of the water
is heard in the water pipes in the walls, under the floor,
under the black and white kitchen tiles,
in the earthenware drainpipe in the yard, under the ground
among the insatiable roots. The sick woman
calls from the inside room. He
wipes his hands quickly on a towel.
He lights the lamp. His hands tremble.
"It's ready," he says. "I'll bring it."
The light flickers on the big bed
on the moulting blankets full of holes.
The water runs in the gutters. They both know it.

REVERSAL

Roots in the air;—two faces between them;
the well was at the bottom of the garden—that's where
they had thrown their rings one day; then
they looked up, very high up, pretending not to see
the old woman shitting in the empty flowerpot
as she bit into the big apple.

Translations by **Nikos Stangos**

EVENING

The olive-trees on the hill, the white-washed enclosure,
the doors, the windows, the bathroom, the terraces,
further below, the beehive tombs—all so quiet
like continuation or repetition. The guard
passed slowly. The shotgun idle on his shoulder.
On his face, still youthful, the sunset
sympathetic, peaceful, blood-red. His shadow
huge on the plain like dead Agamemnon.

Translated by **Paul Merchant**

EVENING

Agamemnon: in Greek legend, King of Mycenae, murdered by his wife Clytemnestra on his return from the Trojan War.

GEORGE SEFERIS

(GEORGE SEFERIADHIS)

1900–1971

George Seferis was born in Smyrna, Turkey. At the onset of the First World War in 1914, his family moved to Athens, where he attended high school. His father was a lawyer who wrote poetry, and Seferis himself studied law and literature in Paris (1918–24). He went to Cairo in 1926 in the Greek diplomatic service, and later became ambassador to England. In 1953 he received the Nobel Prize for Literature. Seferis spent the last fourteen years of his life on the Smyrnan seacoast. In September 1971, 25,000 people walked in his funeral procession, which became a protest march against the military dictatorship. The following day his last poem, "Against Woodwaxen," was published on the front pages of the newspapers *To Vima* and *Ta Nea.* His books of poetry include *Turning Point* (1931), *The King of Asine* (1948), *Poems 1924–1955* (1967), and *Three Secret Poems* (1969).

The poems of George Seferis are myth-histories, death testaments, race recollections. Seferis's voice speaks from his poems as if he had entered another world from which everything in this life is now seen clearly. He allows the rarest glimpses into our own lives: fragments of the past grow into summers, an evening summons all the twilights we have known. The poems warm us, the way the blood rushes in and comforts our arms after they have been asleep.

MYTHISTOREMA

III

Remember the baths where you were slain

I awoke with this marble head between my hands
Which tires my elbows out. Where can I put it down?
It was falling into the dream as I rose from the dream
And so our lives grew one, hard now to be separated.

Mythistorema: from *mythos* (myth, mythology) and *istoria* (history, story); colloquially, a novel.

Remember the baths . . . : Aeschylus, *Choephoroe (The Libation Bearers)*, l. 491. Orestes is invoking the spirit of his murdered father, Agamemnon (see note, p. 125).

I peer into the eyes, neither shut nor open,
I speak to the mouth which is always trying to speak,
I hold the cheeks which have grown beyond the skin.
I can do no more.

My hands are lost, my hands come back to me,
Maimed.

STRATIS THE SAILOR DESCRIBES A MAN

3

ADOLESCENT

In the summer of my sixteenth year a strange voice sang in my
ears.
I was standing, I remember, by the sea's edge, among the red nets
and the shell of an abandoned boat like a skeleton.
I tried to get nearer to that voice by putting my ear down on the
sand.
The voice vanished
But a shooting star
As though I had never seen a shooting star before,
And on my lips the salt taste of the waves.
That night the roots of the trees no longer came.
Next day a voyage unfolded in my mind, then shut again like a
picture book.
I thought of going down every evening to the shore
To learn first about the shore and then to take to the sea.
On the third day I fell in love with a girl on a hill;
She had a little white house like a mountain chapel;
An old mother by the window, spectacles bent over the knitting
Never a word,
A pot of basil, a pot of carnations.
She was called, I think, Vasso, Frosso or Bilio;
So I forgot the sea.
One Monday in October
I found a broken jar in front of the little white house.
Vasso (let us say for short) appeared in a black dress,
Her hair disordered, her eyes red.

To my question she replied:
'She is dead; the doctor says she died because we didn't slaughter
the black cock on the foundations. . . . How could we get
hold of a black cock here? . . . There is nothing except white
flocks . . . and the poultry in the market are sold already
plucked.'
This was not how I had imagined grief and death.
I left and went back to the sea.
That night on the deck of the *St. Nicholas*
I dreamed of a very old olive tree in tears.

MATHIOS PASCHALIS AMONG THE ROSES

I have been smoking since morning without a break;
If I stop the roses will take me in their embrace,
With thorns and with fallen petals they will choke me.
They grow crookedly all of them with the same pink color;
They are staring; they are waiting for someone; no one comes.
Behind the smoke of my pipe I watch them
On a bored stalk, without scent;
In the other life a woman used to say to me: you can touch this
hand
And it is yours this rose, it is yours you can take it
Now or later, whenever you like.

Still smoking, I go down the garden steps
And the roses come down with me. They are excited;
They have something in their manner of that voice
At the root of the cry, at the point where man begins
To shout out 'Mother!' or 'Help!',
Or the small white cries of love.

It is a small garden full of roses,
A few square yards that come along down with me
As I descend the steps, without the sky.
And her aunt was saying to her 'Antigone,
Today you forgot to do your exercises.

MATHIOS PASCHALIS AMONG THE ROSES
Mathios Paschalis: like Stratis the Sailor, a recurrent persona in Seferis's poems.

At your age I never wore a corset. Not in my time'.
Her aunt was a poor old body,—veins in relief,
Many wrinkles round her ears, a nose about to die:
Yet her words always full of wisdom.
One day I saw her touching Antigone's breast,
Like a child stealing an apple.

Will I perhaps meet the old woman as I keep descending?
When I left she said to me 'Who knows when we shall meet
again?'
Then I read of her death in some old newspapers
And of Antigone's wedding and the wedding of Antigone's
daughter
Without an end of the steps or of my tobacco
Which imparts to me the taste of a haunted ship
With a mermaid crucified, when still beautiful, to the wheel.

THE LAST DAY

The day was cloudy. No one could make up his mind.
A light wind blew. 'North east' someone said 'a touch of south'.
A few slim cypresses nailed on the slope; the sea,
A little further, was grey with shining pools.
The troops were presenting arms as it started to drizzle.
'The wind is not north-east; it is south east——';
That was the only definite thing that was heard.
And yet we knew that tomorrow there would be left to us
Nothing at all, not even the woman beside us drinking sleep,
Not even the memory that once we were men,
By tomorrow's dawn nothing at all any more.

'This wind reminds me of the spring' she said,
My friend walking beside me, looking into the distance, 'the
spring
That suddenly came in winter by the shut-in sea.
So unexpected. So many years have passed
Since then. How shall we die?'

A funeral march moved by in the thin rain.
How does a man die? Strange that no one thought of this.
Or if one did, it was as a recollection from ancient chronicles,

The Crusades, perhaps, or the sea-battle fought at Salamis.
And yet death is a thing that happens. How does a man die?
And yet one wins one's death, which is one's own and nobody else's,
And this kind of game is life.
The light was sinking from the clouded day. No one made up his mind.
Tomorrow there would be left to us nothing at all,—
Everything surrendered,—not even our hands,
And our women working for strangers at the water springs,
Our children at the quarries.
My friend, walking beside me, was singing a snatch of song
'In spring, in summer, slaves. . . .'
One could remember old teachers who left us orphaned.
A couple passed us, talking,
'I am sick and tired of the dusk. Let's go.
Let us go home now and turn on the light.'

Translations by **Rex Warner**

ON STATE

3

You, what were you seeking? Your face grimaced.
You had just arisen,
leaving the sheets to grow cold
and the avenging baths.
Drops rolled over your shoulders,
over your belly,
your feet bare on the ground,
on the cut grass.
They,
the three faces of bold Hecate,

THE LAST DAY

Salamis: an island near Athens where the Persian fleet was destroyed by the Greeks in 480 B.C.

ON STATE

Hecate: an ancient chthonian goddess associated with the spirits of the dead, with night, and with magic. She has power to bestow success and wealth, benefit one in courts of law, and grant victory in war and athletics. Often represented with three bodies standing back to back, especially in statues placed at crossroads, which she was supposed to haunt.

they sought to take you with them.
Your eyes were two tragic shells,
and on the nipples of your breasts you had
two small cherry-red pebbles—
stage props, I suppose.
They,
they howled,
but you remained rooted to the ground;
their gestures tore the air.
Slaves brought them knives,
but you remained rooted to the ground,
a cypress.
They drew the knives from the scabbards
and probed where to strike you.
Only then did you cry out:
"Let whoever wishes come sleep with me:
am I not the sea?"

SUMMER SOLSTICE

7

The poplar tree in the little garden,
its breathing marks your hours
night and day:
a sky-filled clepsydra.
Under the moon's brightness its leaves
drag black footsteps across the white wall.

On the border, a few pines,
then fragments of marble and the lights of the city
and people—the way people usually are.
Yet the blackbird twitters
when it comes to drink,
and at times you hear the voice of the ringdove.

Ten steps in the little garden:
you can see the sunlight

SUMMER SOLSTICE
clepsydra: a glass instrument used by the ancients to measure time by the fall or flow of water; a water clock.

fall on two red carnations,
on an olive tree and a bit of honeysuckle.

Accept who you are.
The poem,
do not cast it down under the thick plane trees;
nourish it with the earth and rock you have.
For better things—
dig the same ground to find them.

11

The sea that they call calm,
ships and white sails,
sea breeze from the pines and the Mount of Aéghina,
panting breath;
your skin slippery on hers,
easy and warm;
thought almost half-formed and at once forgotten.

But in the shallows
a speared octopus pulsed out its ink,
and in the depths—
if you could think where the beautiful islands end.

I watched you with all the light and darkness I have.

Translations by **Walter Kaiser**

"AGAINST WOODWAXEN . . ."

Sounion was beautiful on that day of the Annunciation
once more with spring
a handful of green leaves round the rusted stones

SUMMER SOLSTICE

Aéghina: an island in the Sinus Saronicus, near the coast of Argolis. On Mt. Aéghina still stands the Doric temple of Pallas Athena, one of the oldest temples in Greece.

"AGAINST WOODWAXEN . . ."

"against woodwaxen": a quotation from Plato's *Republic,* Bk. X; the same phrase appears in the poem (l. 16), translated slightly differently.

Sounion: a cape south of Athens, site of remnants of an ancient temple. The first piece of the Attic coast visible to returning sailors.

the red earth and the woodwaxen,
showing at ready their long thorns and yellow flowerings.
Not far off, the ancient columns, chords of a harp,
    echo still . . .

Peaceful.
—What could have reminded me of Ardiaios? that man.
—A word in Plato, I believe, lost in the brain furrows.
The name of the yellow bush
has never changed since those days.
During the night I found the missing link:
"They bound him hand and foot," he tells us,
"they cast him down and flayed him
and dragged him out of the open road, torn;
carding him over the woodwaxen thorns,
they took him to Tartaros and threw him there, ragged."

So, in the world below he was paying for pitiless acts
this Pamphylios Ardiaios, the miserable Tyrant.

Translated by **John Chioles**

Ardiaios: see Plato's *Republic,* Bk. X, where Ardiaeus the Great, tyrant of Pamphylia, who killed his father and elder brother, is described as having "done many other unholy things."

Tartaros: the underworld, Hades.

FRENCH GUIANA

LÉON DAMAS

1912–

Léon Damas was born in the city of Cayenne. As a child he suffered from chronic asthma and was bedridden almost constantly until he was six. Damas met Aimé Césaire at the Lycée Schoelcher in Martinique, later left his studies of law and oriental languages in Paris because of his interest in black culture, and returned to school on a scholarship given to him by an organization of black students. With Césaire and Léopold Senghor he started the journal *L'Etudiant noir.* His first collection of poems, *Pigments* (1937), was banned by the French government. During World War II Damas was decorated for his services with the French armed forces. In 1948 he returned to Paris as a deputy to the National Assembly from French Guiana; he has since been a cultural diplomat to Haiti and French West Africa. Other books of poems include *Graffiti* (1952), *Black-Label* (1956), and *Neuralgias* (1965).

The poems of Léon Damas are like tightly stretched catgut, reverberating. At times nostalgic, at times acidic, sardonic, Damas declares negritude: enough of white table manners, enough of the Frenchman's French, enough glossed-down hair. His deliberate rhythms and his imperative voice underscore social images that both decry colonialism and affirm black dignity.

IN SINGLE FILE

And the hooves
of the beasts of burden
hammering out in Europe
the still uncertain dawn
remind me
of the strange renunciation
of early-morning trayloads
brimming

that give a rhythm in the Antilles
to the hips of women
in single file

And the strange renunciation
of early-morning trayloads
brimming
that give a rhythm in the Antilles
to the hips of women
in single file
reminds me
of the hooves
of the beasts of burden
hammering out in Europe
the still uncertain dawn

Translated by **Norman Shapiro**

POSITION PAPER

The days
shape themselves: African masks
aloof
from the quick-lime obscenities
enraging
a piano pounding with the same old wheeze—
Breathless Moonlight
in the shrubbery
in the gondolas
etc.

Translated by **Robert Bagg**

SOCIAL GRACES

They don't yawn at home
the way they yawn here
with
their hand over their mouth

I want to yawn without airs
my body hunched
into the perfumes tormenting the life
I've made for myself
from their dog-faced winter
from their sun that couldn't
even
warm
the coco milk that would gurgle
in my belly when I'd wake up

Let me yawn,
my hand
there
on my heart,
at the obsession with everything that
in one single day I
turned my back on

Translated by **Michael S. Harper**

HAITI

RENÉ DÉPESTRE

1926–

René Dépestre was born in Jacmel, on the southern coast of Haiti. When he was nineteen he published his first book of poems, *Sparks*. At about the same time he also cofounded the magazine *La Ruche* (The Beehive), which was closed down by the government for its Marxist views. After the fall of the Lescot regime in 1946, Dépestre went into exile in Paris and Africa. He returned to Haiti briefly in 1958 but soon left because of hostile pressure from the government and has since lived mostly in Cuba. Seven books of poems include *Vegetations of Clarity* (1951), *Black Ore* (1956), and *A Rainbow for the Christian West* (1967).

The poems of René Dépestre speak in images of black spit, black swamps, black flesh, "black ore." They burn, excoriate; poems of high fever. With snakelike accuracy, the voice in the poems strikes at the culture of capitalism.

VIOLENCE

Rotten the world rotten the flesh   rotten the life
rotten all things seen   rotten all things heard
rotten the beaks of birds   the mouths of men
rotten the muzzles of women   the claws of beasts
breath of my words   cleaves the air
above the black swamps   above all rottenness
above the dying leaves   above the burnt lips
above the lifted wings   above the twisted limbs
these are weapons in my hands
these are weapons deployed   in the water running from my
    eyes
arms high as our palm trees
arms at the vulture's neck   on the syllables' crest

weapons to mow down the empty harvests   the bloodied workers
these are the fine deeds of tenderness
these are the fine deeds of crime   high deeds of injury
high deeds which open   sluice-gated odds
to those who possess   the foetus of a younger crop
to those who have no fangs
to those whose sap mounts   from the soles of their feet to their hair
to those of the shadows those of the plagues   those of the rotting odors
to these the way is open   to these the air is pure
here is the earth   her rotten crust lopped off
the new flesh comes   and the joy, new in their hearts.

MOUTH OF LIGHTS

My mouth mad with systems
mad with adventures
the lighthouse point
where it's a risk to turn

My mouth black with want
with black spit
black of black night
drinks from its bowl of lights

My mouth heavy with song
heavy with snakebite
with my newborn cry
puts in a word
sawing the moon in two

And it's my mouth
filled with rumors
come to tell men
the pain in a world
which opens its veins

Translations by **James Scully** *and* **Susanna Lang**

BLACK ORE

When the sun, and it was abrupt, had dried up the sweat of the
Indian
When gold fever had drained the last drop of Indian blood into
the marketplace
So that, on the grounds of the gold mines, there wasn't an Indian
left
They looked then to the muscular African river
Sure to be relieved of their despair
Then began the rush on the inexhaustible
Treasure of black flesh
Began then the mad scramble
Into the gleaming black tropical body
And throughout the earth echoed the clamor of picks
In packed black ore
Which would have been all wrong, if chemists hadn't thought up
Ways to make some precious alloy
With black metal, all wrong if ladies hadn't
Dreamed of a battery of cooks
In negrony from Senegal, of a tea service
In hulking niggerboy from the West Indies
All wrong if some priest
Hadn't promised his parish
A bell surging with the resonance of black blood
Or, again, if an irreproachable Santa Claus hadn't considered
For his annual visit
Little soldiers in black lead
Or if some brave captain
Hadn't sharpened his sword in the petrified ebony
And throughout the earth quivered with drills
In the bowels of my race
In the muscular strata of the black man
And so many centuries gone on quarrying
Marvels from this race
O metallic seams, veins of my people
Inexhaustible ore of human dew
How many pirates have forced
The dark depths of your flesh
How many marauders hacked a road

Through the lush vegetation of lights on your body
Strewing your years with dead stalks
Small pools of tears
A people plundered, a people turned over top to bottom
Like a laboring land
A people broken up to enrich
The great fair grounds of the world
Brood, deep in your flesh-and-blood night, on what will erupt
No one will dare cast cannon or pieces of gold
From the black metal of your wrath pouring out

Translated by **James Scully**

GYULA ILLYÉS

1902–

Gyula Illyés was born at Rácegres, between the Danube and Lake Balaton, into a family of estate servants. In 1919, in the confusion following the First World War, he left his studies for the Hungarian Red Army, and when the Republic fell that year he went to Paris to study. When he returned to Hungary he served as assistant editor and then editor until 1944 of the literary magazine *Nyugat* (West), which became *Hungarian Star* when he took over the editorship. Illyés is a vice-president of P.E.N., an international organization of writers, and has several times been nominated for the Nobel Prize. His *Collected Poems* appeared in 1940 and 1947, and his *Selected Poems* in 1961.

The poems of Gyula Illyés are like markings on lead weights: a heaviness surrounds images from nightmare journeys, details from childhood, life in Old Hungary. Illyés is as skilled in identifying the subtle political overtones that entwine our lives as he is in evoking the deeply personal relationships that enmesh them. In the poems below, "Brazilian Rain Forest," while describing a drunken girl in the streets of Old Buda, contemplates the relationships of men and women. "Work," which Illyés wrote in memory of his father's craft, is the poet's *Ars Poetica*.

SUCCESSFUL EFFORT

The ship sank, it reached the sea bottom with a great jolt, then turned over onto its side. It had been a country, now it was clear, a nation. 'After the tempest.' I was a passenger, but in some way or another—either through accident or because I had come up on deck to look around despite the storm—a current whirled me up to the sea surface. I clung in vain to the hand-rail. The sun shone. A regatta was taking place on the abated water. My friends flew past on a boat. They were shouting in a language foreign to me, yet as intelligibly and with words as clear-shining as the brilliant glitter of the sun on the ripples. They knew nothing about the shipwreck, not even about the storm. I was laughing, I was drinking—the divine *banyuls*—and since, also through mere accident, I was handy with sails, I was immediately taken on as a happy member of the *équipage* and together we wore the victor's laurel.

. . . It has cost me five years and a thousand tricks to get back again to the ship deep under water, where those who have not yet perished have gone mad.

Translated by **Frederic Will** *and* **Julia Kada**

BRAZILIAN RAIN FOREST

In Old Buda, a street almost as wide as a square coming down from Újlak Church. The one-story houses here are even lower than usual. The pavement once swelled to the level of the windows, and remained there as in some frozen flood. From such a house, a tavern still privately owned, a tall slender young woman who is well-dressed comes out into the Friday twilight. Her eyes are glazed; she is dead drunk. She sways gracefully. The basalt cobble-stones of the broad street mock her by pretending to be the stepping stones across a mountain stream, and that's why she may only step on every second one. Since the stones are wet, the scene is made all the more probable. It is raining, fully and evenly, as in the tropics, although it is November. The pouring rain is broken into threads by the light of the street lamps. The woman's dishevelled hair drips also into so many threads. She is soaked to the skin.

She is soaked to the skin, but does not feel a thing. Otherwise she would not push away the threads of rain as if she were parting the reeds of a marsh or thrusting aside the bead curtain of some southern barber shop. But after this bead curtain comes another and then another, ten, twenty, a hundred, thousand upon wondrous thousand.

SUCCESSFUL EFFORT
banyuls: an ancient Hungarian liquor.
BRAZILIAN RAIN FOREST
Old Buda: the oldest part of the city of Budapest.

All this, of course, is illusion. The situation and reality: the woman walks amid the lianas, the hanging tendrils of a Brazilian rain forest, and above her are trees teeming with bright-colored parakeets, snarling monkeys, serpents, and other creatures that do not even exist in South America, but have come here only for this occasion. At such a time who would not think of coming to her aid? As Chateaubriand says, this is how the most exciting adventures with native women really begin. Yes, but there is something rarely taken into account—the distances in a rain forest! Between the two of us, my sailor's eye tells me, a thousand miles at least.

DO YOU REMEMBER?

Do you remember—when you were skating—
the long grass on the shallow
bottom, under a thin membrane
of ice; and the fish darting up below?

The green ice cracked: you raced ahead.
Around your foot there burst a star.
You raced ahead; with sparkling thunder,
racing with you, went the star.

You raced against danger: for as long
as you glided on ice you would not sink.
The braver you were, the safer by far;
safer always the greater the risk.

WORK

They stuck pigs in the throat. Might I not have done it myself? They tossed chickens with their heads cut off out into the courtyard. With a child's thirst for knowledge, I watched their

BRAZILIAN RAIN FOREST

Chateaubriand: François-René (1768–1848), French writer. While visiting America in 1791, he spent several months among the Indian tribes of New York State and "the Floridas"; his experiences inspired the writing of his famous romantic tales *Atala* and *René,* and are described in his *Memoirs*.

final spasms with a heart hardly touched. My first really shattering experience came when I watched the hooping of a cartwheel.

From the huge coal fire, with pincers at least a yard long, the apprentices grabbed the iron hoop, which by then was red hot up and down. They ran with it to the fresh-smelling oak wheel that had been fixed in place in the front of the blacksmith's shop. The flesh-colored wooden wheel was my grandfather's work; the iron hoop, which gave off a shower of sparks in its fiery agony, was my father's. One of the apprentices held the sledge hammer, the other the buckets. Places, everyone. As on shipboard. As at an execution. The hoop, which in its white-hot state had just expanded to the size of the wheel, was quickly placed on it; and they began to pry it out with their tongs. My father swung the hammer with lightning speed, giving orders all the while. The wood caught fire; they poured a bucket of water on it. The wheel sent up steam and smoke so thick you couldn't see it. But still the hammer pounded on, and still came the "Press hard!" uttered breathlessly from the corner of the mouth. The fire blazed up again. Water flung again as on a tortured man who has sunk into a coma. Then the last flourishing bush of steam evaporated while the apprentices poured a thin trickle from a can on the cooling iron which, in congealing, gripped lovingly its life-long companion to be. The men wiped the sweat from their brows, spat, shook their heads, satisfied. Nothing—not the slightest flicker of a movement—could have been executed differently.

Translations by **William Jay Smith**

FERENC JUHÁSZ

1928–

Ferenc Juhász was born in Bia, a small Transdanubian village near Budapest. He studied business, and was introduced to science and technology at Budapest University, which he left in order to join a publishing house as a sub-editor. In autumn 1944 he fled Budapest to avoid conscription. After the war (1947) he entered the Attila József College of Literature, where he met and married Erzsébet Severénczi. Juhász's first collection of poems, *The Winged Colt* (1949), was followed by such books as *The*

Breeding Country: Collected Poems (1957), *The Flowering World Tree: Selected Poems* (1965), and *Legends of the Holy Flood of Fire* (1969).

The poems of Ferenc Juhász are sensuous, sinewy, many-armed: steaming poems of stew and golden-floating onions, insect and reptile poems of turtle-sized beetles and chrome-green Gigantosauruses, poems of sleeping snails and blossoming peonies, scraggy geese and porcelain colors. Juhász roams through the twilight of the preconscious and discovers a world of folk pleasures and human isolations.

from POWER OF THE FLOWERS

You saw the armored Gigantosaurus' bloody battles,
the rending jaws of chrome green, thorn-crested reptiles,
how the Tri-Corn pushed his bone pike far into the breast of the
  Lizard King,
whose yellow-purple lung-clots and fats welled out with the flood
  of blood mingling,
the swish of the first birds on squealing wings, the awkward
roaring also of turtle-sized beetles you heard,
you felt the procreating storms of love-symbol marked moths of
  great size,
you saw the painful slow trek of the turtles, heard their death
  sighs,
you felt the wind of man's flashing metal arrow,
you saw the pursed sweet smile of the Avar baby, and long ago
the Huns' rushing cloud of horse, huge-chested whirlwind of a
  thousand nostrils,
in your dew the Thracian virgin washed her blood-gummed
  nipples,
a love-sick Latin maiden gazed up from where she lay at the axes
  of your petals,
and you set upon the gypsy's nose, when he bent over you, a
  yellow pimple,
you heard the bellowing of bullocks when from the dust-cloud
  they raised

Avar: refers to the Avars on the Danube, whose empire was broken by Charlemagne.
Huns: The Huns invaded the Eastern Roman empire about A.D. 372–453.

the Magyars swooped, harassed behind, longing for the beeches' shade
in that wanderers' apocalypse, the battle-axes, death rattles,
wailings, and spears, are preserved in your parts with the great lost battles
iron flowers of silence, glass-tongued flowering clubs, grasses like wires,
you have preserved the possible conceiving of curses, kisses, prairie-fires,
and the dust-veiled dirge of every ragged devout procession
that carries the green-stone form nailed onto wood, the Second Person,
you hold the wilted suffering of all guilty rebels,
the mail-clad stallions' grey-green lips of rheumy piles,
beneath the passing shadowed roar of the bomber each of you trembles,
collapsing stone-woods, burning blood bubble-sprays stain your petals,
you have heard the soft addresses of stern poets,
life-giving mothers' ecstatic screams, cursings of prophets,
flowers, crucibles of scent, in the moonlight here trembling,
shining like money, like divination, tender shadows throwing,
oh in the steaming mooncake's white glimmer, the brooding Narcissus
blooms beside sleeping saurians and blue lizards,
I hardly know whether small moths or petals, mongrel-descendants,
are flooding the little brook with quicksilver blue radiance,
under films of nickel the in-motion for eternity sleeping foliage floats,
in and out dance the tiny scintillating fishes with pulsing white throats.
I know only this, that I am human and from instincts of seaweed,
hot primeval muds, mortal and eternal, I have risen indeed,
consciousness purified in flame, a cell arrived at man's estate;
I do not know, world, your ways, but I manage, I estimate
what is to be done with courage and as you, world, would have it done,

Magyars: The Magyars crossed the Carpathians into Hungary in A.D. 898.
saurians: an order of reptiles including lizards and crocodiles.

this you can in no way understand, Violet, Viburnum.
You can in no way understand that what is brought through me
to blossom among us
is a flower that can speak, and is fairer far than the moonlight
Narcissus,
its stalk grows up towards space, giving its scent to time's future,
meteoric time dusts its stamens, its petal's root will not wither,
thinking back to the first cleaving evokes pain and impurity in
turn,
I carry within me the scales, dragon-crests, gills, fins, skin,
feathers, star-mists, seas, plants, fires, iron, lime, sand,
oh this, flowers in the moonlight trembling, you in no way
understand!
You do not fathom it, Iris and Rue, though you outlive me,
Rose and Hyacinth, Honeysuckle and Peony.

from CROWN OF HATRED AND LOVE

Frost covers the rose-trees; a few scraggy geese stand
with lead-laced wings trailing forlornly on the ground.
Octopus arms of plants wetly catch at bullfrogs.
Like dried-up jellyfish a few torn snowy rags;
long potato-stalks straggle out, limp and brown
like chicken's entrails that dried where they were thrown;
parsley alone stands out green, that frost stiffens
in porcelain feathers of color and silence.

The brown towers of burrs from hawthorn and thistle
are like tatters of mourning in a burned-out chapel,
like an empty wasps' nest's smoked-out architecture.
Thistles and saplings just out from the plastered wall,
and propped there, stick-limbs knotted, helm of mossy metal,
skeleton-membrane shirted, a locust's empty shell,
image of knight's armor in dusty mother-of-pearl.

One tree still stands leaning, lightning-stallion torn,
dreaming on, while a crow caws from its glass crown.
Down from the picket-fence some rusted wreath-wires hang,

POWER OF THE FLOWERS
viburnum: a shrub of the honeysuckle family, with white flowers.

and a broken bucket lies musing on a plank.
The lilacs are creatures guided by other stars.
Hollow-toothed white hen-coops stagger with doors ajar,
just one hen left scratching about in blue manure,
picking at the bones of the cock who had her.

Proud I was, too stupid to be good, a thickhead,
not once did I listen to what my father said,
I left this house behind, with no goodbyes from me.
Slowly, humility put out leaves within me!
My heart, with birds' whirrings once inoculated,
yearned to fly away, into infinity melted,
spending itself in shame, and untrue to its nest.
Now I can only weep, here in my grief wordless.

Where is he who stayed here, and would not renounce me?
In his hot coffin he's fermenting, mould-furry!
He who poured out new wine lazily, who suffered
on his pearl-crusted face my prickly bobbing head,
scolding me so I'd weep, gazing at the smoke-palms,
to whom I would recite 'The Death of György Dózsa'?
The carrion-larvaed star has drunk him up, while I
was lulled in the god's lap who always was to lie.

Where's my father now? Where? Where's my pride of those days?
I became a rainbow, and he maggoty clay.

VIOLET-EYED LITTLE SISTER

By my violet-eyed little sister
I sent home, saying I'd be coming,
that I'd do some work on the fences
and put the rose-bushes to bed.

CROWN OF HATRED AND LOVE

György Dózsa: a peasant captain in the Hungarian Peasants War; executed by nobles who seated him on a red-hot throne, crowned him with a red-hot iron crown, and thus burned him alive. His story is treated at length in a novel by József Eötvös (1813–71), *Hungary in 1514.*

I heard that my mother baked some cakes,
sieving flour for them from
the bottom of the sack, the drawer's corners,
and dusted off her floury apron.
She laid the table with a clean cloth,
warm goat's milk was in the mug,
my white shirt, spread out freshly ironed
shone waiting for me on the bed.
My father sliced tobacco leaves
for me to blow smoke-rings; he'd gathered up
a basketful of dry stalks and shavings
and lit a fire, so I wouldn't shiver:
white paper won't keep out the cold.
From early morning they stood at the gate,
shuffling their feet, coughing now and then,
looking up at the sky, then down the street,
they smiled at the boy herding the cattle,
they'd picked a bouquet of numb Michaelmas daisies.
As I didn't come, they stood there felled
by frost, only their sighs rustling;
the autumn wind was breaking loose
scattering thick rime down on their heads.

Translations by **Kenneth McRobbie** *and* **Ilona Duczynska**

SILVER

The traveller stands in the freezing cold
surrounded by drowsy old men.
His moustache is ice, his eyelashes
inhuman half-moons of silver.
He stands watching the horses,
the snow dusting under their hooves
like a cloud of millions of comets
misting the milky star-roads.
His ears are silver, his hair is silver.
The horses twitch their manes and tails.
Silver the velvet nostrils, the steaming flanks.

GOLD

The woman touches her bun
of thinning hair. She laughs,
and drops a spoon and a hunk of bread
in their reaching, grubby hands.
Like roses divining water
the circle of thin red necks
leans over the steaming plates;
red noses bloom in the savory mist.

The stars of their eyes shine
like ten worlds lost in their own light.
In the soup, slowly circling
swim golden onion rings.

THEN THERE ARE FISH

Forever confusing smoke with weeds,
clouds and sky with water.

Born with no lungs, just a blister
floating in a cage of splinters,
listless fins and hyperthyroid eyes.

Even the smallest fry
chase their hunger as boldly as carp—
mouths, nostrils, eyes
burst on a rising scream like a shoal of bubbles.

A world of nothing but water!

Houses and trees
float up like giant bubbles.

Translations by **David Wevill** *and* **Flora Papastavrou**

MIKLÓS RADNÓTI

1909–1944

Miklós Radnóti was born in Budapest; his mother died giving birth to him and his dead twin brother. He graduated from the University of Szeged, but had difficulty finding work because of his Jewish background. Radnóti spent part of 1937 in Paris. In 1940 he began serving time in various work camps as a miner, explosives expert, and forced laborer. After being taken to a concentration camp in Bor, Yugoslavia, in 1944, he was forced across the Hungarian border to Abda, where he and others were beaten to death and dumped into a mass grave. In 1946 his wife found his body; his last poems were still in his trenchcoat pocket. During his lifetime Radnóti not only translated Shelly, Cocteau, and La Fontaine, but also published six books of poems, including *Pagan Toast* (1930) and *Man Sentenced to Death, Keep Walking* (1936). Two collections appeared posthumously: *Clouded Sky* (1946) and *Collected Poems* (1948).

The poems of Miklós Radnóti are vivid, anguished, tender; their clarities are the clarities of the condemned man. Radnóti's images are at once exquisite and heart-rending, as when he tells us that the Allied bombers overhead have no instruments to detect the stone at his feet that he purposely tripped over as a child to keep from going to school. The poems are of peasants, workers, sufferers, and the dying, and his final postcards from the edges of his own death memorialize the uncountable victims of mass murders unable to speak for themselves.

RED SHORE

The road has grown silent, a crow
wobbles across it like a pregnant woman.
"Well crow, finally!" the road sighs,
and babbles about its grief.

In the ground, wounded seeds listen.
The battlescarred landscape's eyelashes flicker—
even though the evening rocks it more and more
gently now, it still hasn't forgotten.

A small mine hides in a small hole,
it glitters angrily, wants to explode,
but it's afraid. Cabbages stare
at it darkly and hold it down.

There at the foot of a young tree,
behind the sunflowers hanging their wise heads,
a steel-blue fog stretches across in straight lines—
thick barbed wire waiting for blood.

But at dawn, when dew weighs it down
(its stem is a delicate fuse),
carefully the golden blossom of
the squash creeps through the wire and opens.

And in time, silence drizzles again.
Sometimes a stork stands on top of a trench.
Florian plows over the approach trenches
that are rabbit holes now.

And the workers come back.
Weavers weave again.
They dream about fine thread
until the crystals of dawn wake them.

And women bend down again and again,
a new world grows at their feet.
Vain little girls in dresses red as poppies
and boys, like little butting goats, make noise.

And soaked in the bearded light of the stars,
the wise order of the world returns,
the order of animals and ears of corn,
the stern but still gentle service regulations.

January 17, 1941

GOATS

Veils are slipping across the clouds
that lose their color now.
In the grass it's growing dark.
The soft little bodies of
fattening goats still shine
and stand out in the dark.

One gray goat stands around.
The light on her hair goes out,

dreams go on in her eyes,
her big udder bulges
with the force of sun-ripened grass,
and she looks past the calm stable.

Dust hurls its foam
into the air again, and blood,
spilled at the edge of the sky, flares up.
Lecherously a buck bites off
flowers and, standing on its back legs,
laughs and laughs at the moon.

Another walks like a ghost.
He steps carefully through the short grass
and cries in a black wood voice.
His beard shakes, he scatters
bunches of small dark round things
all through the night.

Nagytelekmajor
November 12, 1942

I DON'T KNOW

I don't know what this land means to others, this little country
circled by fire, place of my birth,
world of my childhood, rocking in the distance.
I grew out of her like the fragile branch of a tree,
and I hope my body will sink down in her.
Here, I'm at home. When one by one, bushes kneel at my feet,
I know their names and the names of their flowers.
I know people who walk down the roads and where they're going,
and on a summer evening, I know the meaning of the pain
that turns red and trickles down the walls of houses.
This land is only a map for the pilot who flies over.
He doesn't know where the poet Vörösmarty lived.
For him factories and angry barracks hide on this map.

I DON'T KNOW

Vörösmarty: Mihály (1800–55), anti-classical and anti-Germanic Hungarian romantic poet who nationalized the spirit and language of Hungarian literature. 10,000 marched in the funeral procession to his grave.

For me there are grasshoppers, oxen, church steeples, gentle
farms.
Through binoculars, he sees factories and plowed fields,
I see the worker, shaking, afraid for his work.
I see forests, orchards filled with song, vineyards, graveyards,
and a little old woman who weeps and weeps quietly among the
graves.
The industrial plant and the railway must be destroyed.
But it's only a watchman's box and the man stands outside
sending messages with a red flag. There are children around him,
in the factory yard a sheep dog plays, rolling on the ground.
And there's the park and the footprints of lovers from the past.
Sometimes kisses tasted like honey, sometimes like blackberries.
I didn't want to take a test one day, so on my way to school
I tripped on a stone at the edge of the sidewalk.
Here is the stone, but from up there it can't be seen.
There's no instrument to show it all.

We're sinners, just like people everywhere,
we know what we did wrong, when and how and where.
But innocent workers and poets live here too.
Knowledge grows inside nursing babies
and it shines in there. Hiding in dark cellars, they guard it,
waiting for the day when the finger of peace will mark our land.
And their new words will answer our muffled ones.

Night cloud, you who stay awake, spread your great wings out
over us.

January 17, 1944

THE SEVENTH ECLOGUE

Do you see night, the wild oakwood fence lined with barbed wire,
and the barracks, so flimsy that the night swallowed them?
Slowly the eye passes the limits of captivity
and only the mind, the mind knows how tight the wire is.
You see, dear, this is how we set our imaginations free.
Dream, the beautiful savior, dissolves our broken bodies
and the prison camp leaves for home.

THE SEVENTH ECLOGUE
eclogue: a short, pastoral poem.

Ragged, bald, snoring, the prisoners fly
from the black heights of Serbia to the hidden lands of home.
Hidden lands of home! Are there still homes there?
Maybe the bombs didn't hit, and they *are*, just like when we were "drafted"?
Next to me, on my right, a man whines, another one lies on my left. Will they go home?
Tell me, is there still a home where they understand all this?

Without commas, one line touching the other,
I write poems the way I live, in darkness,
blind, crossing the paper like a worm.
Flashlights, books—the guards took everything.
There's no mail, only fog drifts over the barracks.

Frenchmen, Poles, loud Italians, heretic Serbs, and dreamy
Jews live here in the mountains, among frightening rumors.
One feverish body cut into many pieces but still living the same life,
it waits for good news, the sweet voices of women, a free, a human fate.
It waits for the end, the fall into thick darkness, miracles.

I lie on the plank, like a trapped animal, among worms. The fleas
attack again and again, but the flies have quieted down.
Look. It's evening, captivity is one day shorter.
And so is life. The camp sleeps. The moon shines
over the land and in its light the wires are tighter.
Through the window you can see the shadows of the armed guards
thrown on the wall, walking among the noises of the night.

The camp sleeps. Do you see it? Dreams fly.
Frightened, someone wakes up. He grunts, then turns in the tight space
and sleeps again. His face shines. I sit up awake.
The taste of a half-smoked cigarette in my mouth instead of the taste
of your kisses and the calmness of dreams doesn't come.
I can't die, I can't live without you now.

Lager Heidenau, in the mountains above Žagubica
July, 1944

POSTCARD

1

From Bulgaria the huge wild pulse of artillery.
It beats on the mountain ridge, then hesitates and falls.
Men, animals, wagons and thoughts. They are swelling.
The road whinnies and rears up. The sky gallops.
You are permanent within me in this chaos.
Somewhere deep in my mind you shine forever, without
moving, silent, like the angel awed by death,
or like the insect burying itself
in the rotted heart of a tree.

In the mountains

POSTCARD

2

Nine miles from here
the haystacks and houses burn,
and on the edges of the meadow
there are quiet frightened peasants, smoking.
The little shepherd girl seems
to step into the lake, the water ripples.
The ruffled sheepfold
bends to the clouds and drinks.

Cservenka
October 6, 1944

POSTCARD

3

Bloody drool hangs on the mouths of the oxen.
The men all piss red.
The company stands around in stinking wild knots.
Death blows overhead, disgusting.

Mohács
October 24, 1944

POSTCARD

4

I fell next to him. His body rolled over.
It was tight as a string before it snaps.
Shot in the back of the head—"This is how
you'll end. Just lie quietly," I said to myself.
Patience flowers into death now.
"Der springt noch auf," I heard above me.
Dark filthy blood was drying on my ear.

Szentkiralyszabadja
October 31, 1944

Translations by **Steven Polgar, Stephen Berg,** *and* **S. J. Marks**

"Der springt noch auf": He's getting up again.

INDONESIA

CHAIRIL ANWAR

1922–1949

Chairil Anwar was born of Moslem parents in Medan, on the east coast of Sumatra, one of the major islands of Indonesia. His family's poverty prevented him from continuing his formal education beyond the first two classes of secondary school. In 1940, when Anwar was eighteen, he moved with his mother to Djakarta, on the neighboring island of Java. None of his poems were published during the Japanese occupation, which began in 1942, because they were considered subversive by the censor, but when the Indonesian Republic was founded in 1945 Anwar became the model of young Indonesian writers, the "Generation of '45." Through the British and American information services in Djakarta he read western poetry, and on one occasion he quoted verse after verse of Emily Dickinson to a friend. When he was twenty-seven he entered a hospital suffering from syphilus, typhus, and tuberculosis. At his death he could read Dutch, German, English, French, and Spanish. No volume of poems appeared in his lifetime, but his *Selected Poems* was published in the United States in 1963.

The poems of Chairil Anwar are brash and unaffected. His staccato rhythms and broken images range across the waterfront, Indonesian folk traditions, and his own tormented soul. The upheavals of his life mirror the upheavals of Asia, his own anguish the anguish of Indonesia. Although he wrote no more than eighty poems, they have been a rallying point of contemporary Indonesian poetry since the Second World War.

FOR MRS. N.

That was too high a mountain, last year,
So she's climbing down where it's flat.
She got to the peak and didn't know it,
Strange birds were flitting around her head
And queer bits of forest rubbed their colors on her coat.

Along the way she remembers there was someone
All alone, up on the peak,

Wrapped in the wind and the world, and knowing more about
 death.
But the air stayed empty, she got to the top and didn't know it,
She won't risk that first road again,
From now on there'll be no strange birds, no odd patches of
 fragrant pine.
She's going right down. Lonely.
The great flat plain has no edges.

AT A MOUNTAIN RESORT

Pondering, pondering on you, dear. . . .

It's Sunday morning, here. The excitement
 of the pushing, crowded city, heaping problems
onto problems—whether spinning or spun—
seems to have quieted down; we're lying in bed, naked
We're out of words, now, we've said it all, before,
 in the darkness.
Because we're 6,000 feet up in the air, the crossing
 and crisscrossing of the harbor
looks like nothing at all compared to
the bright green fir trees, the bright green river

So, my love, my darling, I try to cling to your hand
to hug your unknown face, to find your reluctant lips.
You jump out of bed, run to the window that's
stuffed with fog, and there you see, between
the bright green fir trees and the bright green
 mountain stream
the old question still growing, blooming, the old,
 old question, the question.

TWILIGHT AT A LITTLE HARBOR

for Sri Ajati

This time no one's looking for love
between the sheds, the old houses, in the make-believe

AT A MOUNTAIN RESORT
Pondering . . . dear: in English in the original.

of poles and ropes. A boat, a *prau* without water
puffs and blows, thinking there's something it can catch.

The drizzle comes harder and darkens. There's an eagle flapping,
pushing sulkily off, and the day swimming silkily
to meet temptations yet to come. Nothing moves.
And now the sand and the sea are asleep, the waves are gone.

There's no one else. I'm alone. Walking,
combing the cape, still drowning the hope
of just once getting to the end of it and saying goodbye to
everything
from the fourth beach, where the last sob could be hugged tightly
to me.

Translations by **Burton Raffel** *and* **Nurdin Salam**

prau: a swift boat with a lateen sail and one outrigger.

IRELAND

PATRICK KAVANAGH

1905–1967

Patrick Kavanagh was born on a farm in County Monaghan, where he was raised. He was poor all his life and on many occasions almost starved in Dublin. Kavanagh said that he often "borrowed a 'shilling for the gas'" when in fact he "wanted the coin to buy a chop." *The Ploughman,* his first book of poems, appeared in 1938. His attitude toward autobiography and personal drama is best expressed in his own comment that in the summer of 1955 he sat on the bank of the Grand Canal and let the water lap idly on the shores of his mind. Kavanagh wrote two novels: *The Green Fool* (1938) was withdrawn after a libel suit, and *Tarry Flynn* (1949) was banned and then unbanned in Ireland. Books of poems include *The Great Hunger* (1942) and *Come Dance with Kitty Stobling* (1960).

Patrick Kavanagh observes that Homer made *The Iliad* out of "a local row," and he names the names in his own poems: Billy Brennan's barn, Slieve Donard, Islington Green, Ballyrush, Gortin, Gilpin's horse. Kavanagh is the humanist's iconoclast. He takes the big things of the world and shoves them under a microscope; one frame out of a million moving pictures of the moon will do. The ordinary is extraordinary, and when he walks the Inniskeen Road on a July evening he is "king of banks and stones and every blooming thing."

EPIC

I have lived in important places, times
When great events were decided, who owned
That half a rood of rock, a no-man's land
Surrounded by our pitchfork-armed claims.
I heard the Duffys shouting 'Damn your soul'
And old McCabe stripped to the waist, seen
Step the plot defying blue cast-steel—

rood: one-fourth of an acre.

'Here is the march along these iron stones'
That was the year of the Munich bother. Which
Was more important? I inclined
To lose my faith in Ballyrush and Gortin
Till Homer's ghost came whispering to my mind
He said: I made the Iliad from such
A local row. Gods make their own importance.

THE GOAT OF SLIEVE DONARD

I saw an old white goat on the slope of Slieve Donard,
Nibbling daintily at the herb leaves that grow in the crevasses,
And I thought of James Stephens—
He wrote of an old white goat within my remembering,
Seven years ago I read—
Now it comes back
Full of the dreaming black beautiful crags.
I shall drink of the white goat's milk,
The old white goat of Slieve Donard,
Slieve Donard where the herbs of wisdom grow,
The herbs of the Secret of Life that the old white goat has
 nibbled,
And I shall live longer than Methuselah,
Brother to no man.

EPIC

Ballyrush: the names of more than 1000 towns in Ireland begin with "Bally," which simply means "a place." There are several Ballyrushes.

Gortin: a village in county Tyrone, pop. 267. Lewis reports *(Topographical Dictionary of Ireland)* "there is a small distillery in the village, and fairs are held on the first Wednesday in every month, for cattle, sheep, and pigs, and a pleasure fair on Easter-Monday."

THE GOAT OF SLIEVE DONARD

Slieve Donard: (Gaelic) the mountain of Donard. A disciple of St. Patrick, Domhanghard (Donart), founded two churches, one near the base and one near the summit, and the mountain was named Donard in his memory.

James Stephens: Irish poet and novelist (1882–1950) who wrote *The Charwoman's Daughter* and *The Crock of Gold.*

A WREATH FOR TOM MOORE'S STATUE

The cowardice of Ireland is in his statue,
No poet's honored when they wreathe this stone,
An old shopkeeper who has dealt in the marrow-bone
Of his neighbors looks at you.
Dim-eyed, degenerate, he is admiring his god,
The bank-manager who pays his monthly confession,
The tedious narrative of a mediocrity's passion,
The shallow, safe sins that never become a flood
To sweep themselves away. From under
His coat-lapels the vermin creep as Joyce
Noted in passing on his exile's way.
In the wreathing of this stone now I wonder
If there is not somehow the worship of the lice
That crawl upon the seven-deadened clay.

They put a wreath upon the dead
For the dead will wear the cap of any racket,
The corpse will not put his elbows through his jacket
Or contradict the words some liar has said.
The corpse can be fitted out to deceive—
Fake thoughts, fake love, fake ideal,
And rogues can sell its guaranteed appeal,
Guaranteed to work and never come alive.
The poet would not stay poetical
And his humility was far from being pliable,
Voluptuary to-morrow, to-day ascetical,
His morning gentleness was the evening's rage.
But here we give you death, the old reliable
Whose white blood cannot blot the respectable page.

Tom Moore: Thomas Moore, Irish poet (1779–1852), best known for his *Irish Melodies*. He challenged a critic to a duel interrupted at the last minute by the police, befriended Byron in Italy, set some of his own songs to music and sang them at "great houses," was broken by the misconduct of his sons and the death of his last child, and left unfinished his projected *History of Ireland*.

KERR'S ASS

We borrowed the loan of Kerr's big ass
To go to Dundalk with butter,
Brought him home the evening before the market
An exile that night in Mucker.

We heeled up the cart before the door,
We took the harness inside—
The straw-stuffed straddle, the broken breeching
With bits of bull-wire tied;

The winkers that had no choke-band,
The collar and the reins . . .
In Ealing Broadway, London Town
I name their several names

Until a world comes to life—
Morning, the silent bog,
And the God of imagination waking
In a Mucker fog.

COME DANCE WITH KITTY STOBLING

No, no, no, I know I was not important as I moved
Through the colorful country, I was but a single
Item in the picture, the namer not the beloved.
O tedious man with whom no gods commingle.
Beauty, who has described beauty? Once upon a time
I had a myth that was a lie but it served:
Trees walking across the crests of hills and my rhyme
Cavorting on mile-high stilts and the unnerved
Crowds looking up with terror in their rational faces.
O dance with Kitty Stobling I outrageously
Cried out-of-sense to them, while their timorous paces
Stumbled behind Jove's page boy paging me.

KERR'S ASS

Dundalk: a town on the Castletown River near the Irish Sea.

Mucker: a town name that signifies an area frequented by swine for feeding. "Muc" is Irish for "pig."

I had a very pleasant journey, thank you sincerely
For giving me my madness back, or nearly.

TO A LATE POPLAR

Not yet half-drest
O tardy bride!
And the priest
And the bridegroom and the guests
Have been waiting a full hour.

The meadow choir
Is playing the wedding march
Two fields away,
And squirrels are already leaping in ecstasy
Among leaf-full branches.

INNISKEEN ROAD: JULY EVENING

The bicycles go by in twos and threes—
There's a dance in Billy Brennan's barn to-night,
And there's the half-talk code of mysteries
And the wink-and-elbow language of delight.
Half-past eight and there is not a spot
Upon a mile of road, no shadow thrown
That might turn out a man or woman, not
A footfall tapping secrecies of stone.

I have what every poet hates in spite
Of all the solemn talk of contemplation.
Oh, Alexander Selkirk knew the plight
Of being king and government and nation.
A road, a mile of kingdom, I am king
Of banks and stones and every blooming thing.

INNISKEEN ROAD: JULY EVENING

Inniskeen: village in SE county Monaghan on the Fane River, 7 miles west of Dundalk.

Alexander Selkirk: Scottish sailor (1676–1721), the prototype of Robinson Crusoe, was put off at Juan Fernandez Island, west of Valparaiso, where he spent four years and four months alone.

ISRAEL

YEHUDA AMICHAI

1924–

Yehuda Amichai was born in Wurzburg, Germany. When he was thirteen his family moved to Jerusalem, where he later attended Hebrew University. Amichai is a novelist and short story writer as well as a poet, and one of his radio scripts was awarded first prize in a national competition. He has won the Shlonsky Prize and two Acum Prizes for his poetry. In 1971 he taught at the University of California, Berkeley. He now earns his living in Israel as a teacher and is also a sergeant-major in the Israeli army. Books of poems include *Selected Poems* (1968, 1971) and *Jerusalem Songs* (1973).

Yehuda Amichai is a poet of the tired lament, informed by war, softened by fatherhood, embittered by compromisers in high places. The boy in him swings on the chandeliers over the negotiating tables; as a man he knows there are uncrossable enemy borders, and uncrossable borders in love. Old Testament images rise and fall in his poems like clock weights. Amichai is a poet of the new Israel: "Spilt blood isn't roots of trees, but it's the closest to them that man has."

MY MOTHER ONCE TOLD ME

My mother once told me
Not to sleep with flowers in the room.
Since then I have not slept with flowers.
I sleep alone, without them.

There were many flowers.
But I've never had enough time.
And persons I love are already pushing themselves
Away from my life, like boats
Away from the shore.

My mother said
Not to sleep with flowers.

You won't sleep.
You won't sleep, mother of my childhood.

The bannister I clung to
When they dragged me off to school
Is long since burnt.
But my hands, clinging,
Remain
Clinging.

KING SAUL AND I

1

They gave him a finger, but he took the whole hand
They gave me the whole hand: I didn't even take the
little finger.
While my heart
Was weightlifting its first feelings
He rehearsed the tearing of oxen.

My pulse-beats were like
Drips from a tap
His pulse-beats
Pounded like hammers on a new building.

He was my big brother
I got his used clothes.

2

His head, like a compass, will always bring him
To the sure north of his future.

His heart is set, like an alarm clock
For the hour of his reign.
When everyone's asleep, he will cry out
Until all the quarries are hoarse.
Nobody will stop him!
Only the asses bare their yellow teeth
At the end.

3

Dead prophets turned time-wheels
When he went out searching for asses
Which I, now, have found.
But I don't know how to handle them.
They kick me.

I was raised with the straw,
I fell with heavy seeds.
But he breathed the winds of his histories.
He was anointed with the royal oil
As with wrestler's grease.
He battled with olive-trees
Forcing them to kneel.

Roots bulged on the earth's forehead
With the strain.
The prophets escaped from the arena;
Only God remained, counting:
Seven . . . eight . . . nine . . . ten . . .
The people, from his shoulders downwards, rejoiced.
Not a man stood up.
He had won.

4

I am tired,
My bed is my kingdom.

My sleep is just
My dream is my verdict.

I hung my clothes on a chair
For tomorrow.

He hung his kingdom
In a frame of golden wrath
On the sky's wall.

My arms are short, like string too short
To tie a parcel.

His arms are like the chains in a harbor
For cargo to be carried across time.

He is a dead king.
I am a tired man.

Translations by **Assia Gutmann**

JEWS IN THE LAND OF ISRAEL

We forget where we came from. Our Jewish
Names from the exile reveal us,
Bring up the memory of flower and fruit, medieval cities,
Metals, knights that became stone, roses mostly,
Spices whose smells dispersed, precious stones, much red,
Trades gone from the world.
(The hands, gone too.)

The circumcision does it to us,
Like in the Bible story of Shechem and the sons of Jacob,
With pain all our life.

What are we doing here on our return with this pain.
The Longings dried up with the swampland,
The desert flowers for us and our children are lovely.
Even fragments of ships, that sunk on the way,
Reached this shore,
Even winds reached. Not all the sails.

What are we doing
In this dark land that casts
Yellow shadows, cutting at the eyes.
(Sometimes, one says even after forty
Years or fifty: 'The sun is killing me.')

JEWS IN THE LAND OF ISRAEL

Shechem and the sons of Jacob: see Genesis 34:1–31, where Jacob's daughter Dinah is violated by Shechem, who loves her and pleads with his father Hamor to secure Dinah as his wife. Jacob's sons Simeon and Levi exact a bargain from Hamor: in exchange for the circumcision of all the males in Hamor's city they will allow intermarriage between the two houses. On the third day of the circumcision, when all the men were "sore," Simeon and Levi slew all the males including Hamor and Shechem, and took their wives, children, and possessions.

What are we doing with souls of mist, with the names,
With forest eyes, with our lovely children, with swift blood?

Spilt blood isn't roots of trees,
But it's the closest to them
That man has.

Translated by **Harold Schimmel**

ABBA KOVNER

1918–

Abba Kovner was born in Sebastopol in the Crimea while his family was traveling to Palestine. Unable to proceed because of the outbreak of the First World War, they went north to Vilna, where he grew up and graduated from a Hebrew high school. Kovner joined the Zionist Socialist youth movement and worked with the partisans fighting the German occupation. He was caught in 1946 trying to reach Palestine, and imprisoned by the British in Cairo. After his release, Kovner joined the Kibbutz Ein Hahoresh, where he now lives with his wife and two children. During the 1948 war of independence he was an officer of the Givanti Brigade. Winner of the 1971 Israeli Prize for Literature, Kovner has published nine books of poetry, among them *My Little Sister* (1967), *Selected Poems* (1971), and *A Canopy in the Desert* (1973).

In the poems of Abba Kovner an archeologist arranges fragments in such a way that we can see the whole statue. What is undiscovered, what is left unsaid, is part of the body: stases are interstices. The images are personal, biblical, historical; the narrative is arterial but the single poems are bone chips. Poems of the Holocaust, of The War, the wars: sunstruck, chiseled, refractive. *A Canopy in the Desert,* from which the following poems are taken, describes the Israeli army marching and bivouacking across the desert.

AND BELOW US IT FLOWS. SLOWLY.

Forget that anything else exists. Now in the white plain
it twists
around the birds' swaying hill. Tomorrow
it will sweep the hill away

wild in its rocks it spreads its folds and stretches
in a frozen slope, wanders,
closes a circle, returns and makes
a bank
a new wave

like the pages of a long debate

continuing

FROM ANOTHER HOMELAND

And a frozen shriek
like an ice stroke suddenly a spread of wings
pours shadow
falls on sand and pure stone
—a buzzard
a raven from another homeland
someone celebrating at a high altitude.
Close
as a light returned from a lonely island
a single tooth flickers—
maybe the man carved his mother's name
in the sand with a gold tooth
before he collapsed

I HEAR WINGS FLAPPING ON THE SAND

Wings flapping. Endlessly.
The world's a glass door. I see. Picking berries.
Dido lifts his legs over the barbed wire. In his hands
a dark berry. Like the blood of the ram. Dido lowers his legs
from a roof beam. Backward. Dido's crooked legs explore
blind
the wooden ladder. Broken. Its rungs—milk teeth missing in the
center—
it leans against a huge dovecot painted green. Pigeons in the yard
are greenish almost black on their necks and bellies. They must
be
thirsty. He says.

At noon Dido eats in less than a minute. Right away wanders
between the tables. He drags a tin pan banging with his left hand
upsetting time in the dining room. Big Calypso has to
eat well. He smiles.

Calypso's a small soft puppy a kind of damp velvet
pillow and one of us. Calypso will grow up
fast. He'll be the finest dog in the place. Dido says. And Dido
will be a vet. Maybe. A watchman in the fields. One of these
days.

Meanwhile the teachers complain. His feet are muddy. His hair
uncombed. How can you be such a mess
son!

SIXTH GATE:

A SANDSTORM HITS A NEW MOON'S FACE

We went far. The whites of my eyes blink from rock
to rock like a dream of stone.
How the view opens up at me! The wax earth
continues past the sky. Not to go blind. To keep the pupils
spread wide as windows
to see that in it
only in it
something is created in its image and likeness.

A storm plows over Jebel Libni. In the Valley of Nakhl
a wall of white
sand

SIXTH GATE: A SANDSTORM HITS A NEW MOON'S FACE
Jebel Libni: a mountain north of Mitla in the Sinai Peninsula.
Nakhl: a village in Egypt, WNW of Aqaba.

THE EVENING BEFORE

My shoes in the Jiddi Pass

GETTING LATE

The man
is silent. Like one split by the blow of an axe he stands in two
till his lips came together to join
words never separated

go

forth

the desert is yours and the world inside the desert and the desert
inside the world . . . and his murmur blurs.
As sand wilts the edge of a blue balloon
through its thin skin the sea appears
as a violet sea, and he is gone.

Translations by **Shirley Kaufman**

THE EVENING BEFORE
Jiddi Pass: north of the Mitla Pass in the Sinai Peninsula; Brigadier General Yaffi's division broke through to the Suez Canal over the Jiddi Pass in the 1967 War.

ITALY

EUGENIO MONTALE

1896–

Eugenio Montale was born in Genoa. As a young man he studied literature and *bel canto* and served as an infantry officer in the First World War. In 1925 he published his first book of poems, *Bones of the Cuttlefish,* and in 1927 he became curator of the Vieusseux library in Florence, a post he held until he was removed because he refused to join the Fascist Party (1938). Montale stayed in Florence through the Second World War; since 1948 he has lived in Milan, where he has written literary and musical criticism for the periodical *Il Corriere della sera.* He is a skilled translator of Shakespeare's sonnets, Eliot, Hopkins, Dickinson, and Melville. Other books include *Occasions* (1939), *The Storm and Other Things* (1956), and *Selected Poems* (1965). Montale was awarded the Nobel Prize for Literature in 1975.

In the poems of Eugenio Montale ideas and images simplify into human gestures, and the reader is, as Montale says he himself is, stock-still on the edge of understanding. A quiet percipience informs the poet's voice, as nature complements the human moment. In a poem not included below, white mayflies whirl "crazily" when Hitler and Mussulini arrive in Florence. Montale brings news of vigils, posted boundaries, colors in the mist.

BOATS ON THE MARNE

The bliss of cork yielding
to the current
that stipples around the overturned bridges
                Here . . . is the enduring color
of the rat that jumped
through the rushes or the starling's spurt of
poison-green metal vanishing
in the mists on shore
                        Another day done,

you repeat—or what were you saying? And where
does this outlet lead swarming in a single gush?
Evening is like
this. Now we can drift downstream
till the Great Bear kindles.

(Boats on the Marne in Sunday races,
your birthday.)

Translated by **Sonia Raiziss** *and* **Alfredo de Palchi**

NEWS FROM AMIATA

The fireworks of threatening weather
might be murmur of hives at duskfall.
The room has pockmarked beams
and an odor of melons
seeps from the store-room. Soft mists
that climb from a valley
of elves and mushrooms to the diaphanous cone
of the crest cloud over my windows
and I write you from here, from this table,
remote, from the honey cell
of a sphere launched into space—
and the covered cages, the hearth
where chestnuts are bursting, the veins
of saltpetre and mould, are the frame
where soon you will break through.
Life that enfables you is still too brief
if it contains you. The luminous ground
unfolds your icon. Outside it rains.
. . .

Could you but see the fragile buildings
blackened by time and smoke,
the square courtyards with their deep wells

BOATS ON THE MARNE
Marne: a department of old Champagne province in northern France; most of it was a battlefield in World War I.

NEWS FROM AMIATA
Amiata: an extinct volcano in the Apennines, Tuscany.

at center; and could you see
the laden flight of the night birds
and, beyond the ravine, the twinkling
of the Galaxy that soothes all wounds!
But the step that echoes long in the dark
is of one who goes alone and who sees only
this fall of shadows, of arches and of folds.
The stars sew with too fine a thread,
the eye of the tower stopped at two,
even the climbing vines are an ascent of shadows,
and their perfume bitter hurt.
Return tomorrow, colder, wind from the north,
shatter the old hands of the sandstone,
overturn the books of hours in the sunrooms,
and let all be pendulum calm, dominion, prison of sense
which does not know despair! Return still stronger
wind from the north, wind that endears
our chains and seals the spores of the possible!
The paths are too narrow, the hooves of the black donkeys
clicking in file raise sparks,
from the hidden peak magnesium flares reply.
O the slow drip of rain from the dark shacks,
time turned to water,
the long colloquy with the poor dead, the ashes, the wind,
late-coming wind, and death, and death that lives!

. . .

This christian fracas which has no speech
other than shadows or laments,
what does it give you of me? Less
than was snatched from you by the tunnel
plunging gently into its casing of stone.
A mill-wheel, an old tree-trunk,
last boundaries of the world. A heap
of chaff blows off; and, venturing late,
to join my vigil to your deep sleep
that welcomes them, the porcupines
will sip at a thin stream of pity.

Translated by **Irma Brandeis**

IRIS

When suddenly St. Martin's summer topples
its embers and shakes them down low in
Ontario's dark hearth—
snapping of green pine cones in the cinders
or the fumes of steeped poppies
and the bloody Face on the shroud
that separates me from you:
                    this and little else (if very
little is in fact your sign, a nod, in the struggle
goading me into the charnel house, my back
to the wall, where the sapphires of heaven
and palm leaves and one-legged storks don't shut out
the brutal sight from the wretched
strayed Nestorian);
                this is how much of you gets here
from the wreck of my people, and yours,
now that the fires of frost remind me of your
land which you've not seen; and I have
no other rosary to finger, no other flame
has assailed you, if it's not this,
of berries and resin.

The hearts of others are nothing like yours,
the lynx not like the striped tabby, beautiful,
alert for the hummingbird above the laurel;
but do you believe them the same breed, when you
venture outside the sycamore's shade
or maybe that mask on the white cloth
has guided you, that image in crimson?

Iris: feminine name from Greek, meaning rainbow; also the flower. In paintings the iris is often used as the symbol of Christ, the Virgin Mary, or the Immaculate Conception.

St. Martin's summer: Indian summer.

Ontario: a province of SE Canada.

Nestorian: adherent of Nestorius, patriarch of Constantinople who was condemned as a heretic by the Council of Ephesus in 431; believed that Jesus was harmoniously divine and human in his actions but not in his person.

So that your work (a form born of
His) might bloom under new suns
Iris of Canaan, you were gone
in that nimbus of mistletoe and thornbush
ushering your heart through the world's
nighttime, past the mirage
of desert flowers, your first kin.

If you turn up, here's where you'd bring me, the arbor
of stripped vines, next to our river's
pier—and the ferry does not come back again,
St. Martin's sun is blacked out.
But it won't be you, should you return, your earthly
story is changed, you don't wait for
the prow at the crossing,

you have eyes for nothing, and no
yesterdays or tomorrows;
because His work (which translates
into yours) *must be kept going*.

THE STORM

Les princes n'ont point d'yeux pour voir ces grands merveilles,
Leurs mains ne servent plus qu'à nous persécuter . . .
Agrippa D'Aubigné: "A Dieu"

The storm that pelts the tough leaves
of the magnolia with long
March thunders, with hailstones,

(crystal sounds in your nighttime
nest startle you; what's left of the gold

IRIS

Canaan: biblical, the land of milk and honey.

nimbus: a mist or atmosphere, sometimes associated with the rainbow-like radiance surrounding the heads of gods or goddesses or saints in paintings.

THE STORM

"*Les princes n'ont point d'yeux . . .*": Princes have no eyes to see these great marvels; their hands serve only to persecute us."

Agrippa D'Aubigné: (1552–1630), poet and firsthand chronicler of the French court of his time.

doused on the mahogany, on the tooling
of bound books, still burns
a grain of sugar in the shell
of your eyelids)

the lightning blaze that candies
trees and walls surprising them in this
forever of an instant—marble, manna
and destruction—which you bear carved
inside you, your condemnation, and lashes
you to me, strange sister, more than love—
and then the rough crash, rattles, thrill of
timbrels over the hidden pit,
the stamp of the fandango, and beyond it
some groping gesture . . .

The way it was when
you turned, your forehead brushed
of a cloud of hair,

and waved to me—and stepped into darkness.

Translations by **Sonia Raiziss** *and* **Alfredo de Palchi**

CESARE PAVESE

1908–1950

Cesare Pavese was born at Santo Stefano Belbo, a small village in the Piedmontese foothills. He went to school at the classical *liceo* in Turin, where he wrote his thesis on Walt Whitman. His first literary publication was a translation of *Moby Dick* (1932). In 1935 Pavese was arrested by the fascists and confined in a small Calabrian village where he wrote his first book of poetry, *Hard Labor.* During the forties he joined the Communist Party, helped to found Einaudi publishers, and was awarded the Premio Strega (1949) for his novels. Pavese also did brilliant translations of Joyce, Anderson, Steinbeck, Dos Passos, Stein, and Faulkner. He committed

manna: divinely supplied spiritual nourishment.
timbrels: small hand drums or tambourines.
fandango: a lively Spanish or Spanish-American dance performed by a man and a woman with castanets and in triple measure.

suicide in a Turin hotel room. *Poems Published and Unpublished* appeared in 1962.

The poems of Cesare Pavese seem effortless in their simplicity and clarity. Rural village scenes feature a cast of characters with simultaneously narrow and revealing points of view: weary, innocent, embittered. Pavese's style is casually abrupt; small echoes of repetition give the effect of someone watching, thinking. In moments of stillness, while things are ripening, something human happens.

INSTINCT

The old man, disappointed in everything,
stands in the doorway of a house in the warm sun,
watching dog and bitch satisfy their instinct.

The flies keep settling on his toothless gums.
His woman died some time ago. Like all bitches,
she didn't want to know anything about it,
but she had it, the instinct. The old man had a nose for it—
he still had his teeth then—and when it was night,
they went to bed. It was fine, instinct.

What's good about dogs is their great freedom.
From morning till night they roam the street,
sometimes eating, sleeping sometimes, sometimes mounting
the bitches.
The dog doesn't even wait for night. He thinks
the way he smells, and everything he smells is his.

The old man remembers how once, in full daylight,
he did it in a wheatfield, just like a dog.
Who the bitch was, he can't remember; he remembers the hot
sun
and the sweat, and wanting to keep on going forever.
It was like in bed. If only he were young again,
he would like to do it in a wheatfield, always.

A woman comes down the street and stops to watch;
the priest passes and he turns away. On the public square
anything can happen. Even the woman,

who modestly avoids the gaze of the man, stops.
Only a boy cannot bear the play of instinct
and starts throwing stones. The old man is indignant.

GRAPPA IN SEPTEMBER

The mornings run their course, clear and deserted
along the river's banks, which at dawn turn foggy,
darkening their green, while they wait for the sun.
In the last house, still damp, at the field's edge,
they sell tobacco, which is blackish in color
and tastes of sugar: it gives off a bluish haze.
They also have grappa there, the color of water.

There comes a moment when everything is still
and ripens. The trees in the distance are quiet
and their darkness deepens, concealing fruit so ripe
it would drop at a touch. The occasional clouds
are swollen and ripe. Far away, in city streets,
every house is mellowing in the mild air.

This early, you see only women. The women don't smoke,
or drink. All they know is standing in the sun,
letting it warm their bodies, as though they were fruit.
The air, raw with fog, has to be swallowed in sips,
like grappa. Everything here distills its own fragrance.
Even the water in the river has absorbed the banks,
steeping them to their depths in the soft air. The streets
are like the women. They ripen by standing still.

This is the time when every man should stand
still in the street and see how everything ripens.
There is even a breeze, which does not move the clouds
but somehow succeeds in maneuvering the bluish haze
without scattering it. The smell drifting by is a new smell.
The tobacco is tinged with grappa. So it seems
the women are not alone in enjoying the morning.

GRAPPA IN SEPTEMBER
grappa: an almost pure-alcohol spirit distilled from brandy.

SIMPLICITY

The man alone—the former prisoner—goes back to prison
every time he bites into a piece of bread.
In prison he had dreams of the hares bounding across
the plowed winter fields. In the winter fog
the man lives walled in among streets, drinking
his cold water, and biting into his crust of bread.

Someday, you think, your life will begin all over,
that you will breathe in peace, and winter will be back,
bringing the fragrance of wine in the warm tavern,
a blazing fire, a booth, and meals. That's what you think
while you're still inside. Then one night you leave
to find that your hares have been caught, and people are eating
them
steaming hot. You have to stand watching through the window.

The man alone is dying of cold, and musters the strength
to go in and buy a glass of wine. He meditates his wine,
the cloudy color of the wine, its musty smell.
He bites into a piece of bread, which in prison
tasted of wild hares. But now it has no taste of bread
or anything at all. Even the wine tastes only of fog.

The man alone thinks of the fields he dreamed of, content
to know that the plowing is done. In the deserted room
he tries singing, softly. And he sees once more,
along the river's edge, the clumps of naked brambles
which were green in August. He whistles to his bitch,
a hare is suddenly started, and the chill is gone.

FATHERHOOD

A man alone facing the useless sea,
waiting for evening to come, waiting for morning.
There are children playing there, but this man would like
to have a child of his own and watch him playing.
Over the water great clouds build a castle,
which every day is wrecked and remade, coloring
the children's faces. There will always be the sea.

The morning strikes. Over this soggy beach slides
the sun, sticking to nets and stones.
The man steps out into the murky light and walks
along the sea. He does not look at the curving froth
which climbs up the shore and is never at rest.
This is the time when children are still asleep, dozing
in their warm beds. This is the time when a woman lies
dozing in her bed. She would make love
if she were not alone. Slowly, the man strips
naked as the woman in her bed and walks into the sea.

Then the night. The sea disappears and there is only
the sound of emptiness under the stars. Children
in the reddened houses are dropping asleep,
and someone is crying. Tired of waiting, the man
lifts his eyes to the stars, which hear nothing.
This is the time when women are undressing children
and putting them to bed. There is a woman in a bed,
embracing a man. From the black window
comes a hoarse gasping, which nobody hears except
the man who knows by heart all the boredom of the sea.

ATAVISM

Hidden behind the shutters, watching the street,
the boy breathes more easily. Through the bright
chink, he can see the cobbles in the sun. Nobody
in the street. The boy would like to go outside stark
naked—who owns the street?—and soak up the sun.

In the city you can't. You could in the country,
if it weren't for the huge sky overhead, which is scary
and makes you feel small. The grass is cold
and tickles your feet, but the plants just
stare, and the trees and shrubs look so sternly
at your white, skinny body that it makes you shiver.
Even the grass feels funny and shrinks from your touch.

ATAVISM
atavism: resemblance to a remote ancestor.

But the street is empty. If someone went by,
the boy would stare boldly out of the darkness
and think to himself that everyone has a body.
But a horse with rippling muscles goes plodding by,
making the cobbles clatter. It seemed forever—
the horse moving naked and shameless in the sun
right down the middle of the street. A boy
who wanted to be brown and strong as a horse
and even pull a wagon, wouldn't be afraid of being seen.

People with bodies shouldn't hide them. But the boy
isn't sure that everyone has a body. The grizzled
old man who went by that morning is too pale and pitiful
to have a body, to have anything as scary
as a body. And not even grown-ups are naked;
not even mothers who give their breasts to their babies
are really bare. Only boys have bodies.
The boy is afraid to look at himself in the dark,
but he knows for a fact his body must soak up the sun
and get used to the sky, before he can be a man.

Translations by **William Arrowsmith**

GIUSEPPE UNGARETTI

1888–1970

Giuseppe Ungaretti was born in Alexandria, Egypt. His parents, who ran a bakery, were Tuscan. Ungaretti spent much of his youth in Paris, where he studied at the Collège de France and at the Sorbonne. After Italy entered the war in 1915 he served as an infantryman in Italy and France, and wrote his first book of poems in the trenches (*The Buried Port,* 1916). In 1939 his nine-year-old son Antonietto died. Ungaretti was an editor and also a translator of Shakespeare, Blake, Góngora, Mallarmé, and Racine, and became a professor of Italian literature at the universities of São Paulo (Brazil) and Rome. In 1970 he was awarded the first *Books Abroad* International Prize for Literature. Other books of poems include *Sentiments of Time* (1936), *Sorrow* (1947), *A Cry and Landscapes* (1952), and *Life of a Man* (1957).

The poems of Giuseppe Ungaretti come back again and again to the specific details that humanize the conceptual; children's hands in the nests of lapwings tell us it is spring. Quietly dramatic, philosophical, the poems cut through rhetoric to the simplest words and phrases. Nature reveals mankind's poignancies and sadnesses (in a poem not included below Ungaretti says that soldiers remain, like the leaves in autumn). Everything is melody and precision. The decibel-level rarely rises above a whisper.

BITTER CHIMING

Or else on an October afternoon
From the harmonious hills
Amongst thick lowering clouds
The horses of the Heavenly Twins,
At whose hoofs a boy
Had paused enchanted,
Over storm-water launched

(By a bitter chiming of memories
Towards shadows of banana trees
And of giant turtles
Lumbering between masses
Of vast impassive waters:
Under a different order of stars
Among unfamiliar seagulls)

Their flight to the level place where the boy
Rummaging in the sand—
The transparency of his beloved fingers
Wet with driven rain
Turned to flame by splendor of the lightning—
Clutched all four elements.

But death is colorless and without senses
And ignorant of any law, as ever,
Already grazed him
With its shameless teeth.

Translated by **Patrick Creagh**

the Heavenly Twins: in Greek and Roman mythology, Castor and Pollux, also known as the Dioscuri, twin sons of Leda, and according to one tradition, Zeus. During storms, they appeared in the shape of St. Elmo's fire, a glowing electrical discharge at the top of masts, taken by sailors as a friendly sign.

SENSELESS MY STEPS

I pass the usual streets—
senseless my steps
like an automaton's;
they used to move with me in step,
as if possessed.
They no longer know how to open with the large graciousness of time,
they will not unveil the trivial signs that gave them eyes to sum us up,
as they bowed and jumped to each whim.

And when the windows flamed with sunset,
(the houses are joyless now)
I might pause out of habit,
and search through the tactful shadows of withdrawn rooms,
as if I wanted this sop for disillusion.

I do this,
but nothing helps me.
However tender the voice,
not one of the scattered, pressing objects
that have grown old with me,
or were wrapped in some residue of images from something that happened—
none of these can unexpectantly return.
Give me your hand and rescue the word in my heart.

Thus the outstretched hand learned,
though the eye of the flesh was drowned in tears,
and the ear absurd.
I've learned what shaky expectation
drove Michelangelo, he too outstretched to the wall.
In every space, the lightning flash,
one not even allowing the soul
its chance to flash.

With his abandoned shudder,
he gave wings to a city.
The inescapable sky is imprisoned in his feverish, surviving dome.

Translated by **Robert Lowell**

A DOVE

I hear a dove from other floods

Translated by **Andrew Wylie**

FLIGHT

Amsterdam, March 1933

Flocks of lapwing flying over
The dunes and night, like polished glass
Breaking into reflections of metal
Lightning, green, blue, purple.
Having wintered in Sardinia, the lapwings
Paused here, the other day.
I hear them, passing, unseen,
Searching for a stray worm,
And since it is already dark, they shriek, not to get lost.
Return to your nests, tomorrow at dawn
You will find them empty,
and the first dozen little eggs,
Dug out by urchins ("Hush . . . Slow . . .")
Will be carried by bicycle to Wilhelmina,
It is spring.

Translated by **D. M. Pettinella**

JAPAN

TATSUJI MIYOSHI

1900–1964

Tatsuji Miyoshi was born in Osaka. He trained in a military school to be an officer, earned a degree in French literature from Tokyo University (1928), and became an instructor at Meiji University. As a young man he composed haiku but became interested in contemporary poetry and published his first book, *A Survey Ship,* in 1930. He was awarded the Art Academy Prize for *Riding on the Humped Back of a Camel,* has written criticism and essays, and has translated Zola, Baudelaire, James, and Gide. His twelve books of poems include *Flower Basket* (1944) and *Headland in Spring* (1949).

Tatsuji Miyoshi draws pastels with clear, hard edges that suddenly shift. The poems say, look over here for a moment, you haven't seen this before. Images loom and vanish in an atmosphere of quick precision. Landscapes expand our perceptions of the nearby and the far away: in a twenty-five line poem about a volcanic crater, twenty-two lines focus on horses eating in the rain.

SOUVENIR OF WINTER

Let us sit down
on the young grass
as it is spring,
a souvenir of winter.

The pine trees
dance on the sand
for the sand is
a souvenir of the sea.

This is a cove
behind a peninsula
where endless time
comes and moors.

Two sails,
souvenirs of the wind,

loosen their halyards
and they fade.

This talk
of us two—
it is also
one of these.

SPRING

Geese—as there are so many together, they honk lest they should lose themselves.

A lizard—whichever stone I climb up, still my belly is cold.

THE GROUND

Ants
are dragging a wing of a butterfly—
See!
it is like a yacht.

A BOOK

A butterfly, a white book.
A butterfly, a light book.
It dances up a dune
stitching the horizon.

THE SNOW

Putting *Taro* to sleep, the snow lies on *Taro's* roof.
Putting *Jiro* to sleep, the snow lies on *Jiro's* roof.

Translations by **Ichiro Kono** *and* **Rikutaro Fukada**

THE SNOW
Taro, Jiro: common names of Japanese boys.

GOLDEN VENUS

In a sealike evening sky
a golden honeybee makes wing sounds
like buzzing ears. . . .

On the other side of the valley
by the mountain opposite,
poised on top of the thin forest—Venus.

Presently that woman is hidden by a ridge.
I climb up onto a rock.
For a while she is visible.

Presently that woman is hidden by a ridge.
I get up onto a hilltop.
For a while she is visible.

That woman vanishes. That woman goes down.
That woman goes down. She goes away.
Earth is warped. . . . The mountain tilts. . . .

THE DEER

In the morning in a forest a deer is crouching.
Upon his shoulders, the shadow of his horns.
A single deerfly cuts across the space of the breeze and hovers
close to his ears as they listen to a far-off river valley.

GREAT ASO

Horses are standing in rain.
A herd of horses with one or two foals is standing in rain.
In hushed silence rain is falling.
The horses are eating grass.

GREAT ASO
Aso: Aso-san, a volcanic crater in central Kyushu, Japan.

With tails, and backs too, and manes too, completely soaking wet
they are eating grass,
eating grass.
Some of them are standing with necks bowed over absentmindedly
and not eating grass.
Rain is falling and falling in hushed silence.
The mountain is sending up smoke.
The peak of Nakadake is sending up dimly yellowish and heavily
    oppressive volcanic smoke, densely, densely.
And rain clouds too all over the sky.
Still they continue without ending.
Horses are eating grass.
On one of the hills of the Thousand-Mile-Shore-of-Grass
they are absorbedly eating blue-green grass.
Eating.
They are all standing there quietly.
They are quietly gathered in one place forever, dripping and
    soaked with rain.
If a hundred years go by in this single moment, there would be
    no wonder.
Rain is falling. Rain is falling.
In hushed silence rain is falling.

Translations by **Edith Shiffert** *and* **Yuki Sawa**

SHIRO MURANO

1901–

Shiro Murano was born in Tokyo. He began writing haiku while still in junior high school, and later studied German poetry at Keio University, where he graduated with a degree from the Finance Department. Murano published a collection of his own poems, *Trap,* in 1926. He has written a volume of criticism, *Today's Poets,* in addition to ten books of poems, including *Gymnastics* (1937), *A Coral Whip* (1944), *Abstract Castle* (1954) and *A Strayed Sheep,* which won the Yomiuri Award in 1960.

The poems of Shiro Murano are associative, imagistic, visual. Surfaces tremble the way mist rises from a pond. The diver is real, but the water is incidental, and when unexpected images cross over from one reality to another the result is both transformative in effect and matter-of-fact in tone. In Murano's poems the blinders of worldly expectation fall away, and the everyday world emerges—clearer, and more to the point.

AN AUTUMN DOG

As the dark bush of summer peach
is eaten by worms, the sky is peeled
from behind it.

On the streets
cosmoses are in bloom like love
but no one passes by
whom I know.
Among the piled-up stones of a roadside
I squat like a dog,
and on my glass eyeballs
the space blue as bell-flowers is reflected.

Yet I do know
that eternity is nowhere
after all,
that it only exists in me,
together with roundworms.

Something soft
passes by my ear
but I do not trouble myself to turn round—
as I know through numberless misfortunes
that there has been no master for me
from the very beginning.

I am hanging a hot tongue.

DIVING

The dress of clouds opens like a flower.
The reflection of water
prints the stripes on your bare body.
You jump off at last
with the wings of muscles.

O, a little sunburnt bee!
You fall down toward the flower
and dive in it as if to stab.
Soon, from behind a petal of the flower
you come out
drenched through and through
with sweetness.

Translations by **Ichiro Kono** *and* **Rikutaro Fukada**

HORSE ON A CITY STREET

Horse!
Big naked primitive
with blue organs inside!
He often
slipped on the polished artificial marble.
With teeth exposed, he looked back, but
nobody was there.

Poor raw-smelling spirit
that strayed into a peculiar country!
Here
is a transparent hell
where everything evaporates.
First death too,
second death too,
and even the myth.

The horse
recognized a mystic sign
at a strange city corner—
his race's eternal transmigration,
that intense red Pegasus.

Translated by **Edith Shiffert** *and* **Yuki Sawa**

HORSE ON A CITY STREET

Pegasus: in Greek mythology, the winged horse that sprang from Medusa (with whom Poseidon had had intercourse in the form of a horse or a bird) when Perseus struck off her head. Mobil Oil Corporation uses the red Pegasus as a symbol in Japan.

POLE VAULT

He is running like a wasp,
Hanging on a long pole.
As a matter of course he floats in the sky,
Chasing the ascending horizon.
Now he has crossed the limit,
And pushed away his support.
For him there is nothing but a descent.
Oh, he falls helplessly.
Now on that runner, awkwardly fallen on the ground,
Once more
The horizon comes down,
Beating hard on his shoulders.

Translated by **Constance Urdang** *and* **Satoru Sato**

SHINKICHI TAKAHASHI

1901–

Shinkichi Takahashi was born on Shikoku Island, where he attended Yawatahama Middle School. In his teens he went to Tokyo to become a writer, and after several years of poverty, sickness, and work as a waiter and pantry boy he introduced dada poetry to Japan with his first book, *Poems of Dadaist Shinkichi* (1923). In 1928 Takahashi entered a Zen temple where he suffered a nervous breakdown, and was thereafter confined by his family for three years in his bedroom. He wrote poems reflecting the spirit of Zen, and in 1932 returned to Tokyo to attend Zen lectures; in 1935 he began seventeen years of intense training under a Zen master. Takahashi has made his living since then from his writings. He married in 1951. In addition to four books on Zen and a novel, he has published fourteen collections of poems, including *Solar Eclipse* (1934), *Father and Mother* (1934), *The Body* (1956) and *Sparrow* (1966).

The poems of Shinkichi Takahashi are concrete, disciplined, Buddhistic: things apparently moving are standing dead-still within the heart of time. His images move together and apart like seeming coordinates in our memory-banks. In these poems the rituals of daily life form bridges into the world of reflections, space can be reduced to a handful of air, images print the open mind.

FISH

I hold a newspaper, reading.
Suddenly my hands become cow ears,
Then turn into Pusan, the South Korean port.

Lying on a mat
Spread on the bankside stones,
I fell asleep.
But a willow leaf, breeze-stirred,
Brushed my ear.
I remained just as I was,
Near the murmurous water.

When young there was a girl
Who became a fish for me.
Whenever I wanted fish
Broiled in salt, I'd summon her.
She'd get down on her stomach
To be sun-cooked on the stones.
And she was always ready!

Alas, she no longer comes to me.
An old benighted drake,
I hobble homeward.
But look, my drake feet become horse hoofs!
Now they drop off
And, stretching marvellously,
Become the tracks of the Tokaido Railway Line.

STITCHES

My wife is always knitting, knitting:
Not that I watch her,
Not that I know what she thinks.

(Awake till dawn
I drowned in your eyes—
I must be dead:
Perhaps it's the mind that stirs.)

With that bamboo needle
She knits all space, piece by piece,
Hastily hauling time in.

Brass-cold, exhausted,
She drops into bed and,
Breathing calmly, falls asleep.

Her dream must be deepening,
Her knitting coming loose.

RAT ON MOUNT ISHIZUCHI

Snow glitters on the divine rocks
At the foot of Mount Ishizuchi.
Casting its shadow on the mountain top,
A rat flies off.

At the back of the sun,
Where rats pound rice into cakes,
There's a cavity like a mortar pit.

A flyer faster than an airplane,
That's the sparrow.
Mount Ishizuchi, too, flies at a devilish speed,
Ten billion miles a second,
From everlasting to everlasting.

Yet, because there's no time,
And always the same dusk,
It doesn't fly at all:
The peak of Mount Ishizuchi
Has straightened the spine
Of the Island of Futana.

RAT ON MOUNT ISHIZUCHI

Mount Ishizuchi: the highest peak (6,497 ft.) of Shikoku, one of the principal islands of Japan.

Futana: an island eight miles long in the Wallis and Futana Islands protectorate, SW Pacific, which rises to 2,500 feet.

Because there's no space
The airplane doesn't move an inch:
The sun, the plane boarded by the rat,
Are afloat in the sparrow's dream.

AFTERIMAGES

The volcanic smoke of Mount Aso
Drifted across the sea, white ash
Clinging to mulberry leaves
And crowning the heads of sparrows.

An open-mouthed lava crocodile;
A sparrow like a fossil sprig,
The moon filling its eyes;
A colossal water lizard stuck to a dead tree,
Its headland tail quaking.

A cloud floats in my head—beautiful!
When the sparrow opens its eyes,
Nothing but rosy space. All else gone.

Don't tell me that tree was red—
The only thing that moved, ever closer,
Was a girl's nose. All mere afterimages.

Water, coldness itself, flows underfoot.

The sparrow, eyes half closed, lay in an urn
In the pit. Now it fans up. The earth's
Fiery column is nearly extinguished.

Translations by **Lucien Stryk** *and* **Takashi Ikemoto**

KOREA

CHONG CHI-YONG

1903–c. 1951

Chong Chi-yong was born in Okch'on, and graduated from Hwimun High School in Seoul, South Korea. After earning a degree in English literature at Doshisha University in Kyoto, Japan, he worked for the *Kyonghyang Sinmun,* a Seoul newspaper, and taught at Ewha Woman's University in Seoul. Chong opposed Syngman Rhee's regime, and although no exact information about the cause of his death or his whereabouts after 1950 is available, some people say that Chong was among the Korean prisoners of war on Kojedo Island in South Korea, and that he later went to North Korea, where he was presumably killed in the war. Chong wrote at least two books of poems, and discovered and encouraged many young Korean poets.

The poems of Chong Chi-yong are reveries in sharp images. He is a poet of tempered nuances and direct language, of quickened senses and deep color. Chong finds permanence in dreams and memory-pictures. Close your eyes, the past appears. His poetic technique can be illustrated best by one of his own images: wiping and rewiping a frosted window late at night.

SPRING SNOW

The moment I open the door
the far hills coldly strike my brow.

Right on the first day
of the early spring month.

My forehead confronts, cool and bright,
the still snow-covered peak.

The cracked ice and new wind following
make my white coat-tie smell good.

It is now like a dream, rather sad,
to have had such a shrinking time.

Parsley sprouts green,
the once motionless fishes mumble.

For the unseasonable snow before flowering
I long to be cold again without warm clothes.

NOSTALGIA

To the east end of large fields
an old-tale-chattering brook meanders out,
and a piebald ox lows vacantly
a golden idle bellow.
—Even in a dream it remains in me.

As ashes in an earthen brazier grow colder
the night wind drives a horse through the field,
and my old father tired by a dusky drowsiness
raises his straw pillow.
—Even in a dream it remains in me.

I, with a soil-grown mind,
was getting wet to the skin with the grass-dew
looking for an arrow which I shot carelessly
aiming at the long sky's blue.
—Even in a dream it remains in me.

Young sister, flying hair down the lobes
like the waves that dance on the fabled sea,
and my barefoot wife, the ordinary,
gathered ears of corn against the blazing sun.
—Even in a dream it remains in me.

In the sky the dense stars
step towards a mysterious sand castle,
over a poor roof the frosty crows pass cawing,
by the lamplight people chat in a circle.
—Even in a dream it remains in me.

LAKE

A face simply
can be hidden
with two palms . . .

But the desire to see
so large as the lake,
there is nothing for it
but to close my eyes.

Translations by **Ko Won**

MEASLES

A December night quietly sits back
From around the coal fire,
A timeless beauty bursting forth.

There is no gleam on the glass,
The curtains drawn,
The door closed, key left in the lock.

A snow flurry whirls
Like a swarm of humming bees.
The measles, like red azaleas, are rife in a village.

WINDOW PANE

Something cold and sad plays on the pane.
Closer, when I breathe on it and it clouds,
Frozen wings flap half-heartedly—it must be tame.
I wipe and look, wipe and look again;
Pitch black night recedes, surges back,
A wet star flashes, now a set jewel.
Alone at night I wipe a window
For a feeling lonely but luxurious.
The fine veins of your lungs ruptured
You have fled like a wild mountain bird.

Translations by **S. E. Solberg**

LITHUANIA

HENRIKAS RADAUSKAS

1910–1970

Henrikas Radauskas was born in Cracow, Poland. He studied Lithuanian, German, and Russian literature at the University of Kaunas (1930–34), was a radio announcer in the Baltic port-city of Klaipėda (Memel), and an editor in the Lithuanian Ministry of Education (1937–41). He spent the remaining years of the Second World War in Germany. After coming to the United States in 1949, Radauskas worked as a manual laborer for ten years. From 1959 to 1970 he was a member of the staff of the Library of Congress; he died in Washington, D.C. His books include *The Fountain* (1935), *Arrow in the Sky* (1950), *The Winter Song* (1955), and *Lightnings and Winds* (1965).

The poems of Henrikas Radauskas are transformational, shape-shifting, image-floating, prismatic: the unexpected is always vaguely reminiscent. Extraordinary dream phantoms merge with ordinary human terror. In the poems, where art itself constructs the universe, it is as though our lives teeter along the edges of hot wax pools. Before our deaths we count up our lives as casually as we once sang the jump-rope song: one, two, three O'Leary; or counted just before we dove into the water; or as we went under the ether.

THE WINTER'S TALE

Guess what smells so. . . . You didn't guess.
Lilies? Lindens? No. Winds? No.
But princes and barbers smell so,
The evening smells so, in a dream.

Look: a line goes through the glass
Bending quietly; and the hushed
Light, in the tender mist,
Is gurgling like a brook of milk.

Look: it's snowing, it's snowing, it's snowing.
Look: the white orchard is falling asleep.

The earth has sunk into the past.
Guess who's coming. . . . You didn't guess.
Princes and barbers are coming,
White kings and bakers,
And the trees murmur, covered with snow.

THE FIRE AT THE WAXWORKS

In the basement of the waxworks the old guard puts on his glasses. He reads the story of a golden bird that rises each night from the treasure buried in a forgotten tomb. The book and the pipe fall from his hands; the bird, having flown into his dream, swoops down and, ringing like a harp, flings itself over the basement in pieces of gold.

The fire's orange hands creep out from under the bed and gag him; he tries to get up, falls without having screamed; and swimming up slowly, they break through the ceiling with soft blows; instantaneous as a pianist's fingers, skim down the gallery.

The faces of the wax figures begin to glow as they do in surrealist paintings; and the famous poet who, alive, couldn't bear to have a woman near him, sees how with a melting breast, a king's mistress, breaking in two at the waist, leans toward him faster and faster.

He shrieks in a posthumous voice. Making a dreadful face, he falls into her arms and, swimming out of their burning clothes, the two lazily coalesce into a puddle of melted wax.

Translations by **Randall Jarrell**

MARTINIQUE

AIMÉ CÉSAIRE

1913–

Aimé Césaire was born in Basse-Pointe, Martinique, one of seven children. He attended the Lycée Schoelcher in Fort-de-France and won a scholarship to Ecole Normale Supérieure in Paris, where he met Léopold Senghor and renewed his friendship with Léon Damas, whom he had known in Fort-de-France. The three founded *L'Etudiant noir,* a black journal (1934). Césaire returned to Martinique, where during the Second World War he taught at the Lycée and with his wife founded the review *Tropiques.* After the war he went to Paris as a Communist deputy to the Constituent Assembly but soon returned to become mayor of Fort-de-France. Césaire broke with the Communist Party in 1956 and formed his own party, Parti Progressiste Martiniquais. He has written plays, articles, reviews, and historical and political essays. His books of poems include *The Miraculous Weapons* (1946), *Clapped in Irons* (1960) and *Cadastral Survey* (1960).

The poems of Aimé Césaire are proclamative, resonant with images: bullets that aim at the dead center of middleclass-white-francophile values. The sounds they make are the reports of negritude resounding across the Caribbean: the flowering of the third world, the loveliness of black women, the straightforward talk of black people breaking the chains of white Westernism. Dead reefs, storm-struck schooners, villages asleep at the bottom of lakes, all lie in wait; the life of Martinique, the life of Africa, the lives of downtrodden men and women, rise up out of them.

RAINS

Rain
who even in your worst flooding
does not forget the girls of Chiriqui
who will suddenly pull from their
dark breasts a lamp of pure fireflies

Chiriqui: a province of western Panama on the Pacific coast, bounded on the west by Costa Rica; drained by the Chiriqui, David, and Chiriqui Viejo rivers.

Rain
who can wash everything but the blood
flowing over the fingers of those that
murder small nations surprised in
the dark of their innocence.

Translated by **Lucille Clifton**

SAMBA

All the rounds which jelled to form your breasts all the hibiscus
bells all the pearl oysters all the tangled arteries making up a
mangrove all the sunshine stored in the lizards of the sierra all
the iodine you need to make a sea-drenched day all the mother-
of-pearl you need to draw the noise of an underwater conch
If you wanted
  the floating pufferfish would pass by holding hands
If you wanted
  all day long the medusae would turn their tentacles to roads
  and bishop-birds would be so rare you would not be surprised
  to learn they had been devoured by the croziers of the
  trichomanes
If you wanted
  psychic power
  alone would provide the night with aras for beacons
If you wanted
  in those down and out parts of town the buckets of the noria
  would come back up filled with the scents of the very newest
  noises which deep in its infernal folds give the Earth its high
If you wanted
  the wild beasts would drink from the fountains
  and in our heads

SAMBA
trichomanes: a genus of ferns.
ara: a large, brightly colored member of the parrot family; a macaw.
noria: a device for raising water from a river. It involves a series of buckets revolving on a large wheel.

the homelands of violent earth
would stretch like fingers at the birds the motionless presence
of their larch-woods

SON OF THUNDER

And without her deigning to seduce the jailers
a bouquet of hummingbirds peeled away from her breast
from her ears sprouted buds of atolls
she speaks to me in a language so soft that at first I don't
understand but finally I gather she is telling me
spring has come in counter-flow
that all thirst is quenched that autumn is in harmony with us
that the stars in the street have flowered at high-noon
and are letting their fruits hang low so low

Translations by **Emile Snyder** *and* **Sanford Upson**

SUNDRAGON

Snake-eyed sun
fixing my eye   and the sea crawling with lice islands
cracks its fingers   flamethrowing
roses at my safe, thunderstruck body
water raises the glittering carcasses
lost in the unsung strait
vortices of icicles halo the smouldering hearts of crows
our hearts
it's the voice of thunder   harnessed   turning
on deep hinges   iguanas
broadcast   to a country of smashed glass
it is the climb
of vampire flowers   rescuing orchids
distilled from the fire's core
the true fire   the fire of the night mango
disguised under bees
my lust risking tigers   the brimstone shock

but each tin dawn has the gold leaves of childhood
swadling it   and my body is flint   eating
fish   eating doves and sleep   the word
Brazil
is sugar at the deep end of the quagmire

RUINATION

We will smash our warriors' heads at the new air
we will strike sun with our huge open palms
we will strike earth with our barefoot   voices
manflowers will sleep in the haven of mirrors
even the trilobites' armor
will lie low in the endless half-light
on soft breasts swollen with motherlodes of milk—
you think we won't invade that verandah,
the verandah of ruinations?
a virile path runs to the yellow vein-
thin lukewarm stains
where rumble the buffaloes of insolent anger
the path running   the bit of tornadoes
come of age in its teeth
the canefields of the fecund twilight boom boom

Translations by **Robert Bagg**

MEXICO

OCTAVIO PAZ

1914–

Octavio Paz was born in Mexico City. In sympathy with the Spanish Republic he went to Spain during the Civil War, and later in Mexico helped to found the journals *Taller* (Workshop) in 1938, and *El Hijo Prodigo* (Prodigal Son) in 1943, in which many Spanish writers in exile collaborated. Paz won a Guggenheim Fellowship to the United States in 1944. From 1946 to 1948 he was in the Mexican Foreign Service and served in San Francisco, New York, Paris, Tokyo, Geneva, and New Delhi. He was named Ambassador to India in 1962, and won the Grand Prix International de Poésie (Belgium) in 1963. To protest the actions of the Mexican government against students prior to the Olympic games, he resigned his ambassadorship in 1968. Between 1968 and 1972 he was Simón Bolívar professor in Latin American Studies at Cambridge University, was honored by the Third Oklahoma Conference on Writers of the Hispanic World (*Books Abroad*), and served as Charles Eliot Norton Professor of Poetry at Harvard. Published collections include *Savage Moon* (1933), *Sun Stone* (1957) and *Selected Poems* (1960).

The poems of Octavio Paz carry "the infinite weight of light." Philosophical and recapitulative, they range over the physical, spiritual, and human universe. Alone in a dry landscape, Octavio converses with the divine. With mineral-like energy and a laboratory-like concentration he establishes connections between abstract thought and the kingdoms of life. That which is unseen is seen; ideas are particularized. The poems are essays of images, sharpening.

SALAMANDER

Salamander
(the fire wears
black armor)
a slow-burning stove

salamander: See note page 95.

(between the jaws
marble or brick
of the chimney it is
an ecstatic tortoise, a crouched
Japanese warrior:
whatever it is, martyrdom
is repose
impassive under torture)
Salamander
ancient name of fire
(and ancient
antidote to fire)
Flayed sole of the foot walking
on hot coals
Amianthus *amante* amianthus
Salamander
in the abstract city between
dizzy geometries
formidable chimeras appear
raised up by calculus
multiplied by thirst
crystal flanks
rock
aluminum
Sudden poppy
Salamander
Yellow claw (a scrawl
of red letters on a
wall of salt)
Claw of sunlight
on a heap of bones
Salamander
fallen star
in the endlessness of bloodstained opal

amianthus: a greenish stone, like asbestos, with insulating properties; also called "salamander-stone."

amante: lover, sweetheart.

amianthus: from Amianthium, a genus of American herbs of the bunch-flower family; the pounded bulbs of one of the herbs is used as a fly poison.

ensepulchred
beneath eyelids of quartz
lost girl
in tunnels of onyx
in the circles of basalt
buried seed
                grain of energy
                in the marrow of granite
Salamander, you who lay dynamite in iron's
black and blue breast
you explode like a sun
you open yourself like a wound
you speak
              as a fountain speaks
Salamander
                Blade of wheat
daughter of fire
spirit of fire
Condensation of blood
sublimation of blood
Salamander of air
the rock is flame
                    the flame is smoke
red vapor
               straight-rising prayer
lofty word of praise
exclamation
                crown
of fire on the head of the psalm
scarlet queen
(and girl with purple stockings
running dishevelled through the woods)
Salamander, you are
silent, the
black consoler of sulphur tears

One wet summer I heard
the vibration of your
cylindrical tail
between loose tiles of a
dead-calm moonlit patio

Caucasian salamander
                                        (in the rock's
                                        cindery shoulder appears
                                        and disappears
                                        a brief black tongue
                                        flecked with saffron)
Black and brilliant creature
the moss
quivers
you devour
insects
diminutive herald of the rain-shower
familiar spirit of the lightning
(Internal fecundation
Oviparous reproduction
The young live in the water
Once adult they swim sluggishly)
Salamander
hanging bridge between eras
                                                  bridge of cold blood
axis of movement
(The changes in the alpine species
the most slender of all
take place in the mother's womb
Of all the tiny eggs no more than two mature
and until they hatch
the embryos are nourished on a broth
composed of the doughy mass of their aborted brother-eggs)
The Spanish Salamander
black and red mountaineer
(The sun nailed to the sky's center does not throb
does not breathe
Life does not commence without blood
Without the embers of sacrifice
the wheel of days does not revolve
Xólotl refuses to consume himself

Xólotl: an Aztec god; also, in Aztec mythology, the planet Venus, portrayed with a dog's head, one of the forms he assumed when attempting to avoid sacrificing himself for the sake of the sun; became the god of monsters, twins, and double ears of grain. *Xólotl* is the Aztec word for "dog."

He hid himself in the corn but they found him
he hid himself in the maguey but they found him
he fell into the water and became the fish axólotl
the Double-Being
'and then they killed him'
Movement began, the world was set in motion
the procession of dates and names
Xólotl the dog, guide to Hell
he who dug up the bones of the fathers
he who cooked the bones in a pot
he who lit the fire of the years
the Maker of Men
Xólotl the penitent
the burst eye that weeps for us
Xólotl
larva of the butterfly
double of the Star
Sea-shell
other face of the Lord of Dawn
Xólotl the axólotl)
Salamander
solar arrow
lamp of the moon
column of noonday
name of woman
scales of night
the infinite weight of light
a half-drachm on your eyelashes
salamander
back flame
sunflower
you yourself the sun
the moon
turning for ever around you

maguey: any of a variety of fleshy-leaved plants native to tropical America; the leaves are often spiny, with spikes of flowers like candelabra.

axólotl: Mexican name for larval salamanders that live in water and breathe through gills; their heads are fringed with filaments that look like ostrich feathers. Eaten as food since ancient times.

drachm: a unit of weight, a dram.

pomegranate that bursts itself open each night
fixed star on the brow of the sky
and beat of the sea and the stilled light
open mind above the
                    to-and-fro of the sea

The star-lizard, salamandria
saurian scarcely eight centimeters long
lives in crevices and is the color of dust
Salamander of earth and water
green stone in the mouth of the dead
stone of incarnation
stone of fire
sweat of the earth
salt flaming and scorching
salt of destruction and
mask of lime that consumes the face
Salamander of air and fire
                        Wasp's nest of suns
                        red word of beginning

The salamander
a lizard
her tongue ends in a dart
her tail ends in a dart
she rests upon hot coals
queens it over firebrands
If she carries herself in the flame
she burns her monument
Fire is her passion, her *patience*

Salamander   Salamater

Translated by **Denise Levertov**

Salamater: in the original Spanish "*Salamadre,*" a word coined by Paz that unifies the concepts of salamander and motherhood: the great, universal salamander-mother.

XAVIER VILLAURRUTIA

1903–1950

Xavier Villaurrutia was born in Mexico City. After studying at the Yale School of Drama under a Rockefeller Foundation Grant, Villaurrutia co-founded the theater-group and review *Ulises* (1927) and taught literature at the University of Mexico. He was at one time Chief of the Theater Section in the Mexico Ministry of Public Education. He was also an excellent translator of leading European dramatists such as Romains, Chekhov, and Pirandello. In 1953 the Fondo de Cultura Economica of Mexico published his *Complete Poetry and Plays.* Books of poems include: *Reflected Light* (1927), *Nostalgia of Death* (1938), and *Cantos of the Spring* (1948).

In the poems of Xavier Villaurrutia deep broodings give rise to images of silence. At once dusky and philosophical, the poems evoke the deepest human feelings associated with remembered experience. Though it has all slipped through our fingers, Villaurrutia places it again in our hands. He coaxes inanimate things into speech and then suggests that all our voices are only memories.

CEMETERY IN THE SNOW

Nothing is like a cemetery in the snow.
What name is there for the whiteness upon the white?
The sky has let down insensible stones of snow
upon the tombs,
and all that is left now is snow upon snow
like a hand settled on itself forever.

Birds prefer to cut through the sky,
to wound the invisible corridors of the air
so as to leave the snow alone,
which is to leave it intact,
which is to leave it snow.

Because it is not enough to say that a cemetery in the snow
is like a sleep without dreams
or like a few blank eyes.

Though it is something like an insensible and sleeping body,
like one silence fallen upon another

and like the white persistence of oblivion,
nothing is like a cemetery in the snow!

Because the snow is above all silent,
more silent still upon bloodless slabs:
lips that can no longer say a word.

NOCTURNE OF THE STATUE

to Agustín Lazo

To dream, to dream the night, the street, the stair
and the cry of the statue turning back at the corner.
To run toward the statue and to meet the cry only,
to want to touch the cry and only find the echo,
to want to seize the echo and to meet the wall only,
and to run toward the wall and touch a mirror.
To find the statue murdered in the mirror,
to draw it forth from the blood of its shadow,
to dress it, closing the eyes,
to caress it like a sister not foreseen,
and to ply the ends of its fingers,
and to count in its ear a hundred times a hundred hundred times
until one hears it say: "I am dead tired."

Translations by **Donald Justice**

ETERNAL NOCTURNE

When men raise their shoulders and pass on
or when they let their names fall
until the shadow is darkened

when a dust even finer than smoke
adheres to the windows of the voice
and the skin of cheeks and things

NOCTURNE OF THE STATUE
Agustín Lazo: (1900–71), a Mexican painter who also wrote plays in the late forties.

when eyes close their windows
to the rays of the prodigal sun and prefer
blindness to absolution and silence to sobbing

when life or what we futilely call life
and which only comes with an unnamable name
undresses to jump into bed
and drown itself in alcohol or burn in snow

when I when lie when life
wants to surrender in cowardice and darkness
without even telling us the price of its name

when in the loneliness of a dead sky
forgotten stars gleam
and the silence's silence is so great
that we suddenly want it to speak

or when from a nonexistent mouth
there issues an inaudible cry
that hurls its glaring light in our faces
and dies away leaving us in blind deafness

or when everything has died
so terribly and so slowly that we are afraid
to raise our voices and ask "who's alive"

I hesitate to answer
the mute question with a cry
for fear of learning that I no longer exist

because perhaps our voices are not alive either
but are like memories in our throats
and it is not night but blindness
that fills our eyes with shadow

and because perhaps the cry is the presence
of an ancient word
opaque and mute crying out suddenly

because life silence skin and mouth
and solitude memory sky and smoke
are nothing but shadows of words
that issue from us at the night's passing.

Translated by **Rachel Benson**

NETHERLANDS

GERRIT ACHTERBERG

1905–1962

Gerrit Achterberg was born in Langbroek, Netherlands, into a Calvinist peasant family. He trained to be a teacher but never taught, suffering periods of insanity for many years. He is alleged to have been partly responsible for the death of his wife; the image of a wronged dead woman recurs in his poems. Achterberg won the Netherlands State Prize and the Amsterdam Poetry Prize. Twenty-six volumes of poetry include *The Claws of Two Twin Tigers* (1925), *The Book of Forgetting* (1961), *Cryptogamen I-IV* (1961), and *Collected Poems* (1963).

The poems of Gerrit Achterberg occur between two dashes of silence; they move within the quiet verbs: slumber, drift, weigh, creep, slip, skim, curl, whisper. Old farmhouses, old towns, old Octobers, come alive in a way that says: wait, it has all happened—listen, death is coming. Achterberg's tough, lyrical wistfulness asserts private suffering and private endurance.

EBEN HAËZER

Sabbath evening privacy at home.
Mist-footsteps, prowling past the shed.
At that hour, not another soul abroad;
the blue farmhouse a closed hermitage.

There we lived together, man and mouse.
Through cowstall windows an eternal fire
fell ridged from gold lamps on the threshing-floor,
stillness of linseed cakes and hay in house.

There my father celebrated mass:
serving the cows, priestlike at their heads.
Their tongues curled along his hands like fish.

Eben Haëzer: Hebrew for "Stone of Help," a common old name for farmhouses in Holland.

A shadow, diagonal to the rafters.
Worship hung heavy from the loftbeams.
His arteries begin to calcify.

ACCOUNTABILITY

Old oblivion-book, that I lay open.
White eye-corner rounding the page.

Gold lace slips out under the evening,
Green animals creep backwards.

Lifelessness of the experimental station.
Added-up, subtracted sum.

Black night. Over the starlight skims
God's index finger, turning the page.

Death comes walking on all fours
past the room, a crystal egg,

with the lamp, the books, the bread,
where you are living and life-size.

DWINGELO

In the never, still arriving, I find you
again: blue absence keeps knowledge alive,
makes of October an adjusted lens.
The days have almost no clouds left.

Cassiopeia, the Great Bear
let their signals burst by night
to rip into impossibility.
The Pleiades rage silently about.

To wait is the password; and to listen.
In Dwingelo you can hear it whisper,
the void in the radiotelescope.

DWINGELO
Dwingelo: a small town (pop. 893) in NE central Netherlands, a dairy center.

There too the singing of your nerves is gathered,
becoming graphic on a sheet of paper
not unlike this one here.

CITY

Maybe you spoke to someone
and on that hour your face
printed itself for good.
Where is that man? I need
to find him before he dies
and see you drift across his retina.

You have played with children.
They will run up to me
whenever you
come home free in their dreams.

Houses, realized by you,
slumber in that web.

Streets suppose you
in other streets, and call:
Evening papers . . .
Strawberries . . .

The city has changed hands;
the plan you gave it, fallen through.

STATUE

A body, blind with sleep,
stands up in my arms.
Its heaviness weighs on me.
Death-doll.
I'm an eternity too late.
And where's your heartbeat?

The thick night glues us together,
makes us compact with each other.
"For God's sake go on holding me—
my knees are broken,"
you mumble against my heart.

It's as if I held up the earth.
And slowly, moss is creeping
all over our two figures.

Translations by **Adrienne Rich**

NICARAGUA

ERNESTO CARDENAL

1925–

Ernesto Cardenal was born in Granada, Nicaragua. After earning a degree in philosophy and letters in Mexico, he did graduate work at Columbia University in New York, and then, in 1957, entered the Cistercian monastery in Gethsemani, Kentucky, where he was a novice under Thomas Merton. He also lived in a Benedictine monastery in Mexico. Cardenal was ordained a Trappist monk in Nicaragua in 1965 and now directs a monastic community at Archipelago de Solentiname. In addition to a collection of prose meditations, his poetry includes *Psalms of Struggle and Liberation* (1971) and *Homage to the American Indians* (1973).

The voice of Ernesto Cardenal is huge: it speaks for Indian nations who have never put their trust in talk. Cardenal combines the outrage and brilliance of the eighth-century Hebrew prophets, and is as at home in the hip language and glossy images of the contemporary United States as he is with the flowing elegiac chants of the Comanche and the details of the daily life of the Incas. Cardenal is the compatriot of Whitman: the whole world and all of history are crucial.

LOST CITIES

At night owls fly between the stelae,
the mountain lion meows on the terraces,
the jaguar roars in the towers
and the lone coyote barks in the Grand Plaza
to the reflection of the moon in the lakes
that once were ponds in distant katuns.

The stylized animals
on the frescoes are now real

stelae: pillars of stone inscribed for commemorative purposes.
katun: a period of 20 tuns in the Maya calendar; one tun = 360 days (Maya year).

and the princes sell clay pots in the markets.
But how to write anew the hieroglyph,
how to paint the jaguar anew, how to overthrow the tyrants?
How to build our tropical acropolises anew,
our country seats surrounded by milpas?

The underbrush is full of monuments.
There are altars in the milpas.
Among the roots of the *chilamates*, arches with reliefs,
in the forest where one would think no man has ever trod,
where only the tapir and the lone-coati enter
and the quetzal is still dressed as a Maya:
there is a metropolis there.
When the priests climbed the Temple of the Jaguar
with cloaks of jaguar and fans of quetzal tails
and sandals of deer leather and ritual masks,
screams rose from the Ball Game,
the sound of drums, the incense of *copal* burning
in the holy chambers lined with *sapota* wood,
smoke of *ocote* torches . . . and under Tikal
there is another metropolis, a thousand years older.
—Where monkeys now howl in the *sapota* trees.

There are no names of soldiers on the stelae.

In their temples and palaces and pyramids
and in their calendars and chronicles and codices
there are no names of caudillos caciques emperors
nor of priest leader statesman general or chief
and they did not record political events on their stones

milpas: cornfields.
chilamates: fig trees.
tapir: a hoofed, hoglike mammal of Central and South America.
coati: mammal of tropical America, related to the raccoon.
quetzal: a crested, brilliantly colored bird.
copal: resin.
sapota: the sapodilla, a large tree of tropical America; the latex yields *chicle* (see below).
ocote: species of pine.
Tikal: Maya ruins in Peten, northern Guatemala; thought to be the largest and oldest of Mayan cities.
caudillos: leaders, chiefs of state.
caciques: head men, local rulers.

nor administrations, nor dynasties,
nor ruling families, nor political parties.
For centuries you cannot find the glyph of a man's name
and archeologists still don't know how they used to rule
themselves!

The word "Lord" was foreign to the tongue.
And the word "wall." They did not wall in their cities.
Their cities were of temples and they lived in the fields,
among milpas and palm and papaya trees.
The arch of their temples was a copy of their huts.
The roads were only for processions.
Religion was the only tie among them,
but it was a religion freely taken
and neither an oppression nor a burden on them.
Their priests had no earthly power
and their pyramids were built without forced labor.
The peak of their civilization did not lead to an empire.
And they had no colonies. They did not know the arrow.
They knew Jesus as the god of corn
and they offered him simple sacrifices
of corn and birds and feathers.
They had no wars nor knew the wheel
but calculated the synodic revolution of Venus:
every evening they took note of the ascent of Venus
in the horizon, on a distant ceiba tree,
when the couples of *lapa* birds flew back to their nests.
They did not work metals. Their tools were of stone,
and technologically they remained in the Stone Age.
But they computed exact dates that were
400 million years ago.
They did not develop applied sciences. They were not practical.
Their progress took place in religion, in the arts, in mathematics,
in astronomy. They did not know how to weigh.
They worshipped time, that mysterious flowing
and flowing of time.
Time was sacred. The days were gods

ceiba: massive tropical tree with buttress-like ridges; its silky fibers yield kapok.
lapa birds: macaws.

Past and future suffused their songs.
They counted past and future with the same katuns
because they believed time repeats itself
as they saw the rotation of the stars repeat itself
But the time they worshipped stopped suddenly.

There are stelae that were not engraved.
The blocks remained half-cut in the quarries.
—And they are still there.—

Now only the solitary chicle-hunters cross the Peten.
Vampires nest in the stucco friezes
Wild pigs grunt in the evening.
The jaguar roars in the towers—the towers among the roots—
a coyote, far, on a square barks to the moon,
and a plane of the Pan American Airlines flies over the pyramid.
But will the past katuns ever come back?

from THE ECONOMY OF TAHUANTINSUYU

They had no currency
        gold was used to fashion the lizard
and NOT COINS
        the garments
                        which flashed like fire
            in the light of the sun or of the bonfires
the images of the gods
                and the women they had loved
and not coins
            Millions of forges shining in the night of the Andes
and a bounty of gold and silver
                they had no money
they knew how

LOST CITIES

chicle: a gum from the latex of the sapodilla tree, used as the chief ingredient of chewing gum.

Peten: an area in Guatemala bordered on the north and west by Mexico and on the east by British Honduras.

THE ECONOMY OF TAHUANTINSUYU

Tahuantinsuyu: an ethnic group that inhabited the plateau of South America before Columbus discovered the New World.

to cast roll weld carve
gold and silver
gold: sweat of the sun
silver: tears of the moon
Threads beads filigrane
pins
pectorals
jingle bells
but not MONEY
and because there was no money
there was neither prostitution nor plunder
the doors of the houses stayed open
there was no Administrative graft nor embezzlement
every 2 years
they reported to Cuzco
because there was no commerce no money
there was no
sale of Indians
No Indian was ever sold
and there was *chicha* for everybody

They did not know the inflationary power of money
Their coin was the Sun which shines for everybody
the Sun that belongs to everybody and makes everything grow
the Sun without inflation and deflation: and not
those dirty "soles" with which the *peon* is paid
(who will show you his ruins for a Peruvian *sol*)
And they ate twice a day throughout the Empire

Financiers were not
the creators of their myths
Later the gold was stolen from the temples of the Sun
and went into circulation in ingots
with Pizarro's initials

Cuzco: Peruvian city, formerly the capital of the Inca empire, one of the largest and most civilized new-world cities. Captured by Pizarro in 1533. Still populated mostly by Indians and *mestizos* (30,000).
chica: corn liquor.
sol: (1) the sun; (2) the monetary unit of Peru (45 *soles* = 1 dollar).
Pizarro: Francisco (1471–1541), Spanish explorer and conqueror of Peru.

Money brought taxes
and the first beggars appeared with the Colony

The water sings no longer in the stone channels
the roads are torn
lands dry as mummies
as mummies
of happy girls who danced
in *Airiway* (April)
the month of the Dance of the Sweet Corn
now dry and squatting in Museums

Manco Capac! Manco Capac!
Rich in virtues and not in money
(Mancjo: "virtue", Capacj: "rich")
"Man rich in virtues"
A system of economics without CURRENCY
the moneyless society we dream of
They valued gold just
as they valued the pink marble or the grass
and they offered it as food
like grass
to the horses of the conquerors
upon seeing them chew metal (the bridles)
with their foamy mouths
They did not have money
and nobody starved in their whole Empire
and the dye of their *ponchos* has lasted 1,000 years
even princesses spun on their spindles
the blind shelled corn
children hunted birds
KEEP THE INDIANS BUSY
was an Inca slogan
the lame the maimed the old worked
there were neither lazy nor idle men
whoever could not work would be fed
and the Inca worked painting and drawing
When the Empire fell
the Indian squatted
like a pile of ashes

and has done nothing but think . . .
indifferent to skyscrapers
to the Alliance for Progress
To think? Who knows
The architect of Macchu Picchu
in houses of cardboard
and Quaker Oats tin cans

The carver of emeralds, hungry and smelly
(the tourist takes a snapshot)
Lonely as a cactus
as silent as the landscape—in the background—of the Andes
They are ashes
they are ashes
that the wind of the Andes fans
And the crying llama loaded with kindling
silently stares at the tourist
close to its owners

They did not have money
Nobody was ever sold
And they did not exploit the miners
the extraction of mercury with snake movements
(which caused the Indians to tremble)
was FORBIDDEN
The fishing of pearls was forbidden
And the Army was not hated by the people
The function of the State
was to feed the people
The land belonged to whoever worked it
and not to the landlord
And the Pleiades watched over the cornfields
There was land for all
Free water and guano
(there was no guano monopoly)
Compulsory banquets for the people
And when work started each new year
the plots were distributed with songs and *chicha*

Macchu Picchu: prehistoric Inca site on a mountain top in the Urubamba Valley, north of Cuzco.

and to the beat of the drum of tapir hide
and to the sound of the flute of jaguar bone
the Inca plowed the first furrow with his golden plow
Even the mummies took along their pouch of grain
for the trip to the Beyond

There was protection for domestic animals
llamas and vicunas were covered by legislation
even the animals of the jungle had their code
(which now the Sons of the Sun do not have)
. . .

Translated by **Monique** *and* **Carlos Altschul**

NIGERIA

CHRISTOPHER OKIGBO

1932–1967

Christopher Okigbo was born in Ojoto in the Ibo country of Eastern Nigeria. He attended the University of Ibadan and studied classics, taught at the Fiditi Grammar School, was a librarian at the University of Nsukka, became West African manager for Cambridge University Press in Ibadan, and was the West African editor of *Transition* magazine. Okigbo's poems reflect the agony surrounding the Western Nigeria crisis of 1962, the death of Patrice Lumumba, and the death of his own eldest son. With Chinua Achebe he started Enugu publishing company in 1967. Okigbo turned down the first prize of the 1966 Festival of Negro Arts in Dakar saying: "There is no African literature. There is good writing and bad writing—that's all." He was a major in the Biafran army, and was killed on the Nsukka battlefront in the Nigerian Civil War. Books of poems: *Heavensgate* (1962), *Limits* (1964), and *Silences* (1965).

The poems of Christopher Okigbo are ritualistic, elegiac, testimonial, religious. Okigbo's quest is the universal quest, and his images range from totem worship to Greek legend. The voice in the poems shifts emphasis like a choreographer. The poems below are reprinted from the opening section of *Labyrinths* (published posthumously), which Okigbo described as "a ceremony of innocence."

THE PASSAGE

Silent faces at crossroads:
festivity in black . . .

Faces of black like long black
columns of ants,

behind the bell tower,
into the hot garden
where all roads meet:
festivity in black . . .

O Anna at the knobs of the panel oblong,
hear us at crossroads at the great hinges

where the players of loft pipe organs
rehearse old lovely fragments, alone—

stains of pressed orange leaves on pages,
bleach of the light of years held in leather:

For we are listening in cornfields
    among the windplayers,
listening to the wind leaning over
    its loveliest fragment . . .

FRAGMENTS OUT OF THE DELUGE

VII

But the sunbird repeats
Over the oilbean shadows:

'A fleet of eagles,
    over the oilbean shadows,
Holds the square
    under curse of their breath.
Beaks of bronze, wings
    of hard-tanned felt,
The eagles flow
    over man-mountains,
Steep walls of voices,
    horizons;
The eagles furrow
    dazzling over the voices
With wings like
    combs in the wind's hair

Out of the solitude, the fleet,
Out of the solitude,

THE PASSAGE
Anna: Okigbo's mother. In his poems she is his advocate with the Christian faith. Both Okigbo's parents were Catholic.

Intangible like silk thread of sunlight,
The eagles ride low,
Resplendent . . . resplendent;
And small birds sing in shadows,
Wobbling under their bones . . .'

LAMENT OF THE SILENT SISTERS

V

Alternately
Crier: Chorus

Yellow images:
Voices in the senses' stillness . . .

Pointed arches:
Pieces in the form of a pear . . .

Angles, filaments:
Hosts of harlequins in the shadows:

And bearded Judas,
Resplendent among the dancers . . .

I hear sounds as, they say,
A worshipper hears the flutes—

The music sounds so in the soul
It can hear nothing else—

I hear painted harmonies
From the mushroom of the sky—

Silences are melodies
Heard in retrospect:

And how does one say NO in thunder?

One dips one's tongue in the ocean;
Camps with the choir of inconstant
Dolphins, by shallow sand banks
Sprinkled with memories;

Extends one's branches of coral,
The branches extend in the senses'
Silence; this silence distills
in yellow melodies.

HURRAH FOR THUNDER

Whatever happened to the elephant—
Hurrah for thunder—

The elephant, tetrarch of the jungle:
With a wave of the hand
He could pull four trees to the ground;
His four mortar legs pounded the earth:
Wherever they treaded,
The grass was forbidden to be there.

Alas! the elephant has fallen—
Hurrah for thunder—

But already the hunters are talking about pumpkins:
If they share the meat let them remember thunder.

The eye that looks down will surely see the nose;
The finger that fits should be used to pick the nose.

Today—for tomorrow, today becomes yesterday:
How many million promises can ever fill a basket . . .

If I don't learn to shut my mouth I'll soon go to hell,
I, Okigbo, town-crier, together with my iron bell.

NORWAY

ROLF JACOBSEN

1907–

Rolf Jacobsen was born in Oslo, where he later studied philosophy at the university, but he spent half his early life in the nearby rural town of Solor. He studied journalism, was active in the Norwegian Labor Party, and published his first book of poems, *Earth and Iron,* in 1933. Jacobsen is currently the assistant editor of *Hamar Arbeiderblad* (The Hamar Worker), and lives in Hamar. Eleven volumes of poems include *Letters to the Light* (1960), *Headlines* (1969), and *Watch the Doors–They Are Closing* (1972).

The poems of Rolf Jacobsen close the gaps between the things of this world. Images arise from deep within the poems, where nature complements human nature. Chaste, lean, matter-of-fact, the poems elaborate on previously unobserved connections. Jacobsen speaks gently in the declarative voice: now, this is the way it is.

OLD AGE

I put a lot of stock in the old.
They sit looking at us and don't see us,
and have plenty with their own,
like fishermen along big rivers,
motionless as a stone
in the summer night.

I put a lot of stock in fishermen along rivers
and old people and those who appear after a long illness.
They have something in their eyes
that you don't see much anymore
the old, like convalescents
whose feet are still not very sturdy under them
and pale foreheads as if after a fever.

The old
who so gradually become themselves once more
and so gradually break up

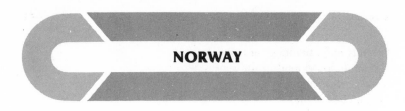

like smoke, no one notices it, they are gone
into sleep
and light.

THE MORNING PAPER

The morning paper is opened out on the 7:35
and suddenly provides all the men with white wings.
They fly off inside a room inside a train
their faces strangely stiff
a procession behind glass
as if to a restricted and private funeral on some star.

THE GLASS SHOP

The glass shop sells the invisible.
It tinkles like spinet music
and is brittle as the floats on dry seaweed.

It is the schizoid's house, those who are
cold as ice inside and have richly developed dreams.
The cut and polished, who are coiled around themselves.

The glass person lives in the kingdom of light,
full of beauty, but sterile
as an aesthetician.

And writing on glass
is like rain in the eyes.

SSSH

Sssh the sea says
sssh the small waves at the shore say, sssh
not so violent, not
so haughty, not
so remarkable.
Sssh
say the tips of the waves

crowding around the headland's
surf. Sssh
they say to people
this is *our* earth,
our eternity.

THE OLD WOMEN

The girls whose feet moved so fast, where did they go?
Those with knees like small kisses and sleeping hair?

In the far reaches of time when they've calmed down,
old women with small hands climb up stairs slowly

with huge keys in their bags and they look around
and chat with small children at cemetery gates.

In that big and bewildering country where winters are so long
and no one understands their expressions any more.

Bow clearly to them and greet them with respect
because they still carry everything with them, like a fragrance,

a secret bite-mark on the chin, a nerve deep in
the palm of the hand somewhere betraying who they are.

MAY MOON

The May moon
goes around like an inspector in a white jacket.

The guests will soon be here.
Is everything in its place? This tapestry
must be brushed, green rugs everywhere
and candles on the tables.

A little music, half muffled,
—one thrush, a little lark, that's better—
and violins. Bring up some more small rivers!

Translations by **Robert Bly**

PERU

CÉSAR VALLEJO

1892–1938

César Vallejo was born in Santiago de Chuco, a medieval Andean town in northern Peru. Both his grandmothers were pure Indian. The youngest of eleven children, César went at eighteen to Trujillo to attend the university, but his studies were interrupted several times by poverty. He taught grade school part time, worked in the mining town of Quiruvilca, and tutored on an estate where he saw Indians beaten and exploited. By 1916 he was publishing poetry in *La Reforma,* and was reading Emerson, Unamuno, Darío, and the French symbolists. In 1920 he served 105 days in a Trujillo jail on the charge of being an "intellectual instigator." Three years later he left Peru for a newspaper correspondent's post in Paris, where he co-edited *Favorables París Poema* and almost starved. In 1928 and 1929 he went to Russia. Vallejo was deported from Spain in 1930 for Communist activities, joined the Party in 1931, and worked for the cause of the Spanish Republic. He died on a rainy day in Paris, as he said he would. In addition to a novel, short stories, plays, and essays, Vallejo wrote four books of poems: *The Black Riders* (1919), *Trilce** (1922), *Human Poems* (1939), and *Spain, Let This Cup Pass from Me* (1940).

The poems of César Vallejo bear witness to the devourings of poverty and the eviscerations of human tyranny. Heightened by wild and agonizing clarities, softened by all-embracing gestures, the poems are sacraments of passionate suffering. Vallejo's images cut through the economic and political darkness of the western world like meteors.

* A word made up by Vallejo when asked by the printer for three extra dollars to change Vallejo's originally chosen pseudonym to his own name. Vallejo was embarrassed and repeated *tres* (three) until he distorted it to *trilce,* which he decided to use for a new title of the book of poems.

TO MY BROTHER MIGUEL

in memoriam

Brother, today I sit on the brick bench outside the house,
where you make a bottomless emptiness.
I remember we used to play at this hour of the day, and mama
would calm us: "There now, boys . . ."

Now I go hide
as before, from all these evening
prayers, and I hope that you will not find me.
In the parlor, the entrance hall, the corridors.
Later, you hide, and I do not find you.
I remember we made each other cry,
brother, in that game.

Miguel, you hid yourself
one night in August, nearly at daybreak,
but instead of laughing when you hid, you were sad.
And your other heart of those dead afternoons
is tired of looking and not finding you. And now
shadows fall on the soul.

Listen, brother, don't be too late
coming out. All right? Mama might worry.

Translated by **John Knoepfle** *and* **James Wright**

THE ANGER THAT BREAKS A MAN DOWN INTO BOYS

The anger that breaks a man down into boys,
that breaks the boy down into equal birds,
and the bird, then, into tiny eggs;
the anger of the poor
owns one smooth oil against two vinegars.

The anger that breaks the tree down into leaves,
and the leaf down into different-sized buds,
and the buds into infinitely fine grooves;
the anger of the poor
owns two rivers against a number of seas.

The anger that breaks the good down into doubts,
and doubt down into three matching arcs,
and the arc, then, into unimaginable tombs;
the anger of the poor
owns one piece of steel against two daggers.

The anger that breaks the soul down into bodies,
the body down into different organs,

and the organ into reverberating octaves of thought;
the anger of the poor
owns one deep fire against two craters.

Translated by **Robert Bly**

BLACK STONE LYING ON A WHITE STONE

I will die in Paris, on a rainy day,
on some day I can already remember.
I will die in Paris—and I don't step aside—
perhaps on a Thursday, as today is Thursday, in autumn.

It will be a Thursday, because today, Thursday, setting down
these lines, I have put my upper arm bones on
wrong, and never so much as today have I found myself
with all the road ahead of me, alone.

César Vallejo is dead. Everyone beat him,
although he never does anything to them;
they beat him hard with a stick and hard also

with a rope. These are the witnesses:
the Thursdays, and the bones of my arms,
the solitude, and the rain, and the roads . . .

Translated by **Robert Bly** *and* **John Knoepfle**

MASSES

When the battle was over,
and the fighter was dead, a man came toward him
and said to him: "Do not die; I love you so!"
But the corpse, it was sad! went on dying.

And two came near, and told him again and again:
"Do not leave us! Courage! Return to life!"
But the corpse, it was sad! went on dying.

Twenty arrived, a hundred, a thousand, five hundred thousand,
shouting: "So much love, and it can do nothing against death!"
But the corpse, it was sad! went on dying.

Millions of persons stood around him,
all speaking the same thing: "Stay here, brother!"
But the corpse, it was sad! went on dying.

Then all the men on the earth
stood around him; the corpse looked at them sadly, deeply moved;
he sat up slowly,
put his arms around the first man; started to walk . . .

November 10, 1937

Translated by **Robert Bly**

LET THIS CUP PASS FROM ME

VIII

Here,
Ramon Collar,
your family goes on from hand to mouth,
it abides,
while far away you visit the seven swords of Madrid,
the Madrid front.

Ramon Collar, ox-driver
and soldier to the extent of being son-in-law to your wife's father,
husband, borderline son of the old Son of Man!
Ramon of sorrows; yes, you, brave Collar,
paladin of Madrid by the hair of your balls. Listen, Roy, here
your folks worry a hell of a lot about your hair-do!

They are really anxious, quick from weeping in a time of tears!
Marching to drums, speaking
in front of your ox in a time of earth!

Ramon! Collar! Think of yourself! If you are hit,
don't go and die on us, restrain yourself!
Here,

LET THIS CUP PASS FROM ME
Let This Cup Pass from Me: Matthew 26:39.
Ramon Collar: Pronounce *Collar* as: *Col-lyár,* with the accent on the last syllable.

your cruel propensity is kept in little boxes;
here,
your dark trousers, with time,
have learned to walk and fade in utter loneliness;
listen, Ramon, here
the old man, your father-in-law,
loses you each time he bumps into his daughter!

I must tell you, they have eaten your flesh here,
unwittingly, of course,
they have devoured your chest without realizing it,
your foot too;
they daydream, crowned in the dust of your footsteps!

They have prayed to God,
here;
they have sat on your bed, talking loudly
in the midst of your solitude and your few little things;
I don't know who has taken up the plow, I don't know
who went to see you, nor who returned with word from your
horse!

Ramon Collar, here, at any rate, is your friend.
Good luck to you, man of God; kill and write!

September 10, 1937

THE SPANISH IMAGE OF DEATH

There she goes! Call her! That's her rib cage!
That's death on her way through Irun,
with her accordion gait, her swear word,
the yard of cloth I've told you about,
the ounce of weight grown silent . . . when it was them!

Call her! Hurry! She looks for me among the guns,
as if she knew well where I could beat her,
which are my best tricks, my specious laws, my awful codes.

THE SPANISH IMAGE OF DEATH
Irun: frontier city of northern Spain, strongly defended by Loyalists in the Spanish Civil War; burned before its surrender to the Nationalists in 1936.

Call her! She walks just like a man, even among beasts,
she leans against that arm wrapped around our leg
as we sleep against the parapets,
she waits by the elastic door of sleep.
And now she's shouted! Shouted her basic, sensorial scream!
She must be shouting with shame,
seeing how she's fallen among plants,
seeing how far she's come from animals,
hearing us say: It's death!
After wounding our vital interests!

(Because that drop I told you about, comrade,
falls and develops its own liver; because it gorges
the neighbor's soul.)
Call her! We must follow her
to the foot of the enemy tanks,
death is a being one becomes by force,
whose beginning and end I carry etched
at the forefront of my hopes
though she may run that ordinary risk that you,
that only you know,
pretending she pretends to ignore me.

Call her! She has no being, this violent death,
she's just barely the most laconic happening;
her style, when attacking,
is closer to a simple tumult without orbit or canticles of joy,
it tends to its own daring bits of timing, to unsure pennies,
full of deaf carats, to despotic applause.
Call her! For in passionately calling her, with figures,
you help her drag her three knees
the way, at times,
those enigmatic, global fractures hurt us, puncture us,
the way, at times, I touch myself and cannot feel a thing.

Call her! Hurry! She's looking for me
with her cognac, her moral cheekbone,
her accordion gait, her swear word.
Call her! We can't lose the thread by which I bewail her.
From her stench upwards; oh dust of mine, comrade!
From her pus upwards; oh whip of mine, lieutenant!
From her magnet down; oh tomb of mine!

FUNERAL TRAIN FOLLOWING THE TAKING OF BILBAO

Wounded and dead, Republican brother,
true creature, they are trampling over your throne,
ever since your spinal column fell so famously;
pale friend, they are trampling on it in your gaunt and annual age
so laboriously absorbed before the wind.

Warrior of both griefs,
sit here to listen, lie down at the foot of the sudden
immediate stick of your throne;
turn around;
those are new, strange sheets there,
trampling, brother, trampling.

They have said, "How? Where . . . ?" expressing
themselves through bits of dove
so that children may climb to your dust without crying.
Ernesto Zuniga, sleep with your hands on,
with the concept,
your peace at rest, your war at peace.

Comrade mortally wounded with life,
comrade horseman,
comrade horse between man and wild beast,
your frail bones of high and melancholic line
create this Spanish pomp
crowned with the laurel of the finest rags.

So, sit down, Ernesto,
and pay attention, for they are trampling on your throne, here,
ever since your ankle bone went grey.
What throne?
Your right shoe! Your shoe!

September 13, 1937

Translations by **Alvaro Cardona-Hine**

Bilbao: city in northern Spain, the seat of the short-lived Basque autonomous government (1936-37), captured by the Nationalists in 1937 after a heroic defense of nine months.

POLAND

ZBIGNIEW HERBERT

1924–

Zbigniew Herbert was born in Lwow. During the Second World War he completed his secondary education in an underground school and began study at an underground university. Herbert wrote his first poems while the Nazis were occupying Poland but was over thirty when his first book appeared (*The Chord of Light,* 1956). After the war he went to the universities at Krakow and Torun, and earned a degree in civil law. Herbert served in the Resistance during the war; later worked in a bank, in a cooperative, and in industry; joined the Polish Writers' Union in 1956; and in the following years traveled to France, England, Italy, Greece, and Austria. He won the Polish Institute of Sciences and Arts in America Award in 1964 and the Austrian Lenau Prize in 1965. Herbert now lives in Warsaw and travels occasionally outside Poland. His other books of poems include *Hermes, Dog and Star* (1957) and *Study of the Object* (1961).

The poems of Zbigniew Herbert are quietly observed dramas in the lives of insects, objects, animals, men and women: the fatigue of the pursued, the clarities of the dying, the patience of the starving. Herbert's poems are stately without being funereal, conversational without being indulgent, sardonic without being petty. Herbert walks with the condemned to the firing squad, strolls through the henyards of villages, and watches from a distance the rituals of human passion.

SHE DRESSED

She dressed her hair to a sleep
and to a mirror.
It lasted endlessly.
Between one and another
bending of her hand
at the elbow
whole ages passed.
From her hair
the soldiers of the III legion

silently poured out
St. Louis with his crusaders
the artillery men from Verdun.

With her strong fingers
she assured the glory above her head.

It lasted so long
that when, at last,
she did begin her balancing march
toward me

my heart, greatly obedient so far,
stopped
and big grains of salt
appeared on my skin.

Translated by **Frederic Will** *and* **Leszek Elektorowicz**

FIVE MEN

1

They were brought out at dawn
into the stone yard
and lined against a wall

five men
two very young
the others middle-aged
no more
can be said of them

2

When the squad takes aim
ready to fire

SHE DRESSED

St. Louis: Louis IX of France, led two crusades and died in Tunisia, A.D. 1270.

Verdun: French city, one of the greatest battlefields of World War I, with more than 700,000 killed or wounded.

everything suddenly stops
in the garish glare
of its obviousness

a yellow wall
a cold blue sky
black wire on the wall—
(their horizon)

this is the moment
for the mutiny of the five senses
which would like to escape
like rats from a sinking ship
before the bullet has reached its destination
the eye sees its coming
the ear registers its metallic whine
the nostrils fill with acrid smoke
petals of blood skim against the palate
the touch shrinks and relaxes

they now lie on the ground
covered with shadow up to the eyes
the firing squad departs
their buttons belts
and steel helmets
are more alive
than those men under the wall

3

This is not something I've just learned
I have known it for some time
so why did I write
those minor poems about flowers

what did the five talk about
that night
before the execution

prophetic dreams
an adventure in a brothel
spare parts for cars
a sea-voyage
and that he shouldn't have bid

when he had all those spades
that vodka is best
as wine gives you a headache
women
fruit
life
thus it seems one can
fill one's poetry with the names of Greek shepherds
fill one's time trying to capture the colors of dawn
one can write about love
but also
in deadly seriousness
offer to the world misled
a rose

Translated by **Jan Darowski**

ELEPHANT

As a matter of fact elephants are very sensitive and nervous. They have a prolific imagination, which allows them now and then to forget about their appearance. When they come down into water, they close their eyes. At the sight of their own legs they are overcome with agitation and weep.

I myself knew an elephant who fell in love with a hummingbird. He lost weight, did not sleep, and finally died of a heart attack. Those who do not know about the nature of elephants have been saying: he was so slobbish.

Translated by **Peter Dale Scott**

APOLLO AND MARSYAS

The real duel of Apollo
with Marsyas
(absolute ear

APOLLO AND MARSYAS

Apollo and Marsyas: In Greek mythology, Marsyas challenged Apollo to a contest of flute with lyre. Apollo won by adding his voice to the strings. King Midas, who voted for Marsyas, was given a pair of donkey ears by Apollo. Marsyas was flayed alive in a cave, his blood the origin of the River Marsyas.

versus immense range)
takes place in the evening
when as we already know
the judges
have awarded victory to the god

bound tight to a tree
meticulously stripped of his skin
Marsyas
howls
before the howl reaches his tall ears
he reposes in the shadow of that howl

shaken by a shudder of disgust
Apollo is cleaning his instrument

only seemingly
is the voice of Marsyas
monotonous
and composed of a single vowel
Aaa
in reality
Marsyas relates
the inexhaustible wealth
of his body

bald mountains of liver
white ravines of aliment
rustling forests of lung
sweet hillocks of muscle
joints bile blood and shudders
the wintry wind of bone
over the salt of memory
shaken by a shudder of disgust
Apollo is cleaning his instrument

now to the chorus
is joined the backbone of Marsyas
in principle the same A
only deeper with the addition of rust

this is already beyond the endurance
of the god with nerves of artificial fiber

along a gravel path
hedged with box
the victor departs
wondering
whether out of Marsyas' howling
there will not some day arise
a new kind
of art—let us say—concrete

suddenly
at his feet
falls a petrified nightingale

he looks back
and sees
that the hair of the tree to which Marsyas was fastened
is white
completely

Translated by **Czeslaw Milosz**

CZESLAW MILOSZ

1911–

Czeslaw Milosz was born in Lithuania and educated in Wilno and Paris. During the Second World War he was a member of the Polish underground and edited in Warsaw a clandestinely printed anthology of anti-Nazi poems. Milosz served the Communist government of Poland as a diplomat from 1946 to 1951 in the Cultural Affairs Division in Washington and Paris. He sought political asylum in Paris in 1951 and lived there for ten years as a freelance writer. Milosz is now Professor of Slavic Languages at the University of California in Berkeley. Books of poems include *Three Deep Winters* (1936), *Escape* (1945), *Daylight* (1953), and *Selected Poems* (1974).

The poems of Czeslaw Milosz are lyrical prophecies, domestic visions, ambient recollections. For Milosz the industrial pollution of contemporary civilization is a second nature created by humankind to mirror its own first nature. The poems are informed by the silent voices of the hamster, the hedgehog, and the mole; peopled by those who tie up tomato plants and gather apples near the pigsty; and colored by the distant lights of the apocalypse. Milosz: "Only this is worthy of praise—the day."

A SONG ON THE END OF THE WORLD

On the day the world ends
A bee circles a clover,
A fisherman mends a glimmering net.
Happy porpoises jump in the sea,
By the rainspout young sparrows are playing
And the snake is gold-skinned as it should always be.

On the day the world ends
Women walk through the fields under their umbrellas,
A drunkard grows sleepy at the edge of a lawn,
Vegetable vendors shout in the street
And a yellow-sailed boat comes nearer the island,
The voice of a violin lasts in the air
And leads into a starry night.

And those who expected lightning and thunder
Are disappointed.
And those who expected signs and archangels' trumps
Do not believe it is happening now.
As long as the sun and the moon are above,
As long as the bumblebee visits a rose,
As long as rosy infants are born
No one believes it is happening now.

Only a white-haired old man, who would be a prophet
Yet is not a prophet, for he's much too busy,
Repeats while he binds his tomatoes:
No other end of the world will there be,
No other end of the world will there be.

1944

A POOR CHRISTIAN LOOKS AT THE GHETTO

Bees build around red liver,
Ants build around black bone.
It has begun: the tearing, the trampling on silks,

It has begun: the breaking of glass, wood, copper, nickel, silver,
foam
Of gypsum, iron sheets, violin strings, trumpets, leaves, balls,
crystals.
Poof! Phosphorescent fire from yellow walls
Engulfs animal and human hair.

Bees build around the honeycomb of lungs,
Ants build around white bone.
Torn is paper, rubber, linen, leather, flax,
Fiber, fabrics, cellulose, snakeskin, wire.
The roof and the wall collapse in flame and heat seizes the
foundations.
Now there is only the earth, sandy, trodden down,
With one leafless tree.

Slowly, boring a tunnel, a guardian mole makes his way,
With a small red lamp fastened to his forehead.
He touches burned bodies, counts them, pushes on,
He distinguishes human ashes by their luminous vapor,
The ashes of each man by a different part of the spectrum.
Bees build around a red trace.
Ants build around the place left by my body.

I am afraid, so afraid of the guardian mole.
He has swollen eyelids, like a Patriarch
Who has sat much in the light of candles
Reading the great book of the species.
What will I tell him, I, a Jew of the New Testament,
Waiting two thousand years for the second coming of Jesus?
My broken body will deliver me to his sight
And he will count me among the helpers of death:
The uncircumcised.

1943

ADVICE

Yes, it is true that the landscape changed a little.
Where there were forests, now there are pears of factories,
cisterns.
Approaching the mouth of the river we hold our noses.

Its current carries oil and chlorine and methyl compounds,
Not to mention the by-products of the Books of Abstraction:
Excrement, urine, and dead sperm.
A huge stain of artificial color poisons fish in the sea.
Where the shore of the bay was overgrown with rushes
Now it is rusted with smashed machines, ashes and bricks.
We used to read in old poets about the scent of earth
And grasshoppers. Now we bypass the fields:
Ride as fast as you can through the chemical zone of the farmers.
The insect and the bird are extinguished. Far away a bored man
Drags the dust with his tractor, an umbrella against the sun.
What do we regret?—I ask. A tiger? A shark?
We created a second Nature in the image of the first
So as not to believe that we live in Paradise.
It is possible that when Adam woke in the garden
The beasts licked the air and yawned, friendly,
While their fangs and their tails, lashing their backs,
Were figurative and the red-backed shrike,
Later, much later, named Lanius collurio,
Did not impale caterpillars on spikes of the blackthorn.
However, other than that moment, what we know of Nature
Does not speak in its favor. Ours is no worse.
So I beg you, no more of those lamentations.

Translations by **Czeslaw Milosz**

THROUGHOUT OUR LANDS

III

If I had to show what the world is for me
I would take a hamster or a hedgehog or a mole
and place him in a theatre seat one evening
and, bringing my ear close to his humid snout,
would listen to what he says about the spotlights,
sounds of the music, and movements of the dance.

ADVICE
shrike: a predatory bird.

XI

Paulina, her room behind the servants' quarters, with one window
    on the orchard
where I gather the best apples near the pigsty
squishing with my big toe the warm muck of the dunghill,
and the other window on the well (I love to drop the bucket down
and scare its inhabitants, the green frogs).
Paulina, a geranium, the chill of a dirt floor,
a hard bed with three pillows,
an iron crucifix and images of the saints
decorated with palms and paper roses.
Paulina died long ago, but is.
And, I am somehow convinced, not just in my consciousness.

Above her rough Lithuanian peasant face
hovers a spindle of hummingbirds, and her flat calloused feet
are sprinkled by sapphire water in which dolphins
with their backs arching
frolic.

XIV

Cabeza, if anyone knew all about civilization, it was you.
A bookkeeper from Castile, what a fix you were in
to have to wander about, where no notion,
no cipher, no stroke of a pen dipped in sepia,
only a boat thrown up on the sand by surf,
crawling naked on all fours, under the eye of immobile Indians,
and suddenly their wail in the void of sky and sea,
their lament: that even the gods are unhappy.
For seven years you were their predicted god,
bearded, white-skinned, beaten if you couldn't work a miracle.
Seven years' march from the Mexican Gulf to California,
the hu-hu-hu of tribes, hot bramble of the continent.
But afterwards? Who am I, the lace of cuffs

Cabeza: Alvar Nuñez Cabeza de Vaca, Spanish explorer (c. 1490-c. 1564); after seven years of heroic exploits in the New World, he was placed under arrest in 1544, and in 1551 was banished to Africa for eight years.

not mine, the table carved with lions not mine, Doña Clara's
fan, the slipper from under her gown—hell, no.
On all fours! On all fours!
Smear our thighs with war paint.
Lick the ground. Wha wha, hu hu.

Translated by **Peter Dale Scott** *and the author*

PORTUGAL

SOPHIA DE MELLO BREYNER

1919–

Sophia de Mello was born in Oporto. She studied classics at Lisbon University and has traveled often to Brazil. In addition to her seven volumes of poems she has written short stories and has translated Dante and Shakespeare. In 1964 Sophia de Mello won the Grand Poetry Prize of the Portuguese Society of Writers for *Sixth Book*. She lives in Lisbon. Other books include *Poems* (1944, 1949), *The Day of the Sea* (1947), *The Gypsy Christ* (1961), and *Geography* (1968).

The poems of Sophia de Mello are distilled explorations into the archetypal vastnesses of space and time—momentary orderings in a fragmented and disordered existence. In these personal visions, she gropes toward a lost and unregainable garden.

LISTEN

Listen:
Everything is calm and smooth and sleeping.
The walls apparent, the floor reflecting,
And painted on the glass of the window,
The sky, green emptiness, two trees.
Close your eyes and rest no less profoundly
Than any other thing which never flowered.

Don't touch anything, don't look, don't recollect.
One step enough
To shatter the furniture baked
By endless, unused days of sunlight.

Don't remember, don't anticipate.
You do not share the nature of a fruit:
Nothing here that time or sun will ripen.

YOU SLEEP CRADLED

You sleep cradled by rocks
And the wind comes and gibbers in my ear.
I listen, seek, call out but you don't answer,
And the world returned to shadow.

I also am trapped, encased, a prisoner
Who wants to break through into daylight,
To resurrect, to breathe, to see again,
But all the world returns to shadows.

And the ocean's voice weighs down the sky and land
A voice which is laden, which falters
And never stops.

White birds violate the windows,
Anemones scintillate upon the rocks:
The terror of my loneliness, of listening
With this dead moment caught between my fingers.

THIS IS THE TIME

This is the time
Of a jungle without meaning

Even the blue air coagulates to gratings
And the sun's light becomes obscene.

This the night
Thick with jackals
Weighted with grief

The time when men give up.

SIBYLS

Sibyls of deep caves, of petrifaction,
Totally loveless and sightless,
Feeding nothingness as if a sacred fire

SIBYLS
sibyl: a female prophetess.

While shadow unmakes night and day
Into the same light of fleshless horror.

Drive out that foul dew
Of impacted nights, the sweat
Of forces turned against themselves
When words batter the walls
In blind, wild swoops of trapped birds
And the horror of being winged
Shrills like a clock through a vacuum.

Translations by **Ruth Fainlight**

ROMANIA

NICHITA STANESCU

1933–

Nichita Stanescu was born in the oil city of Ploesti. He studied at the University of Bucharest, won the Writers Union Poetry Prize in 1964, attended Poetry International in London in 1971, and is currently the assistant editor of *Gazeta Literara.* Stanescu's seven books of poetry include *The Sense of Love* (1960), *Vertical Red* (1967), *The Egg and the Sphere* (1968), and *Alpha* (1968).

In the poems of Nichita Stanescu buzz saws cut off horses' heads in dreams, and leaves stick to the severed necks. One drinks the blood out of glass jugs and soldiers' helmets, and is restored—it is our blood shed for us in remembrance of our own dyings every day. Debunking, satiric, movie-like, the poems seize images from nature and the unconscious, demanding a new idealism.

MARCH RAIN

It was raining like hell
and we were making love in the attic.
By the window, in an oval sky,
clouds hurried. It was March.

The walls of the room were restless
under drawings done with crayon
and our hearts danced,
invisible in a concrete world.

'You will wet your wings,' you said,
'it is raining everywhere in space and time.'
'Lorelei, it does not matter,' I said to you,
'my flying makes the rain, it is the feathers.'

Lorelei: See note, p. 2.

And I got up without knowing
where I had left my room in the world.
You shouted: 'Answer me—
which is more beautiful, man or the rain?'

It was raining like hell
and we were making love in the attic.
I wished that it could have gone on
for ever. It was March.

Translated by **Roy MacGregor Hastie**

SONG

Only the present instant has memories.
What really took place, no one knows.
The dead exchange all the time with each other,
they change their names, their numbers, one, two, three . . .
Only the future really exists,
only the things that did not happen happen,
the events that have not yet taken place
hang from the branch of a tree,
which is not born itself,
a sort of half ghost.
The only body I have that really exists is the body
I will have as an old man, of wood and of stone.

My grief hears the barking of the unborn dogs
barking at the men not yet born.
Oh only those men and dogs will really exist!
We the living are a night dream, elegant,
with thousands of feet, running everywhere!

SECOND ELEGY

A god was set up in every hollow.

If a crack appeared in a stone, they
swiftly brought up a god and laid him in.

If a bridge collapsed, then a god
would appear where that used to be,

and whenever a small hole turned up in the asphalt
it would be filled in with a god right away.

I'm warning you, don't ever slice a hand or a leg
anywhere by accident or for any reason!
They'll lay a god in the wound immediately
as they've already done everywhere else.
They'll set up a god there, just right
for us to worship, because he protects
all things that are separated from themselves.

And soldier, the most important thing of all is, don't ever lose
an eye!
Because someone will requisition a god
and insert it into the socket,
and then he'll sit throned there stiff as a stone
and our souls will all go in circles around him . . .
and even you will convince your soul to worship him
as we worship strangers.

Translated by **Robert Bly** *and* **Alexander Ivasinc**

THE SLEEP CONTAINING SAWS

The sleep containing saws
cuts off the horses' heads,
and the horses run neighing with blood
like red tables which have fled to the streets
from the Last Supper.

And the horses run, jolting shadows
in the red vapors. Phantoms are in their saddles.
Leaves stick to their necks, or else
collapse in on themselves
as the shadow of trees collapses into fountains.

Bring buckets, bring large glass jugs,
bring jugs and cups,
bring old helmets left over from the war,

bring everyone who lacks an eye, or in place
of an arm has an open place which can be filled.

The blood of beheaded
horses flows everywhere freely,
and I who saw this first
tell you that I drank from it, and it tasted
excellent.

Translated by **Peter Jay** *and* **Petru Popescu**

EIGHTH ELEGY: HYPERBOREAN

Then she said to me, seeing the fixed points
of my being:
I would like us to run away to the Far North,
and give birth to you live
on the snow like a bitch
running and howling
at the echoes hanging from the night stars.

Just the two of us in the snow and on the ice.
I would undress
and jump into the water, my soul
unmistaken taking as model
the beats of the sea.

The ocean will swell, surely, will swell
until each one of its molecules
is like the eye of a deer
or
much larger
like the body of a whale.

I would jump into water swollen like this
finding my way into molecular motion
in one movement, desperate
I would zigzag; broken

EIGHTH ELEGY: HYPERBOREAN
Hyperborean: in Greek mythology, an inhabitant of a land of perpetual sunshine beyond the North Wind (Boreas); (adj.) very cold, frigid.

by the vast, dark, cold molecules
Hercules' helpers.

Unable to drown and unable to walk or fly
only zigzag and zigzag and zigzag,
becoming part of a family of ferns
by a fate of spore . . .

I would like us to run away to the Far North
and give birth to you live
howling, running, crushed by
the violet sky
onto ice split into icebergs
scattered beneath the violet sky.

II

Suddenly she made a light gush
near her knee, vertical
under a red hat
and that virginal.

She threw down a book near my ankle
written in cuneiform.
Angels pressed like flowers
were drying out, broken.

Angels blackened by the type
between the page above and the page below,
pressed like flowers, without moisture or freshness
pressed fiercely . . .

To cut myself with their glances,
sent without permission in my direction
while I put on, like a toga,
a sadness sharp as an icicle.

In the Far North, she said to me,
taking hold of each other by the nape
of the right arm, the one which doesn't fly,
we will jump under the ice into the water.

The Far North, home
for life of great minds,

birthplace of stone children,
models for sculptured saints.

Far North, white-black,
gold-silver,
revelation, non-revelation, sadness
running and feeling the way.

III

Suddenly she raised her head
above her ran white globes
and the clouds shredded themselves into green ribbons.
There was a sphere, with dark patches like mountains
turned by birds, beaks to the ground,
with loud beatings of wings.
Surely this is the ideal of flight.
We can see the soft movements of great storks
on the rocks. We can see
immense eagles, heads in stone
beating their wings to deafen you, and we can see
a bird bigger than all the others
with a beak like a bluesteel shaft
around which
the sphere turns at its four seasons.

Surely this is the ideal of flight,
and a green aura heralds
a much more passionate ideal.

Translated by **Roy MacGregor Hastie**

RUSSIA/SOVIET UNION

BELLA AKHMADULINA

1937–

Bella Akhmadulina was born in Moscow during the Stalin purges. She studied, while still a schoolgirl, in the literature study group of the state-owned automobile factory, later attended and was expelled from the Gorky Institute, and has since published mainly in the underground magazine *Sintaxis*. Formerly married to Yevgeny Yevtushenko, she is now married to the writer Yury Nagibin. Akhmadulina has translated into Russian the Georgian poets Klividze, Chikovani, and Chilidze, and became a member of the Soviet Writers' Union as a translator. Her first book of poems, *Chord* (1962), sold out immediately in Russia; her only other collection was published in West Germany (*Shivering*, 1968).

The fierce gentleness of Bella Akhmadulina gathers into a powerful lyrical verse alternately thundering and beckoning and whispering. Her Russian lines tremble with intensity: melodious, aggrieved, ironic, furious, tender. In her poems she invokes the memory of past Russian poets such as Pushkin, Tsvetaeva, and Pasternak, and she transforms her own nerve endings into the nerve endings of man and womankind alike.

I SWEAR

I swear by this summer snapshot
of you, lonely as a gallows
braced on the porch of a stranger,
you were driven out of that house.
That crinkled satin dress
strangles your throat,
and you sit in our past, mute
to our hunger and grief.
It's too much for a beaten horse.

I swear by this picture, by the frail
sharp elbows as small as a child's,

and by the long, drawn, dying smile
like an alibi for children.

I swear by the dark thrusts
wound in the airless griefs
and fevers of your poems,
that I, my throat bleeding,
will also cough and weep.
And I swear by this stolen image,
which I carry and never forget,
that you, a stranger, taboo,
are God's. He misses you.
I swear by your gaunt bones
crawling upon you like rat teeth,
and by holy and blessed Russia
who forgets your deep asylum,
and by that bastard out of Africa
watching over the children,
and the children, by Tversky Boulevard,
and by the sad peace of a heaven
lacking profession and pain.

I'll kill your Yelabuga
and let the new grandchildren sleep,
even though the mothers of mothers
frighten them there in the evenings,
whispering, Yelabuga! she lives!
  "Child, sleep; be still
  Or the blind Yelabuga comes!"
It is ready now! It's coming!
It is stumbling! Quickly, quickly!
And I bring down my boot with its nails
hard on its stretching fingers,
and hard on its throat, and keep
the weight of my heel to its tip.

I swear by the children its blood
will burn my feet like green poison,

bastard out of Africa: the poet Pushkin, whose mother was of African descent; his monument is in the Tversky Boulevard.

Yelabuga: town in Russia; see note on Marina Tsvetaeva below.

and I'll throw to this bottomless earth
the ripe green egg of its tail.
But not one word of that porch
where Marina, homeless, died!
And I swear, though our Yelabuga
should fix me with yellow eyes
and swear in the dark, in the stench
of swamps, by the toad of spring,
that it will kill me. I swear!

Translated by **Joseph Langland, Tamas Aczel,** *and* **Laszlo Tikos**

VERSES ABOUT GEORGIA

The names of Georgian women . . .

There across the sea sails were straying,
and, indifferent to heat,
plane trees blossomed, lazily
shedding December leaves.

The bazaar's noises were strident,
and on the bald heights
the basalt's interlacing stripes
lay black in the snow's lights.

And a little shop in the park by the sea
stood out white and mute,
and the names of Georgian women vaguely
had the scent of grapes just cut.

They turned into a stream of song
running down to the sea,
and then they swam out like a black swan
bending its neck curiously.

I SWEAR

Marina: Marina Tsvetaeva, Russian poet who returned to Russia from Europe in 1939, only to have her daughter arrested, her husband shot, and her son killed in the war. She committed suicide in 1941 in Yelabuga.

VERSES ABOUT GEORGIA

The names of Georgian women: the Russian title of the poem; used as a subtitle by the translators.

A girl called Lamara ran over the stones
toward the edge of the water,
laughing as she jarred her bones,
her lips made up with wine.

In the water Medeya's hair was streaming,
her hands interlaced
in a waterfall of drops striking
the dry air they displaced.

And flowering over the oleanders,
gathering them into one spray,
for a moment the name of Ariadna
hovered and faded away.

Leaning close to the water as a willow,
a mooring by the piles stirred.
"Zissana!" they called down from a window.
"Natela," a voice answered.

THE WAITRESS

But now a queen is walking by,
her earring slowly swaying.
Humbly each young man lowers his eye
and hears what her foot is saying.

She is rustling with the slide of silk.
Her eyes have moist places.
Suddenly everyone is struck
by the shock of her eyelashes.

How splendidly she walks away!
A waitress, never spilling
an arm-high glass, in the café
under the pale blue ceiling.

The customer reading the menu begins
what she can always expand,
and the snowy lances of the napkins
soar up under her hand.

And the unapproachably severe
starched crown upon her curls
floats over her correct coiffure
as white and cool as pearls.

Translations by **Geoffrey Dutton** *and* **Igor Mezhakoff-Koriakin**

JOSEPH BRODSKY

1940–

Joseph Brodsky was born in Leningrad. He entered school when he was seven, left it when he was fifteen, and became in turn a metal-worker, photographer, medical assistant, geologist, sailor, and stocker. Brodsky began to write poems when he was eighteen. In 1964 he was arrested and tried for "social parasitism" and sentenced to five years at hard labor in the northern part of European Russia. Before his trial he spent a short time being examined in a psychiatric prison hospital (the scene of "Sadly and Tenderly," below). Because of protests both inside and outside Russia, Brodsky was released after two years, and he returned to his occupation of translator. In May 1972 Russian authorities proposed that he leave Russia for Israel; instead he came to the United States as poet-in-residence at the University of Michigan. Only four Brodsky poems have been published in the Soviet Union. The first authorized collection of his poems, *A Halt in the Desert,* was published in the United States in 1970, followed by his *Selected Poems* in 1973. Brodsky read at the Poetry International in 1972, and his poems have been translated into French, Italian, German, Czech, Polish, Serbo-Croatian, Hebrew, Spanish, and Greek.

Joseph Brodsky's poems are elegiac, sharply visioned, memorial. To expand one of his own lines, he "transforms the stillness of two pure parallel lines into streams of wavy bones," like an etching needle moving within a prison scene. Chant-like cadences, lyrical outpourings—the poems detail the formal precision of human pain. Brodsky's cantorlike public readings express the elevated rhythms of these poems: eerie tenor recitations reminiscent of tribal convocations.

THE FUNERAL OF BOBÒ

1

Bobò is dead, but don't take off your hat.
No gesture we could make will help us bear it.
Why mount a butterfly upon the spit
Of the Admiralty tower? We'd only tear it.

On every side, no matter where you glance,
Are squares of windows. As for "What happened?"—well,
Open an empty can by way of answer
And say "Just that, as near as one can tell."

Bobò is dead. Wednesday is almost over.
On streets which offer you no place to go,
Such whiteness lies. Only the night river,
With its black water, does not wear the snow.

2

Bobò is dead; there's sadness in this line.
O window-squares, O arches' semicircles,
And such fierce frost that if one's to be slain,
Let blazing firearms do the dirty-work.

Farewell, Bobò, my beautiful and sweet.
These tear-drops dot the page like holes in cheese.
We are too weak to follow you, and yet
To take a stand exceeds our energies.

Your image, as I here and now predict,
Whether in crackling cold or waves of heat,
Shall never dwindle—quite the reverse, in fact—
In Rossi's matchless, long, and tapering street.

3

Bobò is dead. Something I might convey
Slips from my grasp, as bath-soap sometimes does.
Today, within a dream, I seemed to lie
Upon my bed. And there, in fact, I was.

Tear off a page, but read the date aright:
It's with a zero that our woes commence.
Without her, dreams suggest the waking state,
And squares of air push through the window-vents.

Bobò is dead. One feels an impulse, with
Half-parted lips, to murmur "Why? What for?"
It's emptiness, no doubt, which follows death.
That's likelier than Hell—and worse, what's more.

Rossi: K. I. (1775–1849), a well-known designer of palaces, parks, squares, and streets in St. Petersburg.

4

You were all things, Bobò. But your decease
Has changed you. You are nothing; you are not;
Or rather, you are a clot of emptiness—
Which also, come to think of it, is a lot.

Bobò is dead. To these round eyes, the view
Of the bare horizon-line is like a knife.
But neither Kiki nor Zazà, Bobò,
Will ever take your place. Not on your life.

Now Thursday. I believe in emptiness.
There, it's like Hell, but shittier, I've heard.
And the new Dante, pregnant with his message,
Bends to the empty page and writes a word.

Translated by **Richard Wilbur**

SADLY AND TENDERLY

To A. Gorbunov

They served us noodles one more time, and you,
Mickiewicz, pushing back the soup-bowl, said
that you would rather eat nothing at all.
Hence I, too, without risk that the attendant
would think me mutinous, could follow you
to the latrine and stay there till retreat.
'The month of January always yields
to February, then comes March.' Thin scraps
of conversation. Tiles and porcelain
aglow, where water makes a crystal sound.

Mickiewicz lay down, his unseeing eyes
fixed on the orange nightlamp by the door.
(Perhaps he saw his own fate mirrored there.)
Babanov called the attendant to the hall.
Beside the darkened window I stood rooted;
behind my back the television crackled.
'Hey, Gorbunov, just look at that huge tail.'—
'And that queer eye.'—'And there, see that big lump
above the fin.'—'It seems to be an abscess.'

Thus, mouths agape and goggle-eyed, we stared
through winter windows at the starry Fish
and wagged our shaven heads, in that place where
men spit on floors—

where sometimes we are given fish to eat,
but never knife or fork to eat it with.

1964

A WINTER EVENING IN YALTA

He has a sear Levantine face, its pock-
marks hiding under sideburns. As he gropes
for cigarettes, his fingers in the pack,
a dull ring on his right hand suddenly
refracts at least two hundred watts; my eye's
frail crystal cannot tolerate the flash.
I blink, and then he says as he inhales
a mouthful of blue smoke, 'Excuse it, please.'

Crimean January. Winter comes
as though to romp along the Black Sea shore.
The snow loses its grip on the thin-tipped
and spiny-margined leaves of agave plants.
The restaurants are nearly empty now.
Ichthyosaurs belch their black smoke and soil
the roadstead. Rotting laurel permeates
the air. 'And will you drink this vile stuff?' 'Yes.'

A smile and twilight, then, and a carafe.
A barman in the distance wrings his hands,
describing circles, like a porpoise pup
around a fish-filled felucca. Squareness
of windows. Yellow flowers in pots. And snow-
flakes tumbling past. I beg you, moment, stay!

SADLY AND TENDERLY
Fish: the constellation Pisces.

A WINTER EVENING IN YALTA
Yalta: a summer resort on the Crimean coast.
ichthyosaurs: extinct marine reptiles with fishlike bodies and long noses.
roadstead: a place, less enclosed than a harbor, where ships ride at anchor.
felucca: a narrow boat, usually rigged with lateen sails as well as oars.

It's not that you're particularly fair
but rather that you're unrepeatable.

A PROPHECY

We'll go and live together by the shore;
huge dams will wall us from the continent.
A home-made lamp will hurl its warming glow
across the roundness of our centered space.
We shall wage war at cards, and cock an ear
to catch the crashing of the maddened surf.
We'll gently cough, or sigh a soundless sigh,
whenever the wind roars too raucously.

I shall be old, and you will still be young.
But, as the youngsters say, we'll count the time
that's left us till the new age breaks in days,
not years. In our reversed, small Netherland
we'll plant a kitchen-garden, you and I;
and we shall sizzle oysters by the door,
and drink the rays of the sun's octopus,

Let summer rains crash on our cucumbers;
we'll get as tanned as any Eskimo,
and you will run your fingers tenderly
along the virgin V where I'm unburned.
I'll see my collarbone in the clear glass,
and glimpse a mirrored wave behind my back,
and my old Geiger counter, cased in tin,
that dangles from its faded, sweat-soaked strap.

When winter comes, unpitying, it will
twist off the thatch from our wood roof. And if
we make a child, we'll call the boy Andrei,
Anna the girl, so that our Russian speech,
imprinted on its wrinkled little face,
shall never be forgot. Our alphabet's
first sound is but the lengthening of a sigh
and thus may be affirmed for future time.

We shall wage war at cards until the tide's
retreating sinuosities draw us,
with all our trumps, down and away . . .

Our child will gaze in silence at a moth,
not fathoming its urgent moth-motives
for beating at our lamp. But then the time
will come when he must make his way back through
the dam that walls us from the continent.

Translations by **George L. Kline**

ANDREI VOZNESENSKY

1933–

Andrei Voznesensky was born in Moscow. As a child he lived for a time in the ancient Russian city of Vladimir, but during the war he went with his mother to Kurgan, in the Ural mountains. His father was an engineering professor, and his mother, who taught Russian literature, read Severyanin and Pasternak to him as a child. Voznesensky graduated from the Moscow Architectural Institute in 1957, but when his senior project was destroyed in a fire he abandoned his architectural career, moved to Peredelkino, and stayed with Pasternak until Pasternak's death. His first book of poems, *Mosaic and Parabola,* appeared in 1960; two years later 14,000 people heard him read his poetry at a sports stadium and 500,000 subscribed to buy a book of his poems. In 1963, in disfavor with the Khruschev government, he wandered as an exile around the country. Voznesensky regained official approval as the political climate changed, and he has read his poems many times in the United States. Other books include *Achilles Heart* (1966) and *Shadow of Sound* (1970).

In his poems Andrei Voznesensky bears witness to the extraordinary suffering of ordinary people. His eye is keen and his touch deft, and the poems break through their own formal structures with power and clarity. Metaphors of nature expand the boundaries of the merely descriptive, and pictures of Russian life accumulate like an album of remarkable events.

AUTUMN

The flapping of ducks' wings.
And on the pathways in the parks
the shimmer of the last cobwebs
and of the last bicycle spokes.

You should listen to what they are hinting:
go knock at the door of the last house for leavetaking;
in that proper house a woman lives
who does not expect a husband for supper.

She will release the bolt for me
and nuzzle against my coat,
she will laugh as she offers her lips to me;
and suddenly, gone limp, she will understand everything—
the autumn call of the fields,
the scattering of seed in the wind, the breakup of families . . .

Still young, trembling with cold,
she will think about how
even the apple tree bears fruit
and the old brown cow has a calf

and how life ferments in the hollows of oaks,
in pastures, in houses, in windswept woods,
ripening with the grain, treading with woodcocks,
and she will weep, sick with desire,

whispering, "What good are they to me:
my hands, my breasts? What sense does it make
to live as I do, lighting the stove,
repeating my daily round of work?"

And I shall embrace her—
I who can't make sense of it either—
while outside, in the first hoarfrost,
the fields turn aluminum.
Across them—black across them—black and gray
my footprints will march
to the railway station.

Translated by **Stanley Kunitz**

THE LAST TRAIN TO MALÁKHOVKA

Boys with fancy flick knives,
Girls with brassy gold-crowned smiles,
Two conductresses, those stony
Sphinxes, cat-napping . . .

They're all nodding, our workaday citizens,
The coach is blacked out with sleep

THE LAST TRAIN TO MALAKHOVKA
Malákhovka: a town about 18 miles SE of Moscow.

Except at the end of the car where jigs
A hubbub of drunken strings.

I'm there too, near the door,
To get away from the heat and snores.
Around me throbbing like a gypsy camp
Thieves and guitars . . .

I happen to start to say a poem
To some of these toughs in the shadows . . .
Cigarette butts, a litter of
Spat-out sunflower seeds . . .

They've rackets of their own
But I recite to them
About a girl who's crying
In the glassy night of a telephone booth.

They've been up before the judge a hundred times
They don't care what happens to them
They've got away with murder
And figure that they always can

You think they give a damn about that girl
Crying in the telephone booth?
For them she's no more than this one here
All bangs, plastered with powder.

. . .You stand there, you've got
That soggy used-up look,
Your blouse records the fingerprints
Of half the boys in Malákhovka,

Yet it's you who are crying stormily
And shining with tears
Whisper to me obscenely
The purest words

And then from the train
Astounding everyone
You leap to the platform—
Purer than Beatrice.

Translated by **Jean Garrigue**

Beatrice: the woman to whom the Italian poet Dante dedicated most of his poetry; probably Beatrice Portinari, who died in 1290 at the age of 24.

BALLAD OF 1941

To the partisans of the Kerch stone quarries

The piano has crawled underground. Hauled
In for firewood, sprawled
With frozen barrels, crates, and sticks,
The piano is waiting for the axe.

Legless, a black box,
It lies on its belly like a lizard,
Droning, heaving, backed
In an empty mine shaft.

Blood-red, his frozen fingers swollen,
Three lost on one hand, he goes down
On his hands
and knees
To reach the keys.

Seven fingers of an ex-pianist play,
Their frost-bitten skin, steaming, peels away
As from a boiled potato. Their beauty,
Their godliness flame and reply,

Like the great northern lights.
Everything played before is a great lie.
All the reflections of flaming chandeliers,
The white columns, the grand tiers

In warm concert halls—a great lie.
But the steel of the piano howls in me.
I lie in that catacomb,
And I am huge as that piano.

I mirror the soot of the mine. I ape
Hunger, the light of fires, the human shape.
And for my crowning crescendo
I wait for the lick of the axe.

Translated by **Stanley Moss**

partisans of the Kerch stone quarries: On Dec. 25, 1941, a battle occurred between the Russians and the German occupational forces in Kerch, a Ukrainian city near the Black Sea; there are many stone quarries in the area.

FOGGY STREET

The air is gray-white as a pigeon feather.
        Police bob up like corks on a fishing net.
Foggy weather.
What century is it? What era? I forget.

As in a nightmare, everything is crumbling;
        people have come unsoldered; nothing's intact . . .
I plod on, stumbling—
Or flounder in cotton wool, to be more exact.

Noses. Parking lights. Badges flash and blur.
        All's vague, as at a magic-lantern show.
Your hat check, sir?
Mustn't walk off with the wrong head, you know.

It's as if a woman who's scarcely left your lips
        should blur in the mind, yet trouble it with recall—
Bereft now, widowed by your love's eclipse—
        still yours, yet suddenly not yours at all . . .

Can that be Venus? No—an ice-cream vendor!
        I bump into curbstones, bump into passers-by . . .
Are they friends, I wonder?
Home-bred Iagos, how covert you are, how sly!

Why, it's you, my darling, shivering there alone!
        Your overcoat's too big for you, my dear.
But why have you grown
That mustache? Why is there frost in your hairy ear!

I trip. I stagger. I persist.
        Murk, murk . . . there's nothing visible anywhere.
Whose is the cheek you brush now in the mist?
Ahoy there!
One's voice won't carry in this heavy air . . .

When the fog lifts, how brilliant it is, how rare!

Translated by **Richard Wilbur**

Iago: character in Shakespeare's *Othello* who urges Othello in his false accusations of Desdemona.

HUGH MACDIARMID

(CHRISTOPHER MURRAY GRIEVE)

1892–

Hugh MacDiarmid was born in Langholm near the Scottish-English border. As prime mover of the Scottish Renaissance, he revived the Scots vernacular as a contemporary poetic language. In 1922, four years before he published *The Drunk Man Looks at the Thistle* in Scots, he adopted a pseudonym because of his earlier public unfriendliness to the vernacular. MacDiarmid left the Scottish National Party to join the Communist Party, and ran for Prime Minister in the 1964 general election. In 1967 he gave a series of readings and lectures at the University of Massachusetts, Amherst. MacDiarmid now lives near Biggar in Lanarkshire. Other books include *Sangshaw* (Song Glade) (1925), *Penny Beer* (1926), *The Kind of Poetry I Want* (1961), and *Collected Poems* (1967).

The poems of Hugh MacDiarmid are Beethovian, "full of erudition, expertise, and ecstasy." MacDiarmid surrounds objects and experiences and memories with the accumulated insights of contemporary humankind, and his subjects glow in the light of human learning and the warmth of human passion. Wide-angled, efflorescent, particular—MacDiarmid gives us whole choruses of flowers, minerals, languages, geographies, kingdoms, glands, philosophies.

PERFECT

ON THE WESTERN SEABOARD OF SOUTH UIST

Los muertos abren los ojos a los que viven

I found a pigeon's skull on the machair,
All the bones pure white and dry, and chalky,
But perfect,
Without a crack or a flaw anywhere.

South Uist: an island in the Outer Hebrides, Scotland.
Los muertos . . . los que viven: the dead open the eyes of the living.
machair: a flat or low-lying plain or field.

At the back, rising out of the beak,
Were domes like bubbles of thin bone,
Almost transparent, where the brain had been
That fixed the tilt of the wings.

from DIREACH III

And suddenly the flight of a bird reminds me
Of how I once went out towards sunset in a boat
Off the rocky coast of Wigtownshire
And of my glimpse of the first rock-pigeon I saw.
It darted across one of the steep gullies
At the bottom of which our boat lay rocking
On the dark green water—and vanished into safety
In a coign of the opposite wall
Before a shot could be fired.
It swerved in the air,
As though doubtful of its way,
Then with a glad swoop of certainty
It sped forward, turned upward,
And disappeared into some invisible cranny
Below the overhanging brow of the cliff.
So must Euripides have seen a sea-bird
Dart to its nest in the cliffs of Attica.
For an instant, sitting in that swaying boat
Under the red rocks, while the sunset ebbed down the sky
And the water lapped quietly at my side,
I again felt the mind of the poet reaching out
Across the centuries to touch mine.
Scotland and China and Greece!
Here where the colors—
Red standing for heat,
Solar, sensual, spiritual;
Blue for cold—polar, bodily, intellectual;
Yellow luminous and embodied
In the most enduring and the brightest form in gold—

DIREACH III
Euripides: Greek dramatist, c. 484–406 B.C.

Remind me how about this
Pindar and Confucius agreed.
Confucius who was Pindar's contemporary
For nearly half a century!
And it was Pindar's "golden snow"
My love and I climbed in that day.
I in Scotland as Pindar in Greece
Have stood and marvelled at the trees
And been seized with honey-sweet yearning for them;
And seen too mist condensing on an eagle,
His wings "streamlined" for a swoop on a leveret,
As he ruffled up the brown feathers on his neck
In a quiver of excitement;
Pindar, greatest master of metaphor the world has seen,
His spirit so deeply in tune
With the many-sidedness of both Man and Nature
That he could see automatically all the basal resemblances
His metaphors imply and suggest.
Scotland and China and Greece! . . .

WE MUST LOOK AT THE HAREBELL

We must look at the harebell as if
We had never seen it before.
Remembrance gives an accumulation of satisfaction
Yet the desire for change is very strong in us
And change is in itself a recreation.
To those who take any pleasure
In flowers, plants, birds, and the rest
An ecological change is recreative.
(Come. Climb with me. Even the sheep are different

DIREACH III

Pindar: the greatest Greek choral lyricist (c. 518–c. 438 B.C.), master of the ode celebrating an athletic victory.

Confucius: (551–479 B.C.), China's famous teacher, philosopher, and political theorist.

WE MUST LOOK AT THE HAREBELL

harebell: a slender herb with blue flowers; the bluebell.

And of new importance.
The coarse-fleeced, hardy Herdwick,
The Hampshire Down, artificially fed almost from birth,
And butcher-fat from the day it is weaned,
The Lincoln-Longwool, the biggest breed in England,
With the longest fleece, and the Southdown
Almost the smallest—and between them thirty other breeds,
Some whitefaced, some black,
Some with horns and some without,
Some long-wooled, some short-wooled,
In England where the men, and women too,
Are almost as interesting as the sheep.)
Everything is different, everything changes,
Except for the white bedstraw which climbs all the way
Up from the valleys to the tops of the high passes
The flowers are all different and more precious
Demanding more search and particularity of vision.
Look! Here and there a pinguicula eloquent of the Alps
Still keeps a purple-blue flower
On the top of its straight and slender stem.
Bog-asphodel, deep-gold, and comely in form,
The queer, almost diabolical, sundew,
And when you leave the bog for the stag moors and the rocks
The parsley fern—a lovelier plant
Than even the proud Osmunda Regalis—
Flourishes in abundance
Showing off oddly contrasted fronds
From the cracks of the lichened stones.
It is pleasant to find the books
Describing it as "very local."
Here is a change indeed!
The universal *is* the particular.

pinguicula: a butterwort, a carnivorous bog herb that has a thin stem and purple, yellow, or white flowers. Its broad, sticky leaves capture and digest insects with a secretion.

sundew: a carnivorous plant that entraps insects by means of tentacles on the upper surface of its leaves.

Osmunda Regalis: fern that grows in clumps two to ten feet high; some of its leaves bear tufts at the tips.

SCOTLAND SMALL?

Scotland small? Our multiform, our infinite Scotland *small?*
Only as a patch of hillside may be a cliché corner
To a fool who cries "Nothing but heather!" Where in September
 another
Sitting there and resting and gazing round
Sees not only heather but blaeberries
With bright green leaves and leaves already turned scarlet,
Hiding ripe blue berries; and amongst the sage-green leaves
Of the bog-myrtle the golden flowers of the tormentil shining;
And on the small bare places, where the little Blackface sheep
Found grazing, milkworts blue as summer skies;
And down in neglected peat-hags, not worked
In living memory, sphagnum moss in pastel shades
Of yellow, green, and pink; sundew and butterwort
And nodding harebells vying in their color
With the blue butterflies that poise themselves delicately upon
 them,
And stunted rowans with harsh dry leaves of glorious color
"Nothing but heather!"—How marvellously descriptive! And
 incomplete!

from THE KIND OF POETRY I WANT

A poetry full of erudition, expertise, and ecstasy
—The acrobatics and the faceted fly-like vision,
The transparency choke-full of hair-pin bends,
"Jacinth work of subtlest jewellry," poetry *à quatre épingles*—
('Till above every line we might imagine
A tensely flexible and complex curve
Representing the modulation,
Emphasis, and changing tone and tempo
Of the voice in reading;

THE KIND OF POETRY I WANT
"*Jacinth . . . jewellry*": Tennyson, *Morte d'Arthur*, ll. 57–58.
á quatre épingles: meticulously crafted.

The curve varying from line to line
And the lines playing subtly against one another
—A fineness and profundity of organization
Which is the condition of a variety great enough
To express all the world's,
As subtle and complete and tight
As the integration of the thousands of brush strokes
In a Cézanne canvas),
Alive as a bout of all-in wrestling,
With countless illustrations like my photograph of a Mourning
    Dove
Taken at a speed of 1/75,000 of a second.
A poetry that speaks "of trees,
From the cedar tree that is in Lebanon
Even unto the hyssop that springeth out of the wall,"
And speaks also "of beasts and of fowl,
And of creeping things and of fishes,"
And needs, like Marya Sklodowska on her laboratory table,
For its open-eyed wonderment at the varied marvels of life,
Its insatiable curiosity about the mainspring,
Its appetite for the solution of problems,
Black fragments of pitch-blende from Saxony and Bohemia,
Greenish-blue chalcolite from Portugal and Tonkin,
Siskin-green uranium mica from France,
Canary-yellow veined carnotite from Utah,
Greenish-grey tjujamunite from Turkestan,
Pinkish-gray fergusonite from Norway,
Gold-tinted Australian monazite sand,
Greenish-black betafite from Madagascar,
And emerald-green tobernite from Indo-China.
And like my knowledge of, say, interlocking directorships,
Which goes far beyond such earlier landmarks

Cézanne: Paul (1839-1906), post-impressionist French painter who emphasized the structure of the object rather than its emanative light, and who achieved the illusion of depth and volume by juxtaposing articulated planes of paint.

of trees . . . and of fishes: I Kings 4:33.

Marya Sklodowska: (1867-1934), Madame Curie, discoverer of polonium and radium.

As the Pujo Committee's report
Or Louis Stanley's "Spider Chart";
And everywhere without fear of Chestov's "suddenly,"
Never afraid to leap, and with the unanticipatedly
Limber florescence of fireworks as they expand
Into trees or bouquets with the abandon of "unbroke horses."
Or like a Beethovian semitonal modulation to a wildly remote
  key,
As in the Allegretto where that happens with a sudden jump of
  seven sharps,
And feels like the sunrise gilding the peak of the Dent Blanche
While the Arolla valley is still in cloud.
And constantly with the sort of grey-eyed gaiety
So many people feel exalted by being allowed to hear
But are unable to laugh at—as in the case of the don
Who, lecturing on the first Epistle to the Corinthians,
In a note on the uses of αλλα mentioned αλλα *precantis!*
Which an undergraduate took down as *Allah precantis!*

. . .

Pujo Committee: a subcommittee of the House Committee on Banking and Currency that carried out an investigation (1912-13) into the U.S. financial structure and its operations to determine whether concentration of banking control existed. The majority held that concentration of credit control was an accomplished fact, and influenced subsequent legislation such as the Federal Reserve Act of 1913.

Louis Stanley's spider chart: Lewis Stanley was an American Socialist writer whose pictorial chart, "The Spider Web of Wall Street," depicted the interlocking directorates on July 1, 1932, between the eight leading banking institutions in New York City and 120 major corporations; published in *The New Leader.*

Chestov: Leon Shestov (1866-1938), Russian philosopher and religious thinker who believed that "the fundamental property of life is daring; all life is creative daring and thus an eternal mystery."

Allegretto: in Beethoven's 7th Symphony, the 2nd Movement, measures 134–38.

Dent Blanche: peak in the Pennine Alps, Switzerland (14,304 ft.)

Arolla valley: village and resort in the Pennine Alps (6,570 ft.)

αλλα *precantis, Allah precantis:* the first phrase is a grammarian's term to describe one use of the Greek "but" (αλλα), to begin a wish or prayer (i.e., "the 'but' of praying"). The second phrase means "Allah of the man praying."

CRYSTALS LIKE BLOOD

I remember how, long ago, I found
Crystals like blood in a broken stone.

I picked up a broken chunk of bed-rock
And turned it this way and that,
It was heavier than one would have expected
From its size. One face was caked
With brown limestone. But the rest
Was a hard greenish-gray quartz-like stone
Faintly dappled with darker shadows,
And in this quartz ran veins and beads
Of bright magenta.

And I remember how later on I saw
How mercury is extracted from cinnebar
—The double ring of iron piledrivers
Like the multiple legs of a fantastically symmetrical spider
Rising and falling with monotonous precision,
Marching round in an endless circle
And pounding up and down with a tireless, thunderous force,
While, beyond, another conveyor drew the crumbled ore
From the bottom and raised it to an opening high
In the side of a gigantic grey-white kiln.

So I remember how mercury is got
When I contrast my living memory of you
And your dear body rotting here in the clay
—And feel once again released in me
The bright torrents of felicity, naturalness, and faith
My treadmill memory draws from you yet.

SENEGAL

DAVID DIOP

1927–1960

David Diop was born in Bordeaux. Before he was eight, when his father died and the family returned to France, he lived in both Cameroon and Senegal. During the Second World War and the Occupation, he lived in France. Because of bad health, Diop left medical school. He contributed articles, reviews, and poems to *Présence Africaine,* and in 1957–58 taught at the Lycée Maurice Delafosse in Dakar. When Guinea gained its independence he taught school there for two years in the inland town of Kindia. Returning from a holiday in Paris, Diop and his wife were killed in a plane crash on the approach to Dakar, and all Diop's unpublished manuscripts were burned. His only collection of poems, *Poundings,* appeared in 1956.

The poems of David Diop celebrate the gentleness of family life, the grace of black women, the ferocity of black anticolonialism. Poems of drums resonating with uprising, of vulture plantations, and of the body's "black pimento spice."

AFRICA

Africa my Africa,
Africa of proud warriors reaming
my grandfathers' plains,
Africa of my grandmother singing
on the banks of her far river,
I have never known you
but my eyes see with your blood
your sweet black blood
flowering the fields,
blood of your sweat
sweat of your slavery
slavery of your bondage
bondage of your children.
Africa tell me Africa
can this bent back be you,
this back bearing humility

trembling with red stripes that
nod yes to the noon sun's lash?

I heard a grave voice answer,
rash son, this strong young tree
this splendid tree
apart from the white and faded flowers
is Africa, your Africa
patiently stubbornly growing again
and its fruits are carefully learning
the sharp sweet taste of liberty.

Translated by **Lucille Clifton**

RAMA KAM

Song for a Black Woman

I'm made happy by your wild animal gaze
And your mouth with its taste of mango
Rama Kam
Your body's the black pepper
That spurs desire to sing
Rama Kam
When you walk by
Even the prettiest girl
Envies the warm rhythm of your hip
Rama Kam
When you dance
To the tom-tom Rama Kam
The tom-tom stretched tight like a hymen
Breathes heavily under the scop's leaping fingers
And when you make love
When you make love Rama Kam
The tornado itself twists
In the sparkling night of your flesh
And leaves me deeply breathing you
Ah Rama Kam!

Translated by **Henry Braun**

RAMA KAM
scop: bard or poet.

LÉOPOLD SÉDAR SENGHOR

1906–

Léopold Sédar Senghor was born on the Senegalese coast, of Catholic parents who belonged to the Serer tribe. He attended a mission school at Ngazobil, a seminary, and the Lycée in Dakar. In 1928 Senghor went to France on a scholarship, studied at the Lycée Louis-LeGrand and the Sorbonne, and became a French citizen—the first African to obtain the prerequisite diploma for *lycée* and university teaching in France. Senghor fought in the French army in World War II, and was a German prisoner of war from 1940 to 1942. In 1948 he published the most important anthology of negritude writing, *Anthologie de la Nouvelle Poésie Nègre et Malgache* (Anthology of New Black and Malagasgan Poets). In 1959 Senghor became head of the Union Progressiste Sénégalaise, and when the alliance of Senegal and Sudan in the Federation of Mali was severed in 1960 he became president of Senegal. He has won the Prix International des Amitiés Française (1961), the Grand Prix International de Poésie (1962), the Prix de la Langue Française (1963), and the Peace Prize at the International Book Fair (Frankfurt, Germany, 1968). Books of poems include *Songs of the Shade* (1945), *Black Victories* (1948), *Nocturnes* (1961), and *Selected Poems* (1964).

The poems of Léopold Senghor are richly textured, passionate, rhapsodic: oboe-like remembrances of Old Africa, flute-like celebrations of sensual love, trumpetings of black glory—and always the drums "moaning under the conqueror's fingers." Reading Senghor's poems is like drifting on a great arterial river through Senegal, from Joal to Cayor and Baol, from the flats of Dyilor to "the pastoral heart of Sine." Senghor's elegance and grace is like the elegance of huge animals.

BLACK WOMAN

Naked woman, Black woman
robed in the color of life, the shape of beauty,
I bloomed in your shade, and your soft hands
veiled my eyes.
Now in the heart of a summer noon, I come upon you,
Land of Promise,
high on a sun hill and your beauty
stops my heart, like the eagle's flash.

Naked woman, fathomless woman
flesh of ripe fruit, dark ecstasy of dark wines,
mouth making lyric my mouth,
savannah of peerless horizons, savannah quaking
in the fervent caress of the East Wind,
sculptured tom-tom

taut tom-tom
moaning under the conqueror's fingers
your full contralto is the sacred chant of the Beloved.

Naked woman, fathomless woman
oil unruffled by the wind, smooth oil on the athlete's flanks,
oil of the princess of Mali,
gazelle of celestial limbs
pearls are stars on the night of your skin,
delights of the mind at play, red gold rippling
your shimmering skin,
in the shade of your hair, my care
lightens to the nearing suns of your eyes.

Naked woman, Black woman
I sing your beauty as it passes
and fix your shape forever
before jealous destiny burns you to ash
to feed the roots of life.

Translated by **Lucille** *and* **Fred Clifton**

FOR ORGAN FLUTES

It is noon. It is evening. I hear the voices near far-off in the mist
And I lament her face. Not the sun, simply her smile
Not the jubilant burst of her *wai!* Ah! the crowned bird's trumpet!
Ave Maria in the evening, smell of sapodillas in the daytime
Color of *Ave Maria* on the Portuguese stones of the Fort
And the cinnamon sweetness of old lullabies and tears of
 childhood in flat hands.

The *Ave Maria* of Joal and the voices far and near
At six o'clock across the flats of Dyilor—things are without
 thickness or weight.

FOR ORGAN FLUTES

sapodillas: evergreen trees, the bark of which forms the basis of chewing gum; the fruit looks like an Irish potato but tastes like a pear with brown sugar.

Joal: Senghor's home village, on the Atlantic, 55 miles from Dakar.

Dyilor: a village where Senghor's father had a big house.

Are they the voices of Peul angels or of singers who died at
twenty?
Voices of royal nurses? Repeat the serpent-charm upon the tombs.
Where are the wild ducks' trumpets? People come home from the
wells and the fields and the hunt.

I tell only of her smile singing the *Ave Maria*
Making the close to an immemorial lament. And it was the
foretime of the world.

FOR TWO HORNS AND A BALAFONG

She flies she flies through the white flat lands, and patiently I take
my aim
Giddy with desire. She takes her chances to the bush
Passion of thorns and thickets. Then I will bring her to bay in the
chain of hours
Snuffing the soft panting of her flanks, mottled with shadow
And under the foolish Great Noon, I will twist her arms of glass.
The antelope's jubilant death rattle will intoxicate me, new palm
wine
And I will drink long long the wild blood that rises to her heart
The milk blood that flows to her mouth, odors of damp earth.

Am I not the son of Dyogoye? Dyogoye the famished Lion.

ALL DAY LONG

All day long along the long straight rails
(Unbending will on the listless sands)
Across the dryness of Cayor and Baol where the arms of the
baobabs twist in anguish

FOR ORGAN FLUTES
Peul: the Fula people of northern Nigeria and adjacent areas.
FOR TWO HORNS AND A BALAFONG
balafong: a sort of xylophone consisting of about 15 wooden laths.
Dyogoye: Senghor's father, Basile Diogoye.
ALL DAY LONG
Cayor: ancient native kingdom and region in NW Senegal.
Baol: region of western Senegal.
baobab: an African tree that often grows to a diameter of 30 feet; bark used to make cloth and ropes.

All day long, all along the line
Through tiny stations, each exactly like the last, chattering little
black girls uncaged from school
All day long, roughly shaken on the benches of the clanking,
dust-covered wheezing, antique train
I come seeking to forget Europe in the pastoral heart of Sine.

SPRING SONG

For a black girl with a pink heel

I

Bird songs rise up washed in the primitive sky
The green smell of grass rises, April.
I hear the breath of dawn stirring the white clouds of my curtains
I hear the sun's song on my melodious shutters
I feel a breathing and the memory of Naett on my bare neck that
tingles
And my blood's complicity in spite of me whispers down my
veins.
It is you my darling, O listen to the breeze already warm in the
April of another continent
O listen when the wings of migrating swallows slip by, glazed with
blue
Listen to the black and white rustle of the storks at the tips of
their unfolded sails
Listen to the message of spring from another age, another
continent
Listen to the message from distant Africa and the song of your
blood!
I listen to the sap of April, singing in your veins.

II

You said to me:
'Listen my friend to the far-off, muffled, precocious rumble of the
storm like a fire rolling through the bush
My blood shouts with pain in the frenzy of my head, heavy,
delivered over to electric currents.

ALL DAY LONG
Sine: region of west-central Senegal; the Sine River flows from central Senegal SW to the Atlantic.

Down there the sudden storm, the firing of the white coasts of the
white peace of my Africa.
And in the night when there is thunder of rending metal
Hear, closer to us, for two hundred miles, all the howlings of
moonless jackals and the catlike mewings of bullets
Hear the sharp roar of the guns and the trumpeting of hundred-
ton monsters.

Translations by **John Reed** *and* **Clive Wake**

CONGO

Oho! Congo, oho! To rhyme your great name upon the waters,
upon the rivers, upon all remembrance
Let me invoke the voices of the *koras* of Koyaté! The ink of the
writer does not endure.

Oho! Congo, couched in your forest bed, queen over subdued
Africa,
Let the phalli of the mountains bear your pavillion high
For you are woman in my mind, on my tongue, for you are
woman by my belly,
Mother of all things which breathe, crocodiles, hippopotamuses,
Manatees, iguanas, fish, birds, mother of the floods, nurse of the
harvests,
Great woman! Water so open to the oar and to the stem of the
dugouts,
My Sao, my woman with raging thighs, with long arms clad in
calm waterlilies,
Treasured woman of *ouzougou*, body of oil incorruptible on the
skin of the diamond night.

CONGO

kora: a West African harp made from a gourd and from sixteen to thirty-two strings.

Koyaté: the name of a poet.

manatees: aquatic mammals about ten feet long with broad round tails.

Sao: a people who inhabited the region of Chad between the seventh and sixteenth centuries.

ouzougou: black wood, ebony-like in color.

Calm creature, goddess of the slack smile, at the dizzying rush of
 your blood,
Oh malarious by your lineage, deliver me from the uprising of my
 blood.
Tom-tom you, you tom-tom the panther's leap, the strategy of
 ants,
Of the sticky hates on the third day rising from the wallows of the
 marshes,
Ha! above all things, the spongy earth and the soapy songs of the
 white man,
But deliver me from the joyless night, and watch over the silence
 of the forests.
Then let me be the splendid keel and the leap of 26 cubits
In the soft wind let me be the flight of the dugout on the smooth
 swell of your belly.
Glades in your bosom isles of love, hills of amber and *gongo*,
Breezes of boyhood in Joal, and those of Dyilor in September,
And an Ermenonville night in September—it had been so fair
 and so mild.
Serene flowers of your hair, petals as fair as your lips,
Above all the charming discourse during the new moon, on into
 the midnight of the blood.
Deliver me from the night of my blood, because you watch the
 silence of the forests.

My mistress at my side whose ivory-like oil gentles my hands, my
 soul,
My strength is prepared in abandonment, my honor in
 submission,
And my learning in the instinct of your rhythm. The coryphée
 binds his vigor
To the prow of his sex, in sight of the bull, like the Slayer with
 eyes blazing.
Ring handbells, sing tongues, swing oars, the dance of the
 Boatswain.

gongo: a perfume used by Senegalese women.
Ermenonville: a town in the Congo.
coryphée: leader of the chorus in Greek tragedies; lead dancer (ballet); (fig.) leader, chief.

Ah! his dugout is worthy of triumphant choirs of Fadyoutt
And I cry for twice two hands on the tom-toms, forty virgins to
carol his deeds.
Rhyme the shining shaft, the pounce at high-noon,
Rhyme, the rattle of cowries, the roaring of the open sea
And death on the crest of exultation, at the irrefusable summons
of the gulf.

But the dugout is reborn from the white waterlilies of the foam
To float on the fragrance of bamboo one luminous morning in
this life.

Translated by **George Keithley**

JOAL

Joal!
I remember.

I remember the *signares* in the verandahs' green shade
The *signares* with surrealist eyes like moonlight on the shore.

I remember the pomp at Sunset
When Coumba N'Doffene came to have his royal mantle made.

I remember the funeral feasts steaming with the blood of
slaughtered herds
With the din of disputes, with the rhapsodies of *griots*.

CONGO

Fadyoutt: Senghor often went to the sandy island of Fadioutt near Joal to hear the poet Marone N'Diaye (1890–1950), whose poems he later translated. Senghor was influenced by her chants of sorrow and joy, and later said that the great lesson he learned from Marone was that poetry is song and music.

cowries: the brightly polished and colored shells of any of a variety of warm-sea mollusks.

JOAL

signare: a word of Portuguese origin *(senhora)* used to refer to well-born Senegalese women; originally the term used to designate a mulatto mistress of a white man.

Coumba N'Doffene: a king (1853–71) from the Sine Saloun, a west coastal section of Senegal, south of Dakar.

griot: a combination musician-historian who sings the praises of the family to whom he is attached and in whose repertoire is stored genealogy, past exploits, and oral tradition.

I remember the pagan voices chanting a rhythmic *Tantum Ergo,*
And the processions and the palms and the triumphal arches.
I remember the dance of the nubile girls
The choruses at the wrestling matches—oh! the final dance of
the youths, torsos
Leaning forward, tall and slim, and the women's pure shout of
love—*Kor Siga!*

I remember, I remember . . .
My head beating the rhythm
What a weary trek throughout the days of Europe where now
and then
Appears an orphaned jazz that sobs sobs sobs.

Translated by **Sylvia Washington Bâ**

Tantum Ergo: a Gregorian chant traditionally sung during the rite of Benediction in the Roman Catholic Church. The words are from the last section of St. Thomas Aquinas's Corpus Christi hymn *Pange lingua*. An English version begins: "Therefore we before Him bending, this great sacrament revere."

Kor Siga: a Serer phrase; the word "Kor" means "man," but connotes champion or protector when used to designate an athlete. "Siga" is the name of the athlete's fiancee or sister.

SPAIN

RAFAEL ALBERTI

1902–

Rafael Alberti was born in Puerto de Santa Maria, Cadiz, into a poor Catholic family. Alberti rebelled against his Jesuit teachers and his family's move to Madrid in 1917, became ill, and went to the Guadarrama Mountains to be cured of what was feared to be tuberculosis. He not only became a successful cubist painter, but his first book of poems, *Sailor on Land,* won the National Prize in 1925. In 1927 Alberti underwent a period of deep psychological crisis, and emerged from it in the early thirties as a Marxist. He supported the Republicans in the Spanish Civil War and fled to Buenos Aires when the Republic fell. He has lived there ever since, editing texts, painting, and writing. Twenty-five books of poems include *Concerning Angels* (1929), *Homage to Painting* (1948), *Returns of the Far and the Living* (1952), and *Open at All Hours* (1965).

The poems of Rafael Alberti range from the graphic to the esoteric; the terrain is sometimes earthly, sometimes spatial. Alberti combines philosophical concepts and startling details, and the poems illuminate connections between seemingly dissimilar things, as burstings of light over night canyons reveal the high-tension wires that connect centers of power and civilization, and lonely human dwellings.

RED

1

I strike through the greens of the fruit, and prevail.

2

The apple's full flush in the round.

3

Red in the shoulder's repose

and the haunches of Venus:
the drowsing Giorgione.

4

I climb the king's purples
and descend with El Greco in the scattering
draperies.

5

Purples caught through cut glass—
goblet, decanter, and cup—
in the warmth of the wine.

6

The rose in the frost of Velázquez.

7

I descend to the rose of the rose of Picasso.

8

Carnation explosions, erect
in the ivory round of the tightening nipple.

9

The poppy in fugitive cochineal.

10

Think how I dwindle away
in the least of the violets.

Giorgione: Giorgio del Castelfranco (1477?–1510), Venetian painter, one of the first artists who painted small oil canvases for private collectors, rather than large decorative canvases for public patrons. His landscapes of mood were innovations in Renaissance art. In his famous *Sleeping Venus,* the goddess reclines, with one arm bent above her head, on rich, rusty red cushions.

El Greco: Domenikos Theotokopoulos (1541–1614), Spanish painter. The elongated figures, strong contrasts, rich colors, and undulating movement in his paintings convey a remarkable intensity of emotion. His "Portrait of a King" is now in the collection of the Louvre.

Velásquez: Diego Rodriguez de Silva (1599-1660), Spanish painter who blended realism, characterization, and atmosphere.

cochineal: a red dyestuff made from crushed insects.

11

Brueghel's and Bosch's inferno:
the night-hag that stares
from the eyes of insomniac children.

Translated by **Ben Belitt**

THE ANGEL OF NUMBERS

Virgins with rulers
and compasses were watching
the heavenly blackboards.

And the angel of numbers
was thoughtfully flying
from 1 to 2, from 2
to 3, from 3 to 4.

Cold chalk and sponges
streaked and erased
the light of the heavens.

There was no sun, no moon, no stars,
no sudden green
of lightning,
no air. Only mist.

Virgins without rulers,
without compasses were crying.

And on the dead blackboards
the angel of numbers
was lifeless, shrouded
on the 1 and the 2,
on the 3, on the 4 . . .

RED

Brueghel: Pieter, the Elder (1525–69), Flemish painter who satirized human folly in peasant life.

Bosch: Hieronymus (1450–1516), Dutch painter who concentrated on religious allegories and satires of ordinary life.

inferno: hell—represented with grotesque vividness in Brueghel's *Fall of the Rebel Angels* and in two panels of a four-panel group in the Doge's palace in Venice by Bosch: *Fall of the Damned* and *Hell*.

SONG OF THE LUCKLESS ANGEL

You are what moves:
water that carries me,
that will leave me.

Look for me in the wave.

What moves and doesn't return:
wind that in shadows
dies down and rises.

Look for me in the snow.

What nobody knows:
the floating earth
that speaks to nobody.

Look for me in the air.

THE ANGEL OF SAND

It is true, in your eyes the sea was two boys staring at me,
afraid of harsh words and of being trapped,
two terrible boys of the night, thrown out of heaven,
whose childhoods were a robbing of boats and crimes of suns and
moons.
Close your eyes and try to sleep.

I saw that the real sea was a boy who leaped naked,
inviting me in for a dish of stars and a nap of seaweed.
Yes. Yes. My life was going to be, and already was, a shore set
adrift.
But when you woke up, you drowned me in your eyes.

THE BAD MOMENT

In the days when I used to think
that fields of wheat were the homes of stars and gods
and frost a gazelle's frozen tears,
somebody whitewashed my chest and my shadow,
and I was betrayed.

It was a moment of bullets gone wild,
of the sea's making off with men who wished to be birds,
of the telegram bringing bad news and the finding of blood,
of the death of the water that always had stared at the sky.

TWO CHILDREN

1

Now you need only wait for the appearance of those hidden
springs
that lead to the narrow hallways where foreshadowings of death
discourage the light.
A spirit who still values the earth a little asks you,
Won't heaven be scared by the untimeliness of your journey?

Don't those narrow hallways that lead to the winter of a courtyard
freeze the anguish of eternity that hisses through your blood?
Doesn't the open skylight, suffering because it takes in the pain of
a cloud,
kill in your eyelids any desire for hours without end?
It is early,
much too early for a child to be left to the shadows.

2

You can easily see that the night considers a boy differently
than the day which drowns him in a drop of water.
What does the swallow know of the owl's insomnia?

For God's sake,
kill him without the dawn's having to guess if it will happen or
not.

He has left his head forgotten between two wires.
He has shouted his heart out so that echoes would turn against
him.
Ask the needles that have been lost in sofas for his hands.

Where is that boy going who makes wrong turns?

Translations by **Mark Strand**

JORGE GUILLÉN

1893–

Jorge Guillén was born in Valladolid, Old Castile, where he studied at the Institute of Valladolid before attending the Maison Perreyve of the French Fathers of the Oratory in Switzerland. He received his M.A. degree from the University of Granada in 1913 and lectured at the Sorbonne from 1917 to 1923. Guillén wrote his first poems in Paris in 1918, received his Doctor of Letters from the University of Madrid in 1924, and was subsequently a professor at Oxford, the University of Murcia, and the University of Seville. In 1936 he was jailed as a political prisoner in Pamplona. Since the fall of the Republic he has been a professor at Middlebury, McGill, Wellesley, Yale, the University of California at Berkeley, Ohio State University, Harvard, and the University of Puerto Rico. Guillén received the Award of Merit of the American Academy of Arts and Letters in 1955 and the Grand Prix International de Poésie, Belgium, in 1961. His collection of poems, *Cantico,* grew from 75 poems in 1928 to 334 in 1950.

Jorge Guillén is one of the great masters of the Spanish language. A heavy voice glides over the rhythmic surf of his lines, and his conclusions break over us like beach waves. The poems are cerebral, formal, poised—and the light in them originates from a vision that only the special accuracy of art can reflect.

THE HORSES

Shaggy and heavily natural, they stand
Immobile under their thick and cumbrous manes,
Pent in a barbed enclosure which contains,
By way of compensation, grazing land.

Nothing disturbs them now. In slow increase
They fatten like the grass. Doomed to be idle,
To haul no cart or wagon, wear no bridle,
They grow into a vegetable peace.

Soul is the issue of so strict a fate.
They harbor visions in their waking eyes,
And with their quiet ears participate
In heaven's pure serenity, which lies
So near all things—yet from the beasts concealed.
Serene now, superhuman, they crop their field.

DEATH, FROM A DISTANCE

Je soutenais l'éclat de la mort toute pure
Valéry

When that dead certainty appalls my thought,
My future trembles on the road ahead.
There where the light of country fields is caught
In the blind, final precinct of the dead,
A wall takes aim.
But what is sad, stripped bare
By the sun's gaze? It does not matter now—
Not yet. What matters is the ripened pear
That even now my hand strips from the bough.

The time will come: my hand will reach, some day,
Without desire. That saddest day of all,
I shall not weep, but with a proper awe
For the great force impending, I shall say,
Lay on, just destiny. Let the white wall
Impose on me its uncapricious law.

Translations by **Richard Wilbur**

THE DEVOTED LOVERS

Night is much more itself: love is already a fact.
The calm level of peace extends sleep
Like a perfection of love.
And love's bundle,
Now distant in sleep,
Abandons itself to an island of candor
Still keeping its animal nature.
What an infinity of days over the bed
Of one passion: habit surrounded by mystery!
O night, darker than ever in our arms!

Translated by **Mark Strand**

DEATH, FROM A DISTANCE
Je soutenais l'éclat . . . : I endured the brilliance of pure death.

THE THIRSTER

Torrid desolation!
The shaded sidewalk
Shudders with hidden
Bulls. And they crash head on.

A sun without eaves,
Dough of the afternoon,
The sun changes from
A fury to silence.

Hurry, for before us
The grill has swung wide to offer
Its preserve! From within rise
Odors, odors of honeysuckle.

The window blinds retain
The penumbra of oblivion.
A dream together with a coldness
Which is love, which is water.

Ah, bringing revelation,
The water of an ecstasy
Upon my thirst slakes
Eternity.—Drink!

Translated by **W. S. Merwin**

CEMETERY

Neither grieving nor imprisoned but lying alone
Quiet at last between earth and still more
Earth: the unsuffering skeleton, made bone.
Rest peacefully, freed of our presences, under our war.

Translated by **Norman Thomas di Giovanni**

NATURE ALIVE

The panel board of the table,
That smooth plane precisely

True to a hair, holds up
Its level form, sustained

By an idea: pure, exact,
The mind's image before
The mind's eyes! And yet,
Full assurance needs the touch

That explores and discovers
How the formal idea sags back
Down to the rich heaviness
Of kindling, trunk and timber

Of walnut. The walnut wood,
Secure in its own whorls
And grains, assured of its long
Season of so much strength

Now fused into the heart
Of this quiet vigor, the stuff
Of a table board, remains
Always, always wild!

Translated by **James Wright**

MIGUEL HERNANDEZ

1910–1942

Miguel Hernandez was born in Orihuela, Alicante. His father was a goat herder, and Hernandez worked with the goats and sold milk from house to house. He published his first poems in 1932 in a local newspaper, and his first book, *Expert in Moons,* appeared in 1933. Soon afterwards he went to Madrid and became secretary to an art critic. As a Loyalist in the Civil War, Hernandez fought at the front in the Republican 5th Regiment, and later fought in defense of the capital at Madrid. Some of his poems, written in the trenches, were printed on postcards and circulated among the army. Because he supported the Loyalists he was arrested after the war, and in spite of the fact that he had tuberculosis he was confined for the last three years of his life in Franco's prisons—during which time his young son died of starvation. Other books include *The Unceasing Flash* (1936), *The People's Wind* (1937), and *Songs and Ballads of Absence,* published posthumously.

Miguel Hernandez tore out his poems by their roots. He reached into a deep isolation, a deep loneliness and love, for a heart and voice at once stark and tender. The poems are held together by the bone of human fury and the cartilege of human grief. They demonstrate the measure of post-Republic wretchedness with a power seldom equalled in contemporary world poetry.

THE SOLDIER AND THE SNOW

December has frozen its double-edged breath
and blows it down from icy heavens,
like a dry fire coming apart in threads,
like a huge ruin that topples on soldiers.

Snow where horses have left their hoof-marks
is a solitude of grief that gallops on.
Snow like split fingernails, or claws badly worn,
like a malice out of heaven or a final contempt.

It bites, prunes, cuts through with the heavy
slash of a bloodshot and pale marble ax.
It comes down, it falls everywhere like some ruined hug
of canyons and wings, solitude and snow.

This violence that splits off from the core of winter,
raw hunger tired of being hungry and cold,
hangs over the naked with an eternal grudge
that is white, speechless, dark, starving and fatal.

It wants to soften down forges, hatred, flames,
it wants to stop up the seas, to get all love buried.
It goes along throwing up huge, gauzy drifts,
hostile hunks of glass, statues that say nothing.

I want the heart made of wool in every shop
and textile factory to flood over and cover
the bodies that ignite the morning
with their looks and yells, boots and rifles.

Translated by **Timothy Baland**

LULLABY OF THE ONION

(Lines for his son, after receiving a letter
from his wife in which she said that all she had
to eat was bread and onions.)

An onion is frost
shut in and poor.
Frost of your days
and of my nights.
Hunger and onion,
black ice and frost
huge and round.

My son is lying now
in the cradle of hunger.
The blood of an onion
is what he lives on.
But it is your blood,
with sugar on it like frost,
onion and hunger.

A dark woman
turned into moonlight
pours herself down thread
by thread over your cradle.
My son, laugh,
because you can swallow the moon
when you want to.

Lark of my house,
laugh often.
Your laugh is in your eyes
the light of the world.
Laugh so much
that my soul, hearing you,
will beat wildly in space.

Your laugh unlocks doors for me,
it gives me wings.
It drives my solitudes off,
pulls away my jail.

Mouth that can fly,
heart that turns to
lightning on your lips.

Your laugh is the sword
that won all the wars,
it defeats the flowers
and the larks,
challenges the sun.
Future of my bones
and of my love.

The body with wings beating,
the eyelash so quick,
life is full of color
as it never was.
How many linnets
climb with wings beating
out of your body!

I woke up and was an adult:
don't wake up.
My mouth is sad:
you go on laughing.
In your cradle, forever,
defending your laughter
feather by feather.

Your being has a flying range
so high and so wide
that your body is a newly
born sky.
I wish I could climb
back to the starting point
of your travel!

You laugh, eight months old,
with five orange blossoms.
You have five tiny
ferocities.
You have five teeth
like five new
jasmine blossoms.

They will be the frontier
of kisses tomorrow,
when you feel your rows
of teeth are a weapon.
You will feel a flame
run along under your teeth
looking for the center.

My son, fly away, into the
two moons of the breast:
the breast, onion-
sad, but you, content.
Stay on your feet.
Stay ignorant of what's happening,
and what is going on.

I HAVE PLENTY OF HEART

Today I am, I don't know how,
today all I am ready for is suffering,
today I have no friends,
today the only thing I have is the desire
to rip out my heart by the roots
and stick it underneath a shoe.

Today that dry thorn is growing strong again,
today is the day of crying in my kingdom,
depression unloads today in my chest
a depressed heavy metal.

Today my destiny is too much for me.
And I'm looking for death down by my hands,
looking at knives with affection,
and I remember that friendly ax,
and all I think about is the tallest steeples
and making a fatal leap serenely.

If it weren't for . . . I don't know what,
my heart would write a suicide note,
a note I carry hidden there,
I would make an inkwell out of my heart,

a fountain of syllables, and good-byes and gifts,
and *you stay here* I'd say to the world.

I was born under a rotten star.
My grief is that I only have one grief
and it weighs more than all the joys together.

A love affair has left me with my arms hanging down
and I can't lift them anymore.
Don't you see how disillusioned my mouth is?
How unsatisfied my eyes are?

The more I look inward the more I mourn!
Cut off this pain?—who has the scissors?

Yesterday, tomorrow, today
suffering for everything,
my heart is a sad goldfish bowl,
a pen of dying nightingales.

I have plenty of heart.

Today to rip out my heart,
I who have a bigger heart than anyone,
and having that, I am the bitterest also.

I don't know why, I don't know how or why
I let my life keep on going every day.

Translations by **Robert Bly**

JUAN RAMÓN JIMÉNEZ

1881–1958

Juan Ramón Jiménez was born in Moguer, Andalusia. When he was eighteen he went to Madrid to be near Rubén Darío, published his first book of poems, *Violet Souls* (1900), and returned to Moguer because of bad health. In 1916 he came to the United States to marry Zenobia Camprubí, the sister of a Spanish newspaper owner in New York. Jiménez spent several months there and in Boston, where he and his wife translated Rabindranath Tagore. After many intervening years as a resident of Madrid, he went into exile because of the Spanish Civil War, living for a time in Chevy Chase, Maryland, and then in Puerto Rico. When Jiménez received the Nobel Prize for Literature in 1956, no book of his had been published in the United States. He refused to go to Stockholm and said that his wife, who was dying, should have had the Nobel Prize. He wrote no more poems before his own death. Other books of poems include *Diary of a Newly Married Poet* (1917), *Work* (1917, 1922, 1957), *The Total Season* (1946), and *Deep Animal* (1949).

The poems of Juan Ramón Jiménez are poems of air, of thin spider-threads barely visible that connect everything: trees, streets, human arms, souls of the dead, crickets, basil. Simplicity, purity, silence. Poems of the full moon, of dawn, of lying awake in the dark; poems childlike, yearning; remarkable mumblings of a light sleeper, dreaming.

FULL MOON

The door is open,
the cricket singing.
Are you going around naked
in the fields?

Like an immortal water,
going in and out of everything.
Are you going around naked
in the air?

The basil is not asleep,
the ant is busy.
Are you going around naked
in the house?

OCEANS

I have a feeling that my boat
has struck, down there in the depths,
against a great thing.
And nothing
happens! Nothing . . . Silence . . . Waves . . .

—Nothing happens? Or has everything happened,
and are we standing now, quietly, in the new life?

DAWN OUTSIDE THE CITY WALLS

You can see the face of everything, and it is white—
plaster, nightmare, adobe, anemia, cold—
turned to the east. Oh closeness to life!
Hardness of life! Like something
in the body that is animal—root, slag-ends—
with the soul still not set well there—
and mineral and vegetable!
Sun standing stiffly against man,
against the sow, the cabbages, the mud wall!
—False joy, because you are merely
in time, as they say, and not in the soul!

The entire sky taken up
by moist and steaming heaps,
a horizon of dung piles.
Sour remains, here and there,
of the night. Slices
of the green moon, half-eaten,
crystal bits from false stars,
plaster, the paper ripped off, still faintly
sky-blue. The birds
not really awake yet, in the raw moon,
streetlight nearly out.
Mob of beings and things!
—A true sadness, because you are really deep
in the soul, as they say, not in time at all!

I AM NOT I

I am not I.
I am this one
walking beside me whom I do not see,
whom at times I manage to visit,
and whom at other times I forget;
who remains calm and silent while I talk,
and forgives, gently, when I hate,
who walks where I am not,
who will remain standing when I die.

AT FIRST SHE CAME TO ME PURE

At first she came to me pure,
dressed only in her innocence;
and I loved her as we love a child.

Then she began putting on
clothes she picked up somewhere;
and I hated her, without knowing it.

She gradually became a queen,
the jewelry was blinding . . .
What bitterness and rage!

. . . She started going back toward nakedness.
And I smiled.

Soon she was back to the single shift
of her old innocence.
I believed in her a second time.

Then she took off the cloth
and was entirely naked . . .
Naked poetry, always mine,
that I have loved my whole life!

BEING AWAKE

Night goes away, a black bull—
body heavy with mourning and fear and mystery—
it has been bellowing horribly, monstrously,
in genuine fear of all the dead;
and day arrives, a young child
who wants trust, and love, and jokes,
—a child who somewhere
far away, in the secret places
where what ends meets what is starting,
has been playing a moment
on some meadow or other
of light and darkness
with that bull who is running away . . .

Translations by **Robert Bly**

FEDERICO GARCÍA LORCA

1898–1936

Federico García Lorca was born in Fuentevaqueros. As a young man he studied literature, law, the guitar, and the piano. In 1919 he went to Madrid, where his drama *The Butterfly's Evil Spell* was produced, where his *Book of Poems* appeared in 1921, and where he met Jiménez, Alberti, and Neruda. For the next ten years Lorca was one of the personal centers of a renaissance of Spanish art, music, and literature. In 1929 he studied at Columbia University, where he wrote *Poet in New York.* After travels to Cuba and South America he led a traveling student theater around Spain. Other books of poems include *Gypsy Ballads* (1928) and *Lament for the Death of a Bullfighter* (1935). When he was thirty-eight, Lorca was executed by Franco's troops.

Looking out from each of Federico García Lorca's poems are eyes that have been watching for a long time. The poem begins when the eyes have seen enough, and the voice speaks: "Beneath all the statistics there is a drop of duck's blood." Every thing in Lorca's poems has a life of its own: the tiny animals with broken heads, the olives inside the saddlebag of the distant rider. Lorca's poetry is the heart of Spanish life.

THE GUITAR

The crying of the guitar
starts.
The goblets
of the dawn break.
The crying of the guitar
starts.
No use to stop it.
It is impossible
to stop it.
It cries repeating itself
as the water cries,
as the wind cries
over the snow.
It is impossible
to stop it.
It is crying for things
far off.
The warm sand of the South
that asks for white camellias.

For the arrow with nothing to hit,
the evening with no dawn coming,
and the first bird of all dead
on the branch.
Guitar!
Heart wounded, gravely,
by five swords.

THE QUARREL

For Rafael Méndez

The Albacete knives, magnificent
with stranger-blood,
flash like fishes
on the gully slope.
Light crisp as a playing
card snips out of bitter
green the profiles of riders
and maddened horses.
Two old women in an olive
tree are sobbing.
The bull of the quarrel
is rising up the walls.
Black angels arrived
with handkerchiefs and snow water.
Angels with immense wings
like Albacete knives.
Juan Antonio from Montilla
rolls dead down the hill,
his body covered with lilies,
a pomegranate on his temples.
He is riding now on the cross of fire,
on the highway of death.

The State Police and the judge
come along through the olive grove.

THE QUARREL
Albacete: a province in SE central Spain; manufactures cutlery.

From the earth loosed blood moans
the silent folksong of the snake.
"Well, your honor, you see,
it's the same old business—
four Romans are dead
and five Carthaginians."

Dusk that the fig trees and the
hot whispers have made hysterical
faints and falls on the bloody
thighs of the riders,
and black angels went on flying
through the failing light,
angels with long hair,
and hearts of olive-oil.

LITTLE INFINITE POEM

For Luis Cardoza y Aragón

To take the wrong road
is to arrive at the snow,
and to arrive at the snow
is to get down on all fours for twenty centuries and eat the grasses
of the cemeteries.

To take the wrong road
is to arrive at woman,
woman who isn't afraid of light,
woman who murders two roosters in one second,
light which isn't afraid of roosters,
and roosters who don't know how to sing on top of the snow.

But if the snow truly takes the wrong road,
then it might meet the southern wind,
and since the air cares nothing for groans,
we will have to get down on all fours again and eat the grasses of
the cemeteries.

LITTLE INFINITE POEM
Luis Cardoza y Aragón: Guatemalan poet (b. 1902); a friend of Lorca's.

I saw two mournful wheatheads made of wax
burying a countryside of volcanoes;
and I saw two insane little boys who wept as they leaned on a
murderer's eyeballs.

But two has never been a number—
because it's only an anguish and its shadow,
it's only a guitar where love feels how hopeless it is,
it's the proof of someone else's infinity,
and the walls around a dead man,
and the scourging of a new resurrection that will never end.
Dead people hate the number two,
but the number two makes women drop off to sleep,
and since women are afraid of light,
light shudders when it has to face the roosters,
and since all roosters know is how to fly over the snow
we will have to get down on all fours and eat the grasses of the
cemeteries forever.

January 10, 1930. New York.

GHAZAL OF THE TERRIFYING PRESENCE

I want the water to go on without its bed.
And the wind to go on without its mountain passes.

I want the night to go on without its eyes
and my heart without its golden petals;

if the oxen could only talk with the big leaves
and the angleworm would die from too much darkness;

I want the teeth in the skull to shine
and the yellowish tints to drown the silk.

I can see the night in its duel, wounded
and wrestling, tangled with noon.

GHAZAL OF THE TERRIFYING PRESENCE
ghazal: lyric poem that begins with a rhymed couplet whose rhyme is repeated in all even lines.

I fight against a sunset of green poison,
and those broken arches where time is suffering.

But don't let the light fall on your clear and naked body
like a cactus black and open in the reeds.

Leave me in the anguish of the darkened planets,
but do not let me see your pure waist.

GHAZAL OF THE DARK DEATH

I want to sleep the sleep of the apples,
I want to get far away from the busyness of the cemeteries.
I want to sleep the sleep of that child
who longed to cut his heart open far out at sea.

I don't want them to tell me again how the corpse keeps all its blood,
how the decaying mouth goes on begging for water.
I'd rather not hear about the torture sessions the grass arranges for
nor about how the moon does all its work before dawn
with its snakelike nose.

I want to sleep for half a second,
a second, a minute, a century,
but I want everyone to know that I am still alive,
that I have a golden manger inside my lips,
that I am the little friend of the west wind,
that I am the elephantine shadow of my own tears.

When it's dawn just throw some sort of cloth over me
because I know dawn will toss fistfuls of ants at me,
and pour a little hard water over my shoes
so that the scorpion claws of the dawn will slip off.

Because I want to sleep the sleep of the apples,
and learn a mournful song that will clean all earth away from me,
because I want to live with that shadowy child
who longed to cut his heart open far out at sea.

Translations by **Robert Bly**

ANTONIO MACHADO

1875–1939

Antonio Machado was born in Seville. His father was an anthologist of Andalusian folksong. When Machado was eight the family moved to Madrid, and he later entered the Institución de Libre Enseñanza. He visited France, took courses with Bergson, did translations, and met Rubén Darío. In 1907, Machado took a teaching post in Soria, Castile, and in 1909 was married, but his nineteen-year-old wife Leonor died two years later. When the Republic was declared in 1931 Machado returned to Madrid and supported it during the Civil War. When Catalonia fell he went into exile and died soon after in Collioure, France. His poems include *Solitudes* (1903), *Castilian Countryside* (1912), *New Songs* (1924), and *Eighty Poems of Antonio Machado* (1959).

In his poems Antonio Machado brings the life of Spain to the life of the mind. Memories of childhood, landscapes, philosophic meditations—all filter through the pristine light of Machado's austere poetic vision. He says, "I love the subtle worlds, delicate, almost without weight, like soap bubbles." Sometimes aphoristic, always restrained, the poems express both the formal clarities of pure thought and the emotional intensities of transient human experience. Machado's lyrical prophecies elucidate his own definition of poetry as "the word in time."

SONGS

I

The huge sea drives
against the flowering mountain.
The comb of my honeybees
holds tiny grains of salt.

II

Not far from the black water.
Odor of the sea and of jasmine flowers.
Night of Málaga.

III

The spring has arrived.
No one knows what happened.

Málaga: city in Andalusia, southern Spain, on the Mediterranean.

IV

The spring has arrived.
Snow-white hallelujahs
from the flowering blackberry bushes!

V

Full moon, full moon,
so great, so round,
in this tranquil night
of March, honeycomb of light
that the white bees have made!

MEMORY FROM CHILDHOOD

A chilly and overcast afternoon
of winter. The students
are studying. Steady boredom
of raindrops across the windowpanes.

It is the schoolroom. In a poster
Cain is shown running
away, and Abel dead,
not far from a red spot.

The teacher, with a voice husky and hollow,
is thundering. He is an old man badly dressed,
withered and dried up,
who is holding a book in his hand.

And the whole child's choir
is singing its lesson:
one thousand times one hundred is one hundred thousand,
one thousand times one thousand is one million.

A chilly and overcast afternoon
of winter. The students
are studying. Steady boredom
of raindrops across the windowpanes.

PROVERBS AND TINY SONGS

II

Why should we call
these accidental furrows roads? . . .
Everyone who moves on walks
like Jesus, on the sea.

VI

You walking, your footprints *are*
the road, and nothing else;
there is no road, walker,
you make the road by walking.
By walking you make the road,
and when you look backward,
you see the path that you
never will step on again.
Walker, there is no road,
only wakes in the sea.

VII

I love Jesus, who said to us:
heaven and earth will pass away.
When heaven and earth have passed away,
my word will still remain.
What was your word, Jesus?
Love? Forgiveness? Affection?
All your words were
one word: Wakeup.

XI

All things die and all things live forever;
but our task is to die,
to die making roads,
roads over the sea.

XII

To die . . . To fall like a drop
of sea water into the immense sea?
Or to be what I have never been:

one man, without shadow, without dream,
a man all alone, walking
with no road, with no mirror?

XIV

There is a Spaniard today who wants
to live and is starting to live,
between one Spain dying
and another Spain yawning.
Little Spaniard just now come
to the world, may God keep you.
One of these two Spains
will freeze your heart.

Translations by **Robert Bly**

FIGURES IN THE FIELD AGAINST THE SKY!

Figures in the field against the sky!
Two slow oxen plowing
a knoll in early autumn:
between the black heads
bent below the heavy yoke
hangs a basket made of broom and reed—
a child's cradle.
Behind the team
a man plods, leaning toward the earth;
a woman
throws seed in open furrows.
Under a cloud of flame and crimson
in the green fluid gold of sunset,
these shadows grow gigantic.

AUTUMN DAWNING

For Julio Romero de Torres

A long highway
between gray cliff sides,
and a lowly meadow

where black bulls graze. Blackberries, thickets, rockroses.

The earth is wet
with points of dew,
aspen rows are golden
near the river bend.

Behind the violet forests
first dawn is breaking;
on his shoulder a shotgun,
between his nimble hounds, a hunter walking.

Translations by **Willis Barnstone**

SWEDEN

GUNNAR EKELOF

1907–1968

Gunnar Ekelof was born in Stockholm. His father, a broker, died of syphilis when Gunnar was a child. Ekelof pursued oriental studies in London and Uppsala, then music in Paris where, inspired by Stravinsky's music, he wrote his first book of poems, *Late on the Earth* (1932). He was also an essayist, editor, and critic for the periodicals *Spectrum* and *Caravan,* and translated Eliot, Joyce, Auden, Baudelaire, and Rimbaud. He became a member of the Swedish Academy in 1958, received the Grand Prize for poetry from the Danish Academy in 1964, and the prize from the Scandinavian Council in 1966. Ekelof died of throat cancer, and his ashes were placed at Sardis. Some of his fifteen books of poems: *Sympathies and Stars* (1936), *Ferryboat Song* (1941), *Opus Incertum* (1959) and *A Molna Elegy* (1960).

Reading Gunnar Ekelof's poems is like seeing objects through acetate: nothing is magnified, yet the spun film reveals something we haven't noticed before—fossils of delicate shells, or a new configuration of stars, or a strange buoy-marker offshore. Ekelof himself believed that associations in poetry are a "parallel to music." His poems are psychological, dreamlike, outraged, ruminative, insistent. The landscape is the mind, and when we see and listen, we pass between the visible and invisible worlds.

EVEN ABSENTMINDEDNESS IS A MAGNIFICENT LANDSCAPE

Even absentmindedness is a magnificent landscape:
Fields where they plow with oxen, a dog who barks at nothing
a straw-thatched farmhouse whose well-sweep can be seen
blue hillsides with single pines and cypresses
a background to some absent Madonna
with an absent John and a child Jesus
who grasps at the breast in a gesture of emptiness—
Because not one of them is seen, except

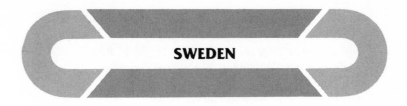

in evening's own transparency—, which might be their
eyes seeing out over fields lying untouched and quiet
when all the visible birds already have left
and only the invisible ones are heard migrating, still, in flights by
night.

TOMBA DEI TORI, TARQUINIA

No researcher into the recondite
no sex-decoder
not even Lawrence, who passed by here
saw that the "bull" on the left is
a long-horned cow—

For me the text reads:

I forced the man to his knees
forced my enemy on all fours
I put his wife on his back
and I took her there
before I gave her to the wild cows

I forced the man to get up
forced my enemy to squat
and I took him from behind
before I gave him to the wild bull
the bull with the face of a man

My prowess.

Translations by **Muriel Rukeyser** *and* **Leif Sjoberg**

TOMBA DEI TORI, TARQUINIA

Tomba dei Tori, Tarquinia: tomb of the bulls; Tarquinia is a town in central Italy overlooking the Tyrrhenian Sea that contains a museum of Etruscan antiquities collected from the nearby necropolis of ancient Tarquinii.

Lawrence: D. H. (1885–1930), English writer; best known for his novels, among them *Sons and Lovers*, *Women in Love*, and *Lady Chatterley's Lover*. He spent his last years in Italy, and his nonfiction includes a small, posthumously published book about the Etruscans and the sites and artifacts of ancient Etruria: *Etruscan Places*.

MONOLOGUE WTH ITS WIFE

Take two extra-old cabinet ministers and overtake them on the
North Sea
Provide each of them with a comet in the rear
Seven comets each!
Send a wire:
If the city of Trondheim takes them in it will be bombed
If the suet field allows them to escape it will be bombed
Now you have to signal:
Larger ships approaching
Don't you see, there in the radio! Larger ship
in converging path. Send a warning!
All small strawberry boats shall be ordered to go into the shore
and lie down

—Come and help me. I am disappearing.
The god is in the process of transforming me, the one in the
corner over there (whispering)

THE SWAN

I

I heard wild geese over the hospital grounds
where many pale people walk back and forth
—one morning in a daze
I heard them! I hear them!
I dreamt I heard—

And nevertheless I did hear them!

Here endless walks circle about
around bottomless dams
Here the days all reflect
one typical day
at the slightest touch
beautiful blossoms close
their strange petals—

The woman on a nurse's arm
she screams incessantly:

Hell Devil Hell
—is led home
hurriedly. . . .
Dusk has come
over the salmon-colored buildings
and outside the wall
the sky reddens in an anemic way over endless suburbs
of identical houses
with some vegetable beds steaming as if in spring between. . . .

They are burning twigs and leaves:
It is fall
and the vegetable beds are attacked by worm-eaten cabbages
and bare flowers—

I heard wild geese over the hospital grounds
one autumnlike spring morning
I heard wild geese one morning
one springautumnmorning
trumpeting—
To the north? To the south?
To the north! To the north!
Far from here—

A freshness lives deep in me
which no one can take from me
not even myself—

II

The moon rises, and night
comes down over the winter fields.
The burning zones of the stars
throw the Swan toward Leda.

Swan, gradually becomes invisible
in the dark, like snowfall in water. He bends
his head over a star, which calls out,
high over the masses of people,
searches with his yellow beak

the Swan . . . Leda: according to Greek legend Leda became (by Zeus in the form of a swan) the mother of Pollux and Helen.

deep in the black ooze:
The black lake is dried.
The name of his food: grubs.
The name of his illness: tedium.

He must swallow living things,
he must kill living things,
feel the hateful things gag him,
feel the hateful things struggle
against the hunger in his gizzard,
feel his hunger fade away,
feel the struggle of the lovers to come together
though they shall never meet.

WHEN ONE HAS COME AS FAR AS I IN POINTLESSNESS

When one has come as far as I in pointlessness
Each word is once more fascinating:
Finds in the loam
Which one turns up with an archeologist's spade:
The tiny word you
Perhaps a pearl of glass
Which once hung around someone's neck
The huge word I
Perhaps a flint shard
With which someone who had no teeth scraped his own
Meat

Translations by **Robert Bly** *with* **Christina Paulston**

TOMAS TRANSTRÖMER

1931–

Tomas Tranströmer was born in Stockholm, the descendant of ship pilots. His first book, *17 Poems,* was published in 1954, while he was still in his early twenties. For several years he was a psychologist at a boy's prison in Linköping. He now lives in Västerås and spends his summers, as he has since childhood, on Runmaro, a small island in the Stockholm skerries. He has led study groups for probation officers on how to treat prisoners, and he currently works with problem cases in occupational psychology and with aptitude tests for the handicapped. Later books of poems include *Secrets on the Road* (1958), *Half-Finished Heaven* (1962), and *Resonance and Foot-Tracks* (1968).

In his poems Tomas Tranströmer gently but firmly opens the lid of the mind's eye, and it is as if we are seeing his personal diary of the most extraordinary things: people playing pianos in dreams, short sonatas of liquid color. Tranströmer objectifies our deepest inner feelings in images of flying, traveling on water, stepping across thresholds, coming close to animals. The past becomes present and our lives merge into a long dream.

THE OPEN WINDOW

I was shaving one morning
by the open window
one flight up.
Switched the razor on.
It began to buzz.
Buzzed louder and louder.
Increased to a roar.
Enlarged to a helicopter,
and a voice—the pilot's—penetrated
the roar, shrieking:
"All eyes open!
You see this for the last time."
We lifted off.
Flew low over summertime.
So many things I loved, have they no significance?
Dozens of dialects of green.
And especially the red of the timbered house-walls.
Beetles that gleamed in dung, in sun.
Cellars pulled up by the roots
came through the air.

UPRIGHT

In a moment of concentration I was able to catch the hen,
and stood with it in my hands. Strange, it didn't feel
really alive: stiff, dry, a white feather-plumed old lady's
hat squawking truths from 1912. Thunder hovered in the air.
From the floorboards wafted an odor like that trapped
between covers of a photo album so ancient that the portraits
can no longer be identified.

I carried the hen to her yard and let her go. She came
suddenly to life, recognized herself, and began racing around
according to the old order. The henyard is full of taboos.
But outside, the ground is loaded with love and *sisu*.
Half overgrown with bushes and vines, a low stone wall.
At dusk the stones begin to emanate light from the century-old
warmth of the hands that piled them.

The winter has been hard, but it is summer now, and the soil
wants us to stay upright. Free but attentive, as when
standing up in a small boat. There leaps to mind a memory
from Africa: the shore at Chari: many boats, a most friendly
atmosphere, the nearly blue black people with three parallel
scars on each cheek (the SARA tribe.) I am welcomed aboard—
a canoe of darkest wood. It is extremely unsteady, even
when I crouch on my heels. The act of balance. If the heart
is on the left, lean the head slightly to the right, keep
your pockets empty, make no big gestures—leave all
rhetoric behind. That's it: rhetoric is impossible here.
The canoe skims over the water.

Translations by **May Swenson** *with* **Leif Sjoberg**

AFTER A DEATH

Once there was a shock
that left behind a long, shimmering
                comet tail.
It keeps us inside. It makes the TV pictures snowy.
It settles in cold drops on the telephone wires.

UPRIGHT
sisu: Finnish, meaning "energy" or "stamina."
Chari: a river in Chad (formerly part of French Equatorial Africa).

One can still go slowly on skis in the winter sun
through brush where a few leaves hang on.
They resemble pages torn from old telephone directories.
Names swallowed by the cold.

It is still beautiful to feel the heart beat
but often the shadow seems more real than the body.
The samurai looks insignificant
beside his armor of black dragon scales.

OUT IN THE OPEN

1

Late autumn labyrinth.
On the porch of the woods a thrown-away bottle.
Go in. Woods are silent abandoned houses this time of year.
Just a few sounds now: as if someone were moving twigs around
carefully with pincers
or as if an iron hinge were whining feebly inside a thick trunk.
Frost has breathed on the mushrooms and they have shrivelled
up.
They look like objects and clothing left behind by people who've
disappeared.
The dusk here already. The thing to do now is to get out
and find the landmarks again: the rusty machine out in the field
and the house on the other side of the lake, a reddish square
intense as a bullion cube.

2

A letter from America drove me out again, started me walking
through the luminous June night in the empty suburban streets
among newborn districts without memories, cool as blueprints.

Letter in my pocket. You wild, raging walking, you are a kind of
prayer for others.
Over there evil and good actually have faces.
For the most part with us it's a fight between roots, numbers,
shades of light.

AFTER A DEATH
samurai: a member of the warrior aristocracy of feudal Japan.

The people who do death's errands for him don't shy from
daylight.
They rule from glass offices. They mill about in the bright sun.
They lean forward over a table, and throw a look to the side.

Far off I found myself standing in front of one of the new
buildings.
Many windows flowed together there into a single window.
In it the luminous nightsky was caught, and the walking trees.
It was a mirror-like lake with no waves, turned on edge in the
summer night.

Violence seemed unreal
for a few moments.

3

Sun burning. The plane comes in low
throwing a shadow shaped like a giant cross that rushes over the
ground.
A man is sitting in the field poking at something.
The shadow arrives.
For a fraction of a second he is right in the center of the cross.

I have seen the cross hanging in the cool church vaults.
At times it resembles a split-second shot of something
moving at tremendous speed.

Translations by **Robert Bly**

STROPHE AND ANTISTROPHE

The outermost circle is the myth's. There the helmsman sinks
upright
among glittering dorsals.
How far from us! When the day
lingers in a close and windless motion—
as the Congo's green shadow holds

STROPHE AND ANTISTROPHE
strophe: the movement of the classical Greek chorus in turning from one side of the orchestra to the other; also, the part of the choral ode sung during this movement. The *antistrophe* is the returning or response of the chorus, in answer to a strophe.

the blue men in its vapor—
when all that driftwood piles up
along the heart's sluggish
winding river.

Suddenly a change: in under the firmament's repose
glide the tethered ones.
High in the stern, with hopeless
bearings, looms the hull of a dream, black
against light-red coastal strip. Abandoned
the years fall, swiftly
and soundlessly—as the sled's shadow, dog-like, large,
travels over the snow,
reaches the woods.

ALLEGRO

I am playing Haydn after a black day
and feel a simple warmth in my hands.

The keys are willing. Soft hammers strike.
The sound is green, lively and soft.

The sound says that freedom exists
and someone will not pay up Caesar's taxes.

I push my hands down in my haydn-pockets
and mimic one who calmly scans the world.

I raise the haydn-flag—it means:
"We won't surrender. But want peace."

The music is a glass house on the slope
where stones fly, where stones roll.

And the stones roll straight through
but every windowpane remains unbroken.

Translations by **Eric Sellin**

TRINIDAD AND TOBAGO

DEREK WALCOTT

1930–

Derek Walcott was born in St. Lucia, Windward Islands. He graduated from University College of the West Indies, and in 1957 received a fellowship from the Rockefeller Foundation to study the American theater. In 1959 Walcott founded the Trinidad Theater Workshop, which he now directs; his plays have been produced in Canada, England, America, and the Caribbean. He has won the Guiness Award for Poetry, a Royal Society of Literature Award, and the Cholmondeley Prize for Poetry. Walcott's first book, *25 Poems,* was published when he was nineteen. He now lives in Port-of-Spain, Trinidad. Other books of poems: *In a Green Night* (1962), *The Castaway* (1965), and *Another Life* (1973).

The poems of Derek Walcott are richly woven tapestries of ideas, images, allusions, and remembrances. An invisible loom shuttles back and forth over autobiography, scenes of passion, classical painting, the lives of fishermen. Walcott is able to concentrate an easy, natural speech within a line tense with vigorous verbs and startling images, interweaving history and personal experience in an atmosphere of relaxed precisions: "Leisurely, the egrit on the mud tablet stamps its hieroglyph."

JUNTA

The sun's brass clamp electrifies a skull
kept shone since he won Individual
of the Year, their first year on the road,
as Vercingetorix and His Barbarous Horde;
lurching from lounge to air-conditioned lounge
with the crazed soldier ant's logistic skill
of pause as capture, he stirs again to plunge,
his brain's antennae on fire through the black ants
milling and mulling through each city fissure;
banlon-cool limers, shopgirls, Civil Servants.

Vercingetorix: Gallic tribal chieftain who led a rebellion against Roman Gaul, was captured and executed by Julius Caesar in 46 B.C.

"Caesar," the hecklers siegheil, "Julius Seizure!"
He fakes an epileptic, clenched salute,
taking their tone, is no use getting vex,
some day those brains will squelch below his boot
as sheaves of swords hoist Vercingetorix!

So that day bursts to bulging cocks, the sun's gong
clangs the coup, a church, a bank explodes,
and, bullet-headed with his cow-horned gang
of marabunta hordes he hits the road.
Dust powders the white dead in Woodford Square;
his black, khaki canaille, panting for orders,
surge round the kiosk, then divide to hear
him clomp up silence louder than the roars
of rapine. Silence. Dust. A microphone
crackles the tinfoil quiet. On its paws
the beast mills, basilisk-eyed, for its one
voice. He clears his gorge and feels the bile
of rhetoric rising. Enraged, that every clause
"por la patria, la muerte!" resounds
the same, he fakes a frothing fit and shows his wounds,
while, as the steel sheaves heighten, his eyes fix
on one black, bush-haired convict's widening smile.

ANOTHER LIFE

from CHAPTER 9

In my father's small blue library
of reproductions I would find
that fine drawn hare of Dürer's, clenched and quivering

JUNTA

marabunta: soldier ants; local name for street gangs.
Woodford Square: a square in Port-of-Spain, Trinidad.
canaille: a pack of dogs; or the lowest type of people, rabble.
kiosk: a stand or booth where information is provided.
basilisk: (1) in classical legend, a creature (serpent, lizard, or dragon) that killed with its look or its breath; (2) a tropical American iguana lizard of the genus *Basiliscus*.
por la patria, la muerte: for the fatherland, death.

ANOTHER LIFE

Dürer: Albrecht (1471–1528), German master of woodcut and copper engraving who introduced Renaissance forms and ideas to the North.

to leap across my wrist,
and volumes of *The English Topographical Draughtsmen,*
Peter de Wint, Paul Sandby, Cotman, and in another
sky-blue book
the shepherdesses of Boucher and Fragonard,
and I raved for
the split pears of their arses,
their milk-jug bubs,
the close and, I guessed, golden
inlay of curls at cunt
and conch-like ear,
and after service, Sunday lay
golden, a fucked Eve
replete and apple-bearing,
and if they were my Muse,
still, out of that you rose,
body downed with the seasons,
gold and white, Anna
of the peach-furred body, light
of another epoch,
and stone-grey eyes.
Was the love wrong that came
out of the Book of Hours,
and the reaper with his scythe,
as your hair gold, dress green,
sickle-armed, you move
through a frontispiece of flowers
eternal, true as Ruth
the wheat-sheaves at her ear,

Boucher: François (1703–70), rococo decorator, friend of Madame Pompadour, painter of "charmingly indelicate mythological scenes" (Murray).

Fragonard: Jean-Honoré (1732–1806), French painter who specialized in gallant and sentimental subjects during the reigns of Louis XV and Louis XVI.

Book of Hours: a medieval book of devotions, illuminated in rich color.

Ruth: In the Old Testament story Ruth leaves her own country to remain with her bereaved mother-in-law Naomi, saying: "Entreat me not to leave thee, or to return from following after thee: for whither thou goest, I will go; and where thou lodgest, I will lodge . . . ." (Ruth 1:16). "Wheat sheaves" refers to Ruth's gleaning in the field of Boaz (see Ruth 2). See also note p. 347.

or gorgonizing Judith
swinging the dead lantern
of Holofernes, that bright year
like all first love, we were
pure and Pre-Raphaelite,
Circe-coil of plaited light
around her, as Gregorias
bent to his handful of earth,
his black nudes gleaming sweat,
in the tiger shade of the fronds.

from CHAPTER 13

Perched on the low stem of the rented shallop,
he watched the barracks on the hill dilate
with every stroke behind the oarsman's ear.
The rower, silent, kept his glaze oblique-
ly fixed on the wharf's receding beacon,
a mannequin with a skirt of lacy iron, and
in the opaque, slowly-coloring harbor
the one sound was the plump plash of the oars,
each stroke concluding with the folded gurgle
of an intaken breath. Weakly protesting,
the oarlock's squeak, the gunwale's heaving lurch,
the pause upheld after each finished stroke,

gorgonizing: mesmerizing, petrifying. In classical mythology, the Gorgons (Medusa and her sisters) were snaky-locked monsters who turned their beholders to stone.

Judith, Holofernes: according to the Apocrypha (Judith VIII-XIV), Holofernes was a general under Nebuchadnezzar (605-562 B.C.) who brought an army to Damascus to fight the Jews. Judith won his favor, beheaded him, and rallied the Israelites. The story was a favorite Renaissance art subject.

Pre-Raphaelite: in the spirit of, or like figures in the works of, the Pre-Raphaelites, anticonventional mid-19th-century English poets and artists such as Dante Gabriel Rossetti and William Morris who emphasized simplicity and fidelity to nature in their attempt to revive the spirit and style of Italian artists before Raphael (1483–1520); artistic, dreamy, sensitive.

Circe: In Greek mythology she was famous for magic. Odysseus, however, took an antidote to her poison and forced her to reconvert his men back from swine.

Gregorias: Nazianzenus (A.D. 329–390), Bishop of Constantinople who resigned in 381 and lived in solitude until his death.

unstudied, easy, pentametrical,
one action, and one thought. Halfway across
the chord between the downstroke of the oar
and its uplifted sigh was deepened
by a donkey's rusty winch, from Foux Lachaud,
a herring-gull's one creak, till the bay grew
too heavy for reflection. The rower veered
precisely, triangulating his approach,
headed for an abandoned rocky inlet
that reeked of butchered turtles, then the shallop
skimmed shallow water, the coast sliding
past easily, easily sliding rocks and trees
over the mossed mosaic of bright stones,
making their arrival secret. He would remember
a child in a canted whaleboat rounding this harbor,
coves chopped in a crescent by the whale's jaw,
with "Boy" or "Babs" Monplaisir at the tiller,
now, lecherous, lecherous, sighed the insucked water,
muttered the wiry writhing sun-shot creeks
and grasses, lecherous, skittered the thin,
translucent minnows from the skiff's shadow,
you with your finger in the pie of sin,
you with an iron in the fire, tell her
that the house could speak. Odor of fish,
odor of lechery. Who spoke? I,
said the Indian woman you finger-poked in the doorway.

I, said the Negro whore on the drawing-room floor
under the silent portraits of your parents,
while Anna slept,
her golden body like a lamp blown out
that holds, just blown, the image of the flame.

from CHAPTER 18

Sunset grew blacker in the fisherman's flesh.
He would resolve into a fish unless he left
the long beach darkening, for the village lamps,
with the claws of the furred sea gripping the high ground,

winch: a machine for hauling or pulling.
Foux Lachaud: a place on the island of St. Lucia.

his eyes would phosphoresce, his head
bubble with legends through the fly-like heads
of fishnets slung between the poles,
where the palm trees were huge spiders stuck on shafts.
Fear rooted him. Run, like a child again, run, run!
The morning bleeds itself away,
everything he touches breaks,
like a child again, he reads
the legend of Midas and the golden touch,
from morning through the afternoon
he feels compelled to read
the enormous and fragile literature
of breakdown. It is like that visit
to that trembling girl, at whose quivering side,
her skin like a plagued foal's,
my own compassion quivered,
dark moons moving under her glazed eyelids,
who answers, "How was it?
It was all trembling."

from CHAPTER 23

I looked from old verandahs at
verandahs, sails, the eternal summer sea
like a book left open by an absent master.
And what if it's all gone,
the hill's cut away for more tarmac,
the groves all sawn,
and bungalows proliferate on the scarred, hacked hillside,
the magical lagoon drained
for the Higher Purchase plan,
and they've bulldozed and bowdlerised our Vigie,
our *ocelle insularum*, our Sirmio

tarmac: the registered trademark of a kind of tar macadam consisting of iron slag mixed with tar and creosote.

Vigie: a three-mile stretch of sand beach in Tobago.

ocelle insularum: "little eye of an island."

Sirmio: a narrow peninsula in Italy where Catullus had his country house; also the subject of a nine-line poem by Tennyson, "Frater Ave Atque Vale" ("Brother, hail and farewell"). At Sirmio a few remains of an ancient building still stand, and on a nearby hill can be seen fragments of Roman baths. Tennyson calls it "sweet Catullus's all-but-island, olive-silvery Sirmio."

for a pink and pastel New Town where the shacks and huts stood
teetering and tough in unabashed unhope,
as twilight like amnesia blues the slope,
when over the untroubled ocean, the moon
will always swing its lantern
and evening fold the pages of the sea,
and peer like my lost reader silently
between the turning leaves
for the lost names
of Caribs, slaves and fishermen?

TURKEY

FAZIL HÜSNÜ DAĞLARCA

1914–

Fazıl Hüsnü Dağlarca was born in Istanbul. His father was an army officer. Fazıl himself graduated from military college and was commissioned a second lieutenant on the day his first book of poems was published (*A World Sketched on Air,* 1935). From 1935 until 1950 he was an infantry officer stationed in various parts of Turkey. Dağlarca retired with the rank of captain, traveled in France and Italy, and became a labor inspector for the Ministry of Labor in 1952. He opened a bookshop in Istanbul in 1959, and still owns and operates it. In 1960 Dağlarca founded the literary periodical *Turkce,* which he edited for five years. He won the Yeditepe Poetry Award (1956), the Turkish Language Society Award (1958), and the International Poetry Forum's Turkish Award (University of Pittsburgh, 1968). Dağlarca has published thirty-one books of poems, among them *Hungry Writing* (1951), *The Agony of the West* (1958), *Open Sesame, Open* (1967), and *Come On* (1968).

Fazıl Hüsnü Dağlarca is a poet of variations: at times aphoristic, at times consecutive. The poems range between philosophical meditations, moral underscorings, lyrical lamentations, epic symphonies. A poet of both intuition and reason, Dağlarca expresses amazement at nature, fury with social injustice, and fascination with the nonrational life of mankind.

IT IS THE SEA

It is the sea.
Each evening
In all thoughts
It comes and goes.

Seven to one—
Its agony,
Its duration,
Its echo.

This deep blue thing is midnight,
The silence
You forgot
Far away.

DRAGGED ALONG

The night
Is a huge bird
Which drags along
A much bigger bird

THE IDIOT

Understanding
Is wisdom
Lack of it
Is ancient wisdom

UNITY

The horse's mind
Blends
So swiftly
Into the hay's mind

FIRE

When
Water forgets—
Whether darkness descends or not—
The flame opens its eyes wide

THOUGHT

I think in fours
The night thinks in sevens and nines
But God thinks
In ones

HOLLOW ECHO

The shepherd plays his flute
He doesn't know
If this silence is for the sheep
Or for the hills

NIGHT OF THE AMNESTY

Prison gates swung open with the amnesty decree.
Out poured big noses, shaven necks, black chins,
Knees bent, shoulders deformed, backs wrenched; they rushed
Out of huge darknesses closed to time.
Huddled together they came,
Tattered, filthy, lice-covered, ugly.
The street resounded with their sweltering spree.

In amazement his palm flitted through his hair again and again.
He had served nine years.

His mother in his arms, his child giving him hugs—
The crowd seethed in front of the prison gate.
Some had rushed all the way from mountain villages,
Some from the seas,
Their hearts clutched by a longing greater than death.
With love they looked for their very own,
Bread in their saddlebags, water in their jugs.

He couldn't believe the sight of all those streets.
He had served twenty years.

The frenzied urge that the heart exudes
Clung to the past with such ardor,
She melted away on the convict's chest.
Remorse for poplars and fields and cattle,
Remorse for ships and weddings and rivers,
Remorse from cradles and ox-carts in silence,
Not by heaven and earth but in multitudes . . .

He embraced all of us like a madman.
He had served five and a half years.

The question of those left in jail invades the blue.
From behind the iron bars,
Both happy and mourning like the wind,
A song of the native land renews the dark.
Time is not light, yet it is.
The empty wards are lying in ambush.
If you ever go back, they will torture you.

In the light his burnt-out eye grew and grew.
He had served eight years.

In bundles, the half sleep of a night or a thousand nights
Walks away from the earth when fatigue takes hold.
Out of the crowd they dispersed in ones and twos, free
To the east and west, to the north and south, free,
An avalanche in their hearts—
Life's joys—
Life's frights.

His stricken side bobbed and throbbed.
He had served seventeen years.

Translated by **Talât Sait Halman**

UNITED STATES

AMIRI BARAKA

(LEROI JONES)

1934–

Amiri Baraka was born in New Jersey and attended school in Newark. He graduated from Howard University when he was nineteen. In 1961 Baraka received a John Hay Fellowship. He is a novelist, an editor of the important anthology of Afro-American writing *Black Fire,* and a renowned playwright, as well as a poet. One of his plays was made into a film by Anthony Harvey. In 1973 Baraka was chairman of the Black National Political Convention in Chicago. Books of poems include *Preface to a 20 Volume Suicide Note* (1961), *The Dead Lecturer* (1964), *Black Magic* (1969), and *It's Nation Time* (1970).

The poems of Amiri Baraka, as he says poems ought to be, are teeth, trees, lemons piled on a step, fists, bullets, daggers: knockoff poems, airplane poems, poems that wrestle cops into alleys. Baraka is acquainted with the pros and cons of the world; he doesn't flinch when the burning black coals are shoved in his face. He talks hip black, jive black, gentle black, straight black: tender love poems, excoriating sermon poems, blue prophecy poems.

LERVE

HAB YOU EBER BEEN BLACK AND SWEATED COME
IN THE DARK BITCH CLUTCHON YOU LIFE WHISPER
SEE HER NOW THE DARK BROWN BLACK LOVE DIDNYU
SEE HER BLACK HANGING CLOTHES IN THE JUNE
DIDN YOU EBER WAKE UP SHITTIFIED AND STRETCHIFIED
AND LAWD LAWD ALL EARTH WORLD DEIFIED, NIGHT DID IT
AND I'M HUMPIN LIKE LORD MOVE MENT HIS SELF, FOR
THE DAY TIME, AND ME THE NIGHT BEING MOVING HIS
    CREATIONS,
AND SHE HANGING UP CLOTHES LONG AND BLACK AND THE WIND
REMEMBERING ALL THE SHIT WE SCREAMED AT IT LAST EVENIN

ARE THEIR BLUES SINGERS IN RUSSIA?

Spies are found wanting. They wanted
in line, on the snow, a love to get high
with, and not, the line, a lie, a circling
tone of merciless involvement, the pushing, the
stomping, an image of green space was what the spy
wanted, standing there being shoved and hurled around
by his nostrils. They cold nights, after waiting, and
worse mornings. When the girls go by, and the lights go off
and on, to forget the clocks, and the counting of cobblestones
to keep pure cellar static off his back. The li'l darling, holding
'is wee wee he gotta pee, a little run down he leg. He pants soiled,
the wind freezed that part of his leg that wanted love most

We stand for tragic emblems when we return to the pros and cons
of the world. The shielding, for nothing. God's contradictions we
speak about as if we knew something, or could feel past what we
describe, and enter the new forms of being. See the door and
 enter,
get in out of the snow, the watermoccasins, and stuff, mud he
carried around in his mouth, or on the ground up to his ankles,
it'll get stupid or boring. So much, so much, to prepare a proper
place, to not exist in.
The day was a bargain.
A jew on the corner was thinking
of bargains. A dog, out back
did not start yet, howling, puny words,
barking in sorrow, a boat, for the spy's family to ride in
while they watched a sinking image of the world, and the spy's
 death
in snow they could really dig as beautiful or cool or somewhere
 else,
or just grimy lace curtains would make them hang against the
 boat's window
dreaming of God. The disappointment would come
after they opened their mouths, or version last
would come, and coparmies would salute the jewish dog
barking the rhythms of embezzled deserts.

We are all spies for god.

We can get betrayed. We ask for it, we ask
so much. And expect the fire the sun set the horizon
to slide through human speech dancing our future dimensions.
We expect some real shit. We expect to love all the things
somebody runs down to us. We want things, and are locked here,
to the earth, by pussy chains, or money chains, or personal
indulgence chains, lies, weak phone calls, attempts to fly when
we know good and fucking well we can't and even the nerve to
get mad, and walk around pretending we are huge magnets for the
most beautiful force in the universe. And we are, but not in the
image of wind spreading the grass, or brown grass dying from a
sudden snow, near the unemployment office where the spy stands
trying to remember just why he wanted to be the kinda spy he was

COPS

flyolfloyd, i kno from barringer,
he used to be the daredevil sax playing
lover of the old sod, near the hip park
where they threw you in, he, with some others,
notably Allen Polite, was a lover, and smooth as anything blowin
in them parts, in that town, in that time
he weighs 400 now
and threatens junkies
on Howard Street, calling them by first or nick
names, really scaring the piss out of them, being
"a nice guy" and all his killings being accidental.
Bowleg Otis played football but was always a prick
he made detective by arresting a dude he knew all his life,
he waited in the cold counting white folks' smiles. Lenny
drives a panel truck, Leon parkd in front of the city hospital
bullshitting, but he'd split yr head. He was a bad catcher w/
Baxter Terrace, you slide home head first you get messed up
strong as a bitch. Herbert Friday, beat up Barry one night,
Herbie was a funnytime cat never played anything. Cats used to

COPS
Howard Street: in Newark.

pop his sister. You wanna stand in front of a bar, with a gun
pointed at you? You wanna try to remember why you liked
    somebody
while the bullet comes. Shit.

INDIANS

Indians. Ride. Hey. Sun's red
dust sprinkled lights moving rock
ahead the slopes of years and time
beating back, water waves snow, in
skin and smokes circling up through
heavy falls. Skins. Silent woman love
me. Indian. Rides. Hey. Night silhouette.
Rides. We cannot make a tongue like that wideness
and fast horse sky. Free, and moving quick. Slide down
to leaps warmth and smokes like eyes big and pretty. Fixed
free chasm 1000 feet spread out and moving, quick. Slide down
the silent woman waits. Her Hands want you, fast, free, wide,
fixed in moving space millions of beautiful shocks she moves
across to pull you. Indians.
                Indians. Hey.
                Ride, as natural warriors
of the lord. God
touch me in clear
heaven. In free clean
skies, moving quick. A warm wet tongue
our boats put out in
take me, bighip girl,
pull me in your dazzle.

Indians. Hey.
Ride. As colored ghosts
and blue jewel feather
touch me, girl and warrior.

That tongue is lost. That way is dead. That heaven sky and God
is beaten, perished from

all warm colored people
trying to live their spiritual
lives.

On 4th Ave Seattle, a twentysix year old king
pulls roaches off his balls. A drunken foam
spits over his gums. On a park bench, a young nigger,
a colored king dies a hundred years.

Indians. Hey.
We see a man getting into his "people car."
He is clean bald and blind. He is white
and "healthy." Clothed in the rent of the planet.

Tonight at 11:30, he will return from his electric cave
to pay homage to the warriors.
Passing close,
he will stop (his old lady cold thighed before
the eye, she sleeps, connected)
approach that chief
and kneel, silently
making his homage, his thin lips,
seeking strength from the young chief's
dick

JOHN BERRYMAN

1914–1972

John Berryman was born in McAlester, Oklahoma. He graduated from Columbia, attended Cambridge (1936–38), and taught at the University of Minnesota, Wayne State University, Harvard, Princeton, and the University of Cincinnati. Berryman won a Rockefeller Fellowship in 1944, the Levinson Prize and a National Institute of Arts and Letters Grant in 1950, a Partisan Review Fellowship in 1957, and the Brandeis University Creative Arts Award in 1959. His books include *Poems* (1940), *Homage to Mistress Bradstreet* (1956), *77 Dream Songs* (1964), *His Toy, His Dream, His Rest* (1968), and *Delusions* (1972). Berryman committed suicide in Minneapolis.

The poems of John Berryman are poems of shorn speech: diary talk, ruminations, inner mutterings. Berryman turns thinking into speaking, and speaking into poems that crackle-glaze with images. His later "dream

songs" drew great praise for their remarkable language and their sustained Berryman-talk voice, but the Anne Bradstreet poems focus the waystations of a woman's life with a psychological intensity seldom surpassed in lyric-narrative poetry.

HOMAGE TO MISTRESS BRADSTREET

9

Winter than summer worse, that first, like a file
on a quick, or the poison suck of a thrilled tooth;
and still we may unpack.
Wolves & storms among, uncouth
board-pieces, boxes, barrels vanish, grow
houses, rise. Motes that hop in sunlight slow
indoors, and I am Ruth
away: open my mouth, my eyes wet: I wóuld smile:

10

vellum I palm, and dream. Their forest dies
to greensward, privets, elms & towers, whence
a nightingale is throbbing.
Women sleep sound. I was happy once.
(Something keeps on not happening; I shrink?)

Mistress Bradstreet: Anne (Dudley) Bradstreet (1612?–1672), first significant poet who wrote in English in America. She was 18 when, with her husband Simon and her parents, she sailed from England in 1630 to settle in the Massachusetts Bay Colony. Both her husband and her father were high officials in the Puritan colonial government. She reared eight children; a ninth died in childbirth. In 1650, as a surprise for her, her brother-in-law arranged to have some of her poems printed in England; these appeared in a first American edition in 1678, but much of her poetry remained unpublished until the mid-19th century.

Ruth: Old Testament heroine who forsook her Moabite people to go to Bethlehem, where she married the landowner Boaz. In his "Ode to a Nightingale," Keats imagines Ruth hearing the song of the "immortal Bird," "when, sick for home, she stood in tears amid the alien corn."

vellum: thin calfskin prepared like parchment, or a manuscript written or printed on it.

greensward: turf that is green with growing grass.

privet: an ornamental shrub used for hedges.

These minutes all their passions & powers sink
and I am not one chance
for an unknown cry or a flicker of unknown eyes.

11

Chapped souls ours, by the day Spring's strong winds swelled,
Jack's pulpits arched, more glad. The shawl I pinned
flaps like a shooting soul
might in such weather Heaven send.
Succumbing half, in spirit, to a salmon sash
I prod the nerveless novel succotash—
I must be disciplined,
in arms, against that one, and our dissidents, and myself.

19

So squeezed, wince you I scream? I love you & hate
off with you. Ages! *Useless*. Below my waist
he has me in Hell's vise.
Stalling. He let go. Come back: brace
me somewhere. No. No. Yes! everything down
hardens I press with horrible joy down
my back cracks like a wrist
shame I am voiding oh behind it is too late

30

And out of this I lull. It lessens. Kiss me.
That once. As sings out up in sparkling dark
a trail of a star & dies,
while the breath flutters, sounding, mark,
so shorn ought such caresses to us be
who, deserving nothing, flush and flee
the darkness of that light,
a lurching frozen from a warm dream. Talk to me.

31

—It is Spring's New England. Pussy willows wedge
up in the wet. Milky crestings, fringed

Jack's pulpits: The most conspicuous part of the woodland plant called jack-in-the-pulpit is the hoodlike green and purple cover that arches over its small flower spike.

yellow, in heaven, eyed
by the melting hand-in-hand or mere
desirers single, heavy-footed, rapt,
make surge poor human hearts. Venus is trapt—
the hefty pike shifts, sheer—
in Orion blazing. Warblings, odors, nudge to an edge—

37

I fear Hell's hammer-wind. But fear does wane.
Death's blossoms grain my hair; I cannot live.
A black joy clashes
joy, in twilight. The Devil said
'I will deal toward her softly, and her enchanting cries
will fool the horns of Adam.' Father of lies,
a male great pestle smashes
small women swarming towards the mortar's rim in vain.

42

When by me in the dusk my child sits down
I am myself. Simon, if it's that loose,
let me wiggle it out.
You'll get a bigger one there, & bite.
How they loft, how their sizes delight and grate.
The proportioned, spiritless poems accumulate.
And they publish them
away in brutish London, for a hollow crown.

45

And they tower, whom the pear-tree lured
to let them fall, fierce mornings they reclined
down the brook-bank to the east
fishing for shiners with a crookt pin,
wading, dams massing, well, and Sam's to be

Orion: the constellation named for the great hunter of Greek mythology; his sword is part of the constellation.

hollow crown: See Shakespeare's *Richard II*, Act III, Sc. ii: "Within the hollow crown/That rounds the mortal temples of a king,/Keeps Death his court; and there the antic sits,/Scoffing his state and grinning at his pomp."

a doctor in Boston. After the divisive sea,
and death's first feast,
and the galled effort on the wilderness endured,

46

Arminians, and the King bore against us;
of an 'inward light' we hear with horror.
Whose fan is in his hand
and he will throughly purge his floor,
come towards mé. I have what licks the joints
and bites the heart, which winter more appoints.
Iller, I, oftener.
Hard at the outset; in the ending thus hard, thus?

52

They say thro' the fading winter Dorothy fails,
my second, who than I bore one more, nine;
and I see her inearthed. I linger.
Seaborn she wed knelt before Simon;
Simon I, and linger. Black-yellow seething, vast
it lies fróm me, mine: all they look aghast.
It will be a glorious arm.
Docile I watch. My wreckt chest hurts when Simon pales.

55

Headstones stagger under great draughts of time
after heads pass out, and their world must reel
speechless, blind in the end
about its chilling star: thrift tuft,
whin cushion—nothing. Already with the wounded flying
dark air fills, I am a closet of secrets dying,
races murder, foxholes hold men,
reactor piles wage slow upon the wet brain rime.

Arminians: rebels against the doctrine of unconditional election. Simon Bradstreet alone opposed the law condemning Quakers to death.
Whose fan . . . floor: Matthew 3:12.
what licks the joints and bites the heart: rheumatic fever.
thrift: the plant, also called Our Lady's cushion.
whin: furze, a prickly evergreen shrub.
wet brain: edema.

56

I must pretend to leave you. Only you draw off
a benevolent phantom, I say you seem to me
drowned towns off England,
featureless as those myriads
who what bequeathed save fire-ash, fossils, burled
in the open river-drifts of the Old World?
Simon lived on for years.
I renounce not even ragged glances, small teeth, nothing,

57

O all your ages at the mercy of my loves
together lie at once, forever or
so long as I happen.
In the rain of pain & departure, still
Love has no body and presides the sun,
and elfs from silence melody. I run.
Hover, utter, still,
a sourcing   whom my lost candle like the firefly loves.

ALLEN GINSBERG

1926–

Allen Ginsberg was born in Paterson, New Jersey. A leader of the Beat Generation of the fifties, he has traveled widely both in the Orient and in the West. Ginsberg graduated from Columbia in 1949, and has worked as a spot welder, a dishwasher on cargo ships, a night porter, a literary agent, a copy boy, a reporter, a market-research consultant, an actor, and a secretary. He won a Guggenheim Fellowship in 1963 and an Academy of American Arts and Letters Award in 1969. Books include *Howl and Other Poems* (1956), *Kaddish* (1961), and *The Fall of America* (1972).

The poems of Allen Ginsberg are ganglia-like, surveyant, homiletical. Ginsberg speaks the rivers and telephone poles and used cars and martinis of America: charms, chants, invocations, psalms—vedas of American

speech. His rhetoric has been weaned on the filibuster and chastened by the oracle: catalogues of sensations, vocables of OOM, lungsfull of justice and mercy for all.

from WICHITA VORTEX SUTRA

I'm an old man now, and a lonesome man in Kansas
but not afraid
to speak my lonesomeness in a car,
because not only my lonesomeness
it's Ours, all over America,
O tender fellows—
& spoken lonesomeness is Prophecy
in the moon 100 years ago or in
the middle of Kansas now.
It's not the vast plains mute our mouths
that fill at midnite with ecstatic language
when our trembling bodies hold each other
breast to breast on a mattress—
Not the empty sky that hides
the feeling from our faces
nor our skirts and trousers that conceal
the bodylove emanating in a glow of beloved skin,
white smooth abdomen down to the hair
between our legs,
It's not a God that bore us that forbid
our Being, like a sunny rose
all red with naked joy
between our eyes & bellies, yes
All we do is for this frightened thing
we call Love, want and lack—
fear that we aren't the one whose body could be
beloved of all the brides of Kansas City,
kissed all over by every boy of Wichita—

vortex: any mass having a circular motion, pulling all elements to its center; here, tornado.

sutra: in Hinduism, a brief aphoristic composition; in Buddhism, a longer exposition in which a doctrine is expounded.

O but how many in their solitude weep aloud like me—
On the bridge over Republican River
almost in tears to know
how to speak the right language—
on the frosty broad road
uphill between highway embankments
I search for the language
that is also yours—
almost all our language has been taxed by war.
Radio antennae high tension
wires ranging from Junction City across the plains—
highway cloverleaf sunk in a vast meadow
lanes curving past Abilene
to Denver filled with old
heroes of love—
to Wichita where McClure's mind
burst into animal beauty
drunk, getting laid in a car
in a neon misted street
15 years ago—
to Independence where the old man's still alive
who loosed the bomb that's slaved all human consciousness
and made the body universe a place of fear—
Now, speeding along the empty plain,
no giant demon machine
visible on the horizon
but tiny human trees and wooden houses at the sky's edge
I claim my birthright!
reborn forever as long as Man
in Kansas or other universe—Joy
reborn after the vast sadness of War Gods!
A lone man talking to myself, no house in the brown vastness to
hear,
imagining the throng of Selves
that make this nation one body of Prophecy
languaged by Declaration as
Happiness!

McClure: Michael, American poet, b. 1932 in Kansas.

I call all Powers of imagination
        to my side in this auto to make Prophecy,
                                        all Lords
                of human kingdoms to come
Shambu Bharti Baba naked covered with ash
                Khaki Baba fat-bellied mad with the dogs
Dehorahava Baba who moans Oh how wounded, How wounded
        Citaram Onkar Das Thakur who commands
                                give up your desire
Satyananda who raises two thumbs in tranquillity
        Kali Pada Guha Roy whose yoga drops before the void
                Shivananda who touches the breast and says OM
Srimata Krishnaji of Brindaban who says take for your guru
        William Blake the invisible father of English visions
        Sri Ramakrishna master of ecstasy eyes

Shambu Bharti Baba: a contemporary Yogi, a Naga sadhu who lived in Manikarnika ghat, the traditional burning ground in Benares, when the author met him in 1963. He walks naked with a vow of silence. Photographs and descriptions of him appear in [Ginsberg's] *Indian Journals* (City Lights, 1970). [AG] Naga is a Hindu sect; a *sadhu* is a Hindu holy man.

Khaki Baba: 19th-century Yogi from Taraphith, Birbhum (area of northern Bengal), home of the Baul sect of devotional poets. He made friends with dogs. [AG]

Dehorahava Baba: a famous contemporary saint whom the author met in 1963 in Benares sitting on a bamboo platform in the Ganges. [AG]

Citaram Onkar Das Thakur: a contemporary Vaishnav saint who suggested to the author, met washing in the Ganges: "Give up desire for children." [AG]

Satyananda: contemporary Calcutta swami with double thumbs, who suggested to the author: "Be a sweet poet of the Lord." [AG]

Kali Pada Guha Roy: contemporary Tantric Yogi, Benares, who commented that, like poetry, yoga also drops before the void. [AG]

Shivananda: the late Swami Shivananda of Rishikesh, Vishnu himself, teacher to Swami Satchitananda, presently in America. [AG]

Srimata Krishnaji: a well-known contemporary saint of Brindaban; she was the teacher of Bankey Behari, author of *Sufis, Mystics and Yogis of India* (translations of Kabir, etc.) (Bhavan's Book University: Bombay, 1962). [AG] Brindaban is the locale of a Krishna cult and according to tradition the scene of many adventures in the life of Krishna.

William Blake: (1757–1827), English mystical poet, painter, and engraver who wrote *Songs of Innocence* and *The Marriage of Heaven and Hell.*

Sri Ramakrishna: (1836–86), the most famous saint of 19th-century India; believed that lust and money ("women and gold") are the chief obstacles to individual enlightenment. Teacher of Swami Vivekenanda (1862–1902), who inspired the Vedanta Society. [AG]

half closed who only cries for his mother
Chaitanya arms upraised singing & dancing his own praise
merciful Chango judging our bodies
Durga-Ma covered with blood
destroyer of battlefield illusions
million-faced Tathagata gone past suffering
Preserver Harekrishna returning in the age of pain
Sacred Heart my Christ acceptable
Allah the Compassionate One
Jaweh Righteous One
all Knowledge-Princes of Earth-man, all
ancient Seraphim of heavenly Desire, Devas, yogis
& holymen I chant to—
Come to my lone presence
into this Vortex named Kansas,
I lift my voice aloud,
make Mantra of American language now,
I here declare the end of the War!
Ancient days' Illusion!—
and pronounce words beginning my own millennium.

Chaitanya: (1485–1534), founder of a Vaishnava sect popular in Bengal and Orissa who stressed singing and dancing as aids to ecstatic communion. Frequent seizures threw him into fits of ecstasy or transfixion. His lineage is now known in the West as the International Society for Krishna Consciousness, which popularized the Hare Krishna Mantra, later recorded by George Harrison. [AG]

Chango: a phallic divinity of creation of the Yoruba tribe of West Africa; a major Oriche (god, totem) of the Santero cult of Cuba. Red in color, like Shiva, he is symbolized by a phallus. [AG]

Durga-Ma: in Hindu mythology, the goddess of battle; one of the many forms of the goddess Sakti, the wife of Siva, usually pictured with eight or ten arms, riding a lion.

Tathagata: the true state of all that exists, synonomous with ultimate reality. Persons who have it within themselves yearn for enlightenment. Also, a title for the historical Buddha, literally translated "he who has passed through."

Harekrishna: According to the Chaitanya cult, Krishna is the supreme personality of the godhead. "Hare" is the pleasure principle of that supreme person. Krishna is an incarnation of Vishnu, the preserver among Indian gods, and the Hare Krishna Mantra is considered to be the most direct path to enlightenment in this Age of Destruction, the *Kali Yuga*. The mantra is as follows: *Hare Krishna Hare Krishna Krishna Krishna Hare Hare Hare Rama Hare Rama Rama Rama Hare Hare.* [AG]

Mantra: in Sanskrit, a prayer, an invocation, a charm.

Let the States tremble,
let the Nation weep,
let Congress legislate its own delight
let the President execute his own desire—
this Act done by my own voice,
nameless Mystery—
published to my own senses,
blissfully received by my own form
approved with pleasure by my sensations
manifestation of my very thought
accomplished in my own imagination
all realms within my consciousness fulfilled
60 miles from Wichita
near El Dorado,
The Golden One,
in chill earthly mist
houseless brown farmland plains rolling heavenward
in every direction
one midwinter afternoon Sunday called the day of the Lord—
Pure Spring Water gathered in one tower
where Florence is
set on a hill,
stop for tea & gas

Cars passing their messages along country crossroads
to populaces cement-networked on flatness,
giant white mist on earth
and a Wichita Eagle-Beacon headlines
"*Kennedy Urges Cong Get Chair in Negotiations*"
The War is gone,
Language emerging on the motel news stand,
the right magic
Formula, the language known
in the back of the mind before, now in black print
daily consciousness
Eagle News Services Saigon—

El Dorado: (1) a legendary king of a northern South American tribe; believed by the 16th-century Spaniards to possess great wealth. His imaginary country abounded in gold. (2) a small town in Kansas.

Headline Surrounded Vietcong Charge Into Fire Fight
the suffering not yet ended
for others
The last spasms of the dragon of pain
shoot thru the muscles
a crackling around the eyeballs
of a sensitive yellow boy by a muddy wall
Continued from page one area
after the Marines killed 256 Vietcong captured 31
ten day operation Harvest Moon last December
Language language
U.S. Military Spokesmen
Language language
Cong death toll
has soared to 100 in First Air Cavalry
Division's Sector of
Language language
Operation White Wing near Bong Son
Some of the
Language language
Communist
Language language soldiers
charged so desperately
they were struck with six or seven bullets before they fell
Language Language M 60 Machine Guns
Language language in La Drang Valley
the terrain is rougher infested with leeches and scorpions
The war was over several hours ago!

Oh at last again the radio opens
blue Invitations!
Angelic Dylan singing across the nation
"When all your children start to resent you
Won't you come see me, Queen Jane?"
His youthful voice making glad
the brown endless meadows
His tenderness penetrating aether,
soft prayer on the airwaves,
Language language, and sweet music too

even unto thee,
hairy flatness!
even unto thee
despairing Burns!

Future speeding on swift wheels
straight to the heart of Wichita!
Now radio voices cry population hunger world
of unhappy people
waiting for Man to be born
O man in America!
you certainly smell good
the radio says
passing mysterious families of winking towers
grouped round a quonset-hut on a hillock—
feed storage or military fear factory here?
Sensitive City, Ooh! Hamburger & Skelley's Gas
lights feed man and machine,
Kansas Electric Substation aluminum robot
signals thru thin antennae towers
above the empty football field
at Sunday dusk
to a solitary derrick that pumps oil from the unconscious
working night & day
& factory gas-flares edge a huge golf course
where tired businessmen can come and play—
Cloverleaf, Merging Traffic East Wichita turnoff
McConnel Airforce Base
nourishing the city—
Lights rising in the suburbs
Supermarket Texaco brilliance starred
over streetlamp vertebrae on Kellogg,
green jewelled traffic lights
confronting the windshield,
Centertown ganglion entered!
Crowds of autos moving with their lightshine,

Burns: another small town in Kansas en route to Wichita.
ganglion: a mass of nerve cells from which impulses are transmitted; a center of energy, activity.

signbulbs winking in the driver's eyeball—
The human nest collected, neon lit,
and sunburst signed
for business as usual, except on the Lord's Day—
Redeemer Lutheran's three crosses lit on the lawn
reminder of our sins
and Titsworth offers insurance on Hydraulic
by De Voors Guard's Mortuary for outmoded bodies
of the human vehicle
which no Titsworth of insurance will customise
for resale—
So home, traveller, past the newspaper language factory
under Union Station railroad bridge on Douglas
to the center of the Vortex, calmly returned
to Hotel Eaton—
Carry Nation began the war on Vietnam here
with an angry smashing axe
attacking Wine—
Here fifty years ago, by her violence
began a vortex of hatred that defoliated the Mekong Delta—
Proud Wichita! vain Wichita
cast the first stone!—
That murdered my mother
who died of the communist anticommunist psychosis
in the madhouse one decade long ago
complaining about wires of masscommunication in her head
and phantom political voices in the air
besmirching her girlish character.
Many another has suffered death and madness
in the Vortex from Hydraulic
to the end of 17th—enough!
The war is over now—
Except for the souls
held prisoner in Niggertown
still pining for love of your tender white bodies O children of
Wichita!

2/15/66

ROBERT LOWELL

1917–

Robert Lowell was born on Revere Street in Boston, and studied at St. Mark's School, Kenyon College, and Harvard University. He was a conscientious objector during World War II and spent five months in a federal penitentiary. James Russell Lowell was his great grandfather's brother; Amy Lowell was a distant cousin. Lowell has been Consultant in Poetry at the Library of Congress, and has taught at Boston University and Harvard. He won the Pulitzer Prize for his second book, *Lord Weary's Castle,* in 1947. Lowell has translated such writers as Racine, Pasternak, Rilke, and Baudelaire. His play *The Old Glory* won the Obie Award for best off-Broadway play of the season in 1965. Other awards include the Boston Arts Festival Award, the National Book Award for *Life Studies* (1959), and another Pulitzer Prize for *The Dolphin* (1973).

The poems of Robert Lowell range from the boiling and breathless to the studied and colloquial. Lowell alternates between stalking and edging around himself, always with burly energy, always keeping close to great caves or trailing a great turbulence. The poetry pulses with ideas, but it is also muscular and idiomatic. Lowell takes on everything from Protestant-capitalist America to himself. In one poem not included below he says: "everyone is tired of my turmoil"; in another place he says "accident threw up subjects, and the plot swallowed them—famished for human chances."

THE QUAKER GRAVEYARD IN NANTUCKET

(For Warren Winslow, dead at sea)

Let man have dominion over the fishes of the sea and the
fowls of the air and the beasts and the whole earth, and
every creeping creature that moveth upon the earth.

I

A brackish reach of shoal off Madaket,—
The sea was still breaking violently and night
Had steamed into our North Atlantic Fleet,
When the drowned sailor clutched the drag-net. Light
Flashed from his matted head and marble feet,
He grappled at the net

Let man have dominion . . . : Genesis 1:26.
Madaket: an area of Nantucket Island.

With the coiled, hurdling muscles of his thighs:
The corpse was bloodless, a botch of reds and whites,
Its open, staring eyes
Were lustreless dead-lights
Or cabin-windows on a stranded hulk
Heavy with sand. We weight the body, close
Its eyes and heave it seaward whence it came,
Where the heel-headed dogfish barks its nose
On Ahab's void and forehead; and the name
Is blocked in yellow chalk.
Sailors, who pitch this portent at the sea
Where dreadnaughts shall confess
Its hell-bent deity,
When you are powerless
To sand-bag this Atlantic bulwark, faced
By the earth-shaker, green, unwearied, chaste
In his steel scales: ask for no Orphean lute
To pluck life back. The guns of the steeled fleet
Recoil and then repeat
The hoarse salute.

II

Whenever winds are moving and their breath
Heaves at the roped-in bulwarks of this pier,
The terns and sea-gulls tremble at your death
In these home waters. Sailor, can you hear
The Pequod's sea wings, beating landward, fall
Headlong and break on our Atlantic wall
Off 'Sconset, where the yawing S-boats splash

Ahab: the monomaniacal captain of the ill-fated Pequod in Melville's *Moby Dick;* namesake of the Old Testament Ahab, king of Israel c. 874–853 B.C., who allowed his wife Jezebel to introduce the worship of Baal in Israel and so brought on himself the bitter hostility of the prophet Elijah (1 Kings 16:29 ff.).

dreadnaughts: large, heavily armored battleships with powerful guns.

Orphean lute: In Greek mythology, Orpheus follows his dead wife Eurydice into the lower world, where the charms of his lute win her back from Hades on the condition that Orpheus not look back until they are both within the upper regions; unfortunately, Orpheus looks back and so loses Eurydice forever.

Pequod: the ill-fated whaling ship in Melville's *Moby Dick* that sails from Nantucket.

S-boats: small German torpedo boats in World War II.

The bellbuoy, with ballooning spinnakers,
As the entangled, screeching mainsheet clears
The blocks: off Madaket, where lubbers lash
The heavy surf and throw their long lead squids
For blue-fish? Sea-gulls blink their heavy lids
Seaward. The winds' wings beat upon the stones,
Cousin, and scream for you and the claws rush
At the sea's throat and wring it in the slush
Of this old Quaker graveyard where the bones
Cry out in the long night for the hurt beast
Bobbing by Ahab's whaleboats in the East.

III

All you recovered from Poseidon died
With you, my cousin, and the harrowed brine
Is fruitless on the blue beard of the god,
Stretching beyond us to the castles in Spain,
Nantucket's westward haven. To Cape Cod
Guns, cradled on the tide,
Blast the eelgrass about a waterclock
Of bilge and backwash, roil the salt and sand
Lashing earth's scaffold, rock
Our warships in the hand
Of the great God, where time's contrition blues
Whatever it was these Quaker sailors lost
In the mad scramble of their lives. They died
When time was open-eyed,
Wooden and childish; only bones abide
There, in the nowhere, where their boats were tossed
Sky-high, where mariners had fabled news
Of IS, the whited monster. What it cost
Them is their secret. In the sperm-whale's slick
I see the Quakers drown and hear their cry:
"If God himself had not been on our side,
If God himself had not been on our side,

spinnaker: a large triangular sail set on a long light pole on the side opposite the mainsail on fore-and-aft rigged yachts and used when running before the wind.
mainsheet: a rope by which the mainsail is trimmed and secured.
blocks: wooden or metal cases enclosing one or more pulleys.
Poseidon: Greek god of the sea.

When the Atlantic rose against us, why,
Then it had swallowed us up quick."

IV

This is the end of the whaleroad and the whale
Who spewed Nantucket bones on the thrashed swell
And stirred the troubled waters to whirlpools
To send the Pequod packing off to hell:
This is the end of them, three-quarters fools,
Snatching at straws to sail
Seaward and seaward on the turntail whale,
Spouting out blood and water as it rolls,
Sick as a dog to these Atlantic shoals:
Clamavimus, O depths. Let the sea-gulls wail
For water, for the deep where the high tide
Mutters to its hurt self, mutters and ebbs.
Waves wallow in their wash, go out and out,
Leave only the death-rattle of the crabs,
The beach increasing, its enormous snout
Sucking the ocean's side.
This is the end of running on the waves;
We are poured out like water. Who will dance
The mast-lashed master of Leviathans
Up from this field of Quakers in their unstoned graves?

MY LAST AFTERNOON WITH UNCLE DEVEREUX WINSLOW

1922: the stone porch of my Grandfather's summer house

I

"I won't go with you. I want to stay with Grandpa!"
That's how I threw cold water
on my Mother and Father's
watery martini pipe dreams at Sunday dinner.

THE QUAKER GRAVEYARD IN NANTUCKET

Clamavimus: Latin, "we called out."

Leviathan: a formidable aquatic animal in the Bible, usually meant to be a crocodile or a whale. Also the political organism or state; cf. Thomas Hobbes' *Leviathan* (1651).

. . . Fontainebleau, Mattapoisett, Puget Sound. . . .
Nowhere was anywhere after a summer
at my Grandfather's farm.
Diamond-pointed, athirst and Norman,
its alley of poplars
paraded from Grandmother's rose garden
to a scarey stand of virgin pine,
scrub, and paths forever pioneering.

One afternoon in 1922,
I sat on the stone porch, looking through
screens as black-grained as drifting coal.
Tockytock, tockytock
clumped our Alpine, Edwardian cuckoo clock,
slung with strangled, wooden game.
Our farmer was cementing a root-house under the hill.
One of my hands was cool on a pile
of black earth, the other warm
on a pile of lime. All about me
were the works of my Grandfather's hands:
snapshots of his *Liberty Bell* silver mine;
his high school at *Stukkert am Neckar*;
stogie-brown beams; fools'-gold nuggets;
octagonal red tiles,
sweaty with a secret dank, crummy with ant-stale;
a Rocky Mountain chaise longue,
its legs, shellacked saplings.
A pastel-pale Huckleberry Finn
fished with a broom straw in a basin
hollowed out of a millstone.
Like my Grandfather, the décor
was manly, comfortable,
overbearing, disproportioned.

What were those sunflowers? Pumpkins floating shoulder-high?
It was sunset, Sadie and Nellie
bearing pitchers of ice-tea,
oranges, lemons, mint, and peppermints,
and the jug of shandygaff,
which Grandpa made by blending half and half
yeasty, wheezing homemade sarsaparilla with beer.

The farm, entitled *Char-de-sa*
in the Social Register,
was named for my Grandfather's children:
Charlotte, Devereux, and Sarah.
No one had died there in my lifetime . . .
Only Cinder, our Scottie puppy
paralysed from gobbling toads.
I sat mixing black earth and lime.

II

I was five and a half.
My formal pearl gray shorts
had been worn for three minutes.
My perfection was the Olympian
poise of my models in the imperishable autumn
display windows
of Rogers Peet's boys' store below the State House
in Boston. Distorting drops of water
pinpricked my face in the basin's mirror.
I was a stuffed toucan
with a bibulous, multicolored beak.

III

Up in the air
by the lakeview window in the billiards-room,
lurid in the doldrums of the sunset hour,
my Great Aunt Sarah
was learning *Samson and Delilah*.
She thundered on the keyboard of her dummy piano,
with gauze curtains like a boudoir table,
accordionlike yet soundless.
It had been bought to spare the nerves
of my Grandmother,
tone-deaf, quick as a cricket,
now needing a fourth for "Auction,"

toucan: a brilliantly colored tropical American bird with a very large beak, often nearly as long as the body and usually as brightly colored.
bibulous: (1) readily taking up fluids; (2) affected by tippling.
Samson and Delilah: a 19th-century opera by the French composer Saint-Saëns, based on the Old Testament story (Judges 14–16).

and casting a thirsty eye
on Aunt Sarah, risen like the phoenix
from her bed of troublesome snacks and Tauchnitz classics.

Forty years earlier,
twenty, auburn headed,
grasshopper notes of genius!
Family gossip says Aunt Sarah
tilted her archaic Athenian nose
and jilted an Astor.
Each morning she practiced
on the grand piano at Symphony Hall,
deathlike in the off-season summer—
its naked Greek statues draped with purple
like the saints in Holy Week. . . .
On the recital day, she failed to appear.

IV

I picked with a clean finger nail at the blue anchor
on my sailor blouse washed white as a spinnaker.
What in the world was I wishing?
. . . A sail-colored horse browsing in the bullrushes . . .
A fluff of the west wind puffing
my blouse, kiting me over our seven chimneys,
troubling the waters. . . .
As small as sapphires were the ponds: *Quittacus*, *Snippituit*,
and *Assawompset*, halved by "the Island,"
where my Uncle's duck blind
floated in a barrage of smoke-clouds.
Double-barrelled shotguns
stuck out like bundles of baby crow-bars.
A single sculler in a camouflaged kayak
was quacking to the decoys. . . .

At the cabin between the waters,
the nearest windows were already boarded.
Uncle Devereux was closing camp for the winter.
As if posed for "the engagement photograph,"

Tauchnitz: Karl Christoph Traugott (1761–1836), German publisher whose firm, established in 1796, specialized in dictionaries, Bibles, and stereotyped editions of the Greek and Roman classics.

he was wearing his severe
war-uniform of a volunteer Canadian officer.
Daylight from the doorway riddled his student posters,
tacked helter-skelter on walls as raw as a board-walk.
Mr. Punch, a water melon in hockey tights,
was tossing off a decanter of Scotch.
La Belle France in a red, white and blue toga
was accepting the arm of her "protector,"
the ingenu and porcine Edward VII.
The pre-war music hall belles
had goose necks, glorious signatures, beauty-moles,
and coils of hair like rooster tails.
The finest poster was two or three young men in khaki kilts
being bushwhacked on the veldt—
They were almost life-size. . . .

My Uncle was dying at twenty-nine.
"You are behaving like children,"
said my Grandfather,
when my Uncle and Aunt left their three baby daughters,
and sailed for Europe on a last honeymoon . . .
I cowered in terror.
I wasn't a child at all—
unseen and all-seeing, I was Agrippina
in the Golden House of Nero. . . .

Near me was the white measuring-door
my Grandfather had pencilled with my Uncle's heights.
In 1911, he had stopped growing at just six feet.
While I sat on the tiles,
and dug at the anchor on my sailor blouse,
Uncle Devereux stood behind me.
He was as brushed as Bayard, our riding horse.
His face was putty.

bushwacked: ambushed.

veldt: grassland of eastern and southern Africa, almost level, often sparsely dotted with shrubs or trees.

Agrippina: "the younger" (A.D. 16–59), Nero's mother, whose intrigues, ambitions, and reputed crimes made her son emperor, and ended in her murder at Nero's orders when she opposed his divorcing Octavia to marry Poppaea Sabina.

the Golden House of Nero: the fabulously expensive palace built by Nero during the reconstruction of Rome after the great fire of A.D. 64.

His blue coat and white trousers
grew sharper and straighter.
His coat was a blue jay's tail,
his trousers were solid cream from the top of the bottle.
He was animated, hierarchical,
like a ginger snap man in a clothes-press.
He was dying of the incurable Hodgkin's disease. . . .
My hands were warm, then cool, on the piles
of earth and lime,
a black pile and a white pile. . . .
Come winter,
Uncle Devereux would blend to the one color.

SYLVIA PLATH

1932–1963

Sylvia Plath was born in the coastal town of Winthrop, Massachusetts. Her father, who died when she was eight, was a professor of biology at Boston University and an authority on bumblebees. Her mother also taught at Boston University. When Sylvia was eight, the *Boston Sunday Herald* published her first poem. She graduated from Smith College and won a Fulbright to Cambridge University, married Ted Hughes in 1956, taught a year at Smith, and returned to England in 1959. A daughter was born in 1960 and a son in 1962. Plath wrote a novel, short stories, reviews, essays, and four books of poems: *The Colossus* (1962), *Ariel* (1966), *Crossing the Water* (1971), and *Winter Trees* (1971). She committed suicide in London.

The poems of Sylvia Plath walk into beehives, tombs, mushrooms, old photographs, gunney sacks, the locked rooms of dreams, the furnaces of crematoria. Plath writes about her own life with a devastating self-scrutiny, and her voice never quivers in the face of her own revelations. She is a priestess of oracular, ritualistic poems that intensify the effects of colloquial speech within formal poetic schemes. The poems enter our feet like sea urchin spines, and work their way up to our throats.

THE MOON AND THE YEW TREE

This is the light of the mind, cold and planetary.
The trees of the mind are black. The light is blue.
The grasses unload their griefs on my feet as if I were God,
Prickling my ankles and murmuring of their humility.

Fumy, spiritous mists inhabit this place
Separated from my house by a row of headstones.
I simply cannot see where there is to get to.

The moon is no door. It is a face in its own right,
White as a knuckle and terribly upset.
It drags the sea after it like a dark crime; it is quiet
With the O-gape of complete despair. I live here.
Twice on Sunday, the bells startle the sky—
Eight great tongues affirming the Resurrection.
At the end, they soberly bong out their names.

The yew tree points up. It has a Gothic shape.
The eyes lift after it and find the moon.
The moon is my mother. She is not sweet like Mary.
Her blue garments unloose small bats and owls.
How I would like to believe in tenderness—
The face of the effigy, gentled by candles,
Bending, on me in particular, its mild eyes.

I have fallen a long way. Clouds are flowering
Blue and mystical over the face of the stars.
Inside the church, the saints will be all blue,
Floating on their delicate feet over the cold pews,
Their hands and faces stiff with holiness.
The moon sees nothing of this. She is bald and wild.
And the message of the yew tree is blackness—blackness and
silence.

DADDY

You do not do, you do not do
Any more, black shoe
In which I have lived like a foot
For thirty years, poor and white,
Barely daring to breathe or Achoo.

Daddy, I have had to kill you.
You died before I had time—
Marble-heavy, a bag full of God,
Ghastly statue with one grey toe
Big as a Frisco seal

And a head in the freakish Atlantic
Where it pours bean green over blue
In the waters off beautiful Nauset.
I used to pray to recover you.
Ach, du.

In the German tongue, in the Polish town
Scraped flat by the roller
Of wars, wars, wars.
But the name of the town is common.
My Polack friend

Says there are a dozen or two.
So I never could tell where you
Put your foot, your root,
I never could talk to you.
The tongue stuck in my jaw.

It stuck in a barb wire snare.
Ich, ich, ich, ich,
I could hardly speak.
I thought every German was you.
And the language obscene

An engine, an engine
Chuffing me off like a Jew.
A Jew to Dachau, Auschwitz, Belsen.
I began to talk like a Jew.
I think I may well be a Jew.

The snows of the Tyrol, the clear beer of Vienna
Are not very pure or true.
With my gypsy ancestress and my weird luck
And my Taroc pack and my Taroc pack
I may be a bit of a Jew.

Nauset: a beach on the east coast of Cape Cod between Eastham and Orleans.

Dachau, Auschwitz, Belsen: German concentration camps in World War II where millions of Jews were murdered.

Taroc: an old and popular card game of central Europe played with a pack containing the 22 tarots plus 40, 52, or 56 cards equivalent to modern playing cards.

I have always been scared of *you*,
With your Luftwaffe, your gobbledygoo.
And your neat moustache
And your Aryan eye, bright blue.
Panzer-man, panzer-man, O You—

Not God but a swastika
So black no sky could squeak through.
Every woman adores a Fascist,
The boot in the face, the brute
Brute heart of a brute like you.

You stand at the blackboard, daddy,
In the picture I have of you,
A cleft in your chin instead of your foot
But no less a devil for that, no not
Any less the black man who

Bit my pretty red heart in two.
I was ten when they buried you.
At twenty I tried to die
And get back, back, back to you.
I thought even the bones would do.

But they pulled me out of the sack,
And they stuck me together with glue.
And then I knew what to do.
I made a model of you,
A man in black with a Meinkampf look

And a love of the rack and the screw.
And I said I do, I do.
So daddy, I'm finally through.
The black telephone's off at the root,
The voices just can't worm through.

Luftwaffe: the German Air Force in World War II.

Aryan: formerly, of or pertaining to the Indo-European language family; misused by the Nazis as a term to describe a fictitiously superior "Nordic" type.

Panzer: German for "armor-plating"; in World War II, the name given to armored tank units of the German Army organized for rapid attack.

a Meinkampf look: from the title of Hitler's book *Mein Kampf* ("My Struggle"), begun in 1923, setting forth his grandiose ambitions and the Nazi "philosophy" of anti-Semitism, dictatorship, and German superiority.

If I've killed one man, I've killed two—
The vampire who said he was you
And drank my blood for a year,
Seven years, if you want to know.
Daddy, you can lie back now.

There's a stake in your fat black heart
And the villagers never liked you.
They are dancing and stamping on you.
They always *knew* it was you.
Daddy, daddy, you bastard, I'm through.

THE BEE MEETING

Who are these people at the bridge to meet me? They are the
villagers—
The rector, the midwife, the sexton, the agent for bees.
In my sleeveless summery dress I have no protection,
And they are all gloved and covered, why did nobody tell me?
They are smiling and taking out veils tacked to ancient hats.

I am nude as a chicken neck, does nobody love me?
Yes, here is the secretary of bees with her white shop smock,
Buttoning the cuffs at my wrists and the slit from my neck to my
knees.
Now I am milkweed silk, the bees will not notice.
They will not smell my fear, my fear, my fear.

Which is the rector now, is it that man in black?
Which is the midwife, is that her blue coat?
Everybody is nodding a square black head, they are knights in
visors,
Breastplates of cheesecloth knotted under the armpits.
Their smiles and their voices are changing. I am led through a
beanfield.

Strips of tinfoil winking like people,
Feather dusters fanning their hands in a sea of bean flowers,
Creamy bean flowers with black eyes and leaves like bored hearts.
Is it blood clots the tendrils are dragging up that string?
No, no, it is scarlet flowers that will one day be edible.

Now they are giving me a fashionable white straw Italian hat
And a black veil that moulds to my face, they are making me one
    of them.
They are leading me to the shorn grove, the circle of hives.
Is it the hawthorn that smells so sick?
The barren body of hawthorn, etherizing its children.

Is it some operation that is taking place?
It is the surgeon my neighbors are waiting for,
This apparition in a green helmet,
Shining gloves and white suit.
Is it the butcher, the grocer, the postman, someone I know?

I cannot run, I am rooted, and the gorse hurts me
With its yellow purses, its spiky armory.
I could not run without having to run forever.
The white hive is snug as a virgin,
Sealing off her brood cells, her honey, and quietly humming.

Smoke rolls and scarves in the grove.
The mind of the hive thinks this is the end of everything.
Here they come, the outriders, on their hysterical elastics.
If I stand very still, they will think I am cow parsley,
A gullible head untouched by their animosity,

Not even nodding, a personage in a hedgerow.
The villagers open the chambers, they are hunting the queen.
Is she hiding, is she eating honey? She is very clever.
She is old, old, old, she must live another year, and she knows it.
While in their fingerjoint cells the new virgins

Dream of a duel they will win inevitably,
A curtain of wax dividing them from the bride flight,
The upflight of the murderess into a heaven that loves her.
The villagers are moving the virgins, there will be no killing.
The old queen does not show herself, is she so ungrateful?

I am exhausted, I am exhausted—
Pillar of white in a blackout of knives.
I am the magician's girl who does not flinch.
The villagers are untying their disguises, they are shaking hands.
Whose is that long white box in the grove, what have they
    accomplished, why am I cold?

BLACKBERRYING

Nobody in the lane, and nothing, nothing but blackberries,
Blackberries on either side, though on the right mainly,
A blackberry alley, going down in hooks, and a sea
Somewhere at the end of it, heaving. Blackberries
Big as the ball of my thumb, and dumb as eyes
Ebon in the hedges, fat
With blue-red juices. These they squander on my fingers.
I had not asked for such a blood sisterhood; they must love me.
They accommodate themselves to my milkbottle, flattening
their sides.

Overhead go the choughs in black, cacophonous flocks—
Bits of burnt paper wheeling in a blown sky.
Theirs is the only voice, protesting, protesting.
I do not think the sea will appear at all.
The high, green meadows are glowing, as if lit from within.
I come to one bush of berries so ripe it is a bush of flies,
Hanging their blue-green bellies and their wing panes in a
Chinese screen.
The honey-feast of the berries has stunned them; they believe in
heaven.
One more hook, and the berries and bushes end.

The only thing to come now is the sea.
From between two hills a sudden wind funnels at me,
Slapping its phantom laundry in my face.
These hills are too green and sweet to have tasted salt.
I follow the sheep path between them. A last hook brings me
To the hills' northern face, and the face is orange rock
That looks out on nothing, nothing but a great space
Of white and pewter lights, and a din like silversmiths
Beating and beating at an intractable metal.

choughs: red-legged crows that frequent the sea-cliffs in many parts of Britain; particularly abundant in Cornwall.

THEODORE ROETHKE

1908–1963

Theodore Roethke was born in Saginaw, Michigan. He briefly attended Harvard to study with I. A. Richards, but returned to graduate from the University of Michigan. His father was a greenhouse florist. Roethke taught at Bennington and the University of Washington, won two Guggenheim Fellowships, the Eunice Tietjens Prize, the Levinson Award, the Pulitzer Prize, and the National Book Award. A film about him made by the San Francisco State College Poetry Center, *In a Dark Time*, was completed shortly before his death. Roethke lived on an island in Puget Sound. His books include *Open House* (1941), *Words for the Wind* (1958), *The Far Field* (1964), and *Collected Poems* (1966).

The poems of Theodore Roethke journey into the interior: his landscapes are the human unconscious. The antennae of Roethke's intuition rise up from his senses like rice shoots growing and reaching from the Michigan greenhouses to the shores of Puget Sound, to inland lakes and streams, across the far reaches of the continent. The poems are larval, mammalian, reptilian. Roethke says that "a poet ought to show as many sides of himself as he, in good conscience, can," and he sways outside himself to embody creatures, stones, and the dark-turned-light.

THE SHAPE OF THE FIRE

1

What's this? A dish for fat lips.
Who says? A nameless stranger.
Is he a bird or a tree? Not everyone can tell.

Water recedes to the crying of spiders.
An old scow bumps over black rocks.
A cracked pod calls.

Mother me out of here. What more will the bones allow?
Will the sea give the wind suck? A toad folds into a stone.
These flowers are all fangs. Comfort me, fury.
Wake me, witch, we'll do the dance of rotten sticks.

Shale loosens. Marl reaches into the field. Small birds pass over
water.

marl: a crumbling earthy deposit of clay mixed with calcium carbonate, often used as a fertilizer.

Spirit, come near. This is only the edge of whiteness.
I can't laugh at a procession of dogs.

In the hour of ripeness, the tree is barren.
The she-bear mopes under the hill.
Mother, mother, stir from your cave of sorrow.

A low mouth laps water. Weeds, weeds, how I love you.
The arbor is cooler. Farewell, farewell, fond worm.
The warm comes without sound.

2

Where's the eye?
The eye's in the sty.
The ear's not here
Beneath the hair.
When I took off my clothes
To find a nose,
There was only one shoe
For the waltz of To,
The pinch of Where.

Time for the flat-headed man. I recognize that listener,
Him with the platitudes and rubber doughnuts,
Melting at the knees, a varicose horror.
Hello, hello. My nerves knew you, dear boy.
Have you come to unhinge my shadow?
Last night I slept in the pits of a tongue.
The silver fish ran in and out of my special bindings;
I grew tired of the ritual of names and the assistant keeper of the mollusks:
Up over a viaduct I came, to the snakes and sticks of another winter,
A two-legged dog hunting a new horizon of howls.
The wind sharpened itself on a rock;
A voice sang:

Pleasure on ground
Has no sound,
Easily maddens
The uneasy man.

Who, careless, slips
In coiling ooze
Is trapped to the lips,
Leaves more than shoes;

Must pull off clothes
To jerk like a frog
On belly and nose
From the sucking bog.

My meat eats me. Who waits at the gate?
Mother of quartz, your words writhe into my ear.
Renew the light, lewd whisper.

3

The wasp waits.
  The edge cannot eat the center.
The grape glistens.
  The path tells little to the serpent.
An eye comes out of the wave.
  The journey from flesh is longest.
A rose sways least.
  The redeemer comes a dark way.

4

Morning-fair, follow me further back
Into that minnowy world of weeds and ditches,
When the herons floated high over the white houses,
And the little crabs slipped into silvery craters.
When the sun for me glinted the sides of a sand grain,
And my intent stretched over the buds at their first trembling.

That air and shine: and the flicker's loud summer call:
The bearded boards in the stream and the all of apples;
The glad hen on the hill; and the trellis humming.
Death was not. I lived in a simple drowse:
Hands and hair moved through a dream of wakening blossoms.
Rain sweetened the cave and the dove still called;
The flowers leaned on themselves, the flowers in hollows;
And love, love sang toward.

5

To have the whole air!
The light, the full sun
Coming down on the flowerheads,
The tendrils turning slowly,
A slow snail-lifting, liquescent;
To be by the rose
Rising slowly out of its bed,
Still as a child in its first loneliness;
To see cyclamen veins become clearer in early sunlight,
And mist lifting out of the brown cattails;
To stare into the after-light, the glitter left on the lake's surface,
When the sun has fallen behind a wooded island;
To follow the drops sliding from a lifted oar,
Held up, while the rower breathes, and the small boat drifts
quietly shoreward;
To know that light falls and fills, often without our knowing,
As an opaque vase fills to the brim from a quick pouring,
Fills and trembles at the edge yet does not flow over,
Still holding and feeding the stem of the contained flower.

THE ROSE

I

There are those to whom place is unimportant,
But this place, where sea and fresh water meet,
Is important—
Where the hawks sway out into the wind,
Without a single wingbeat,
And the eagles sail low over the fir trees,
And the gulls cry against the crows
In the curved harbors,
And the tide rises up against the grass
Nibbled by sheep and rabbits.

THE SHAPE OF THE FIRE

cyclamen: a small plant of the primrose family, with heart-shaped leaves at the base of the stem, and white, pink, or purplish flowers.

A time for watching the tide,
For the heron's hieratic fishing,
For the sleepy cries of the towhee,
The morning birds gone, the twittering finches,
But still the flash of the kingfisher, the wingbeat of the scoter,
The sun a ball of fire coming down over the water,
The last geese crossing against the reflected afterlight,
The moon retreating into a vague cloud-shape
To the cries of the owl, the eerie whooper.
The old log subsides with the lessening waves,
And there is silence.

I sway outside myself
Into the darkening currents,
Into the small spillage of driftwood,
The waters swirling past the tiny headlands.
Was it here I wore a crown of birds for a moment
While on a far point of the rocks
The light heightened,
And below, in a mist out of nowhere,
The first rain gathered?

II

As when a ship sails with a light wind—
The waves less than the ripples made by rising fish,
The lacelike wrinkles of the wake widening, thinning out,
Sliding away from the traveler's eye,
The prow pitching easily up and down,
The whole ship rolling slightly sideways,
The stern high, dipping like a child's boat in a pond—
Our motion continues.

But this rose, this rose in the sea-wind,
Stays,
Stays in its true place,
Flowering out of the dark,

hieratic: a form of ancient Egyptian writing, simpler and more flowing than hieroglyphic.
towhee: a small, North American, ground-feeding sparrow.
scoter: a large, dark-colored sea duck.

Widening at high noon, face upward,
A single wild rose, struggling out of the white embrace of the morning-glory,
Out of the briary hedge, the tangle of matted underbrush,
Beyond the clover, the ragged hay,
Beyond the sea pine, the oak, the wind-tipped madrona,
Moving with the waves, the undulating driftwood,
Where the slow creek winds down to the black sand of the shore
With its thick grassy scum and crabs scuttling back into their glistening craters.

And I think of roses, roses,
White and red, in the wide six-hundred-foot greenhouses,
And my father standing astride the cement benches,
Lifting me high over the four-foot stems, the Mrs. Russells, and his own elaborate hybrids,
And how those flowerheads seemed to flow toward me, to beckon me, only a child, out of myself.

What need for heaven, then,
With that man, and those roses?

III

What do they tell us, sound and silence?
I think of American sounds in this silence:
On the banks of the Tombstone, the wind-harps having their say,
The thrush singing alone, that easy bird,
The killdeer whistling away from me,
The mimetic chortling of the catbird
Down in the corner of the garden, among the raggedy lilacs,
The bobolink skirring from a broken fencepost,
The bluebird, lover of holes in old wood, lilting its light song,
And that thin cry, like a needle piercing the ear, the insistent cicada,
And the ticking of snow around oil drums in the Dakotas,
The thin whine of telephone wires in the wind of a Michigan winter,

madrona: an evergreen tree or shrub, native to the Pacific coast of North America, that has smooth bark, thick shiny leaves, and edible red berries.
killdeer: a small North American plover with a high, piercing cry.
mimetic: imitative, mimicking.

The shriek of nails as old shingles are ripped from the top of a
roof,
The bulldozer backing away, the hiss of the sandblaster,
And the deep chorus of horns coming up from the streets in early
morning.
I return to the twittering of swallows above water,
And that sound, that single sound,
When the mind remembers all,
And gently the light enters the sleeping soul,
A sound so thin it could not woo a bird,

Beautiful my desire, and the place of my desire.

I think of the rock singing, and light making its own silence,
At the edge of a ripening meadow, in early summer,
The moon lolling in the close elm, a shimmer of silver,
Or that lonely time before the breaking of morning
When the slow freight winds along the edge of the ravaged
hillside,
And the wind tries the shape of a tree,
While the moon lingers,
And a drop of rain water hangs at the tip of a leaf
Shifting in the wakening sunlight
Like the eye of a new-caught fish.

IV

I live with the rocks, their weeds,
Their filmy fringes of green, their harsh
Edges, their holes
Cut by the sea-slime, far from the crash
Of the long swell,
The oily, tar-laden walls
Of the toppling waves,
Where the salmon ease their way into the kelp beds,
And the sea rearranges itself among the small islands.

Near this rose, in this grove of sun-parched,
wind-warped madronas,
Among the half-dead trees, I came upon the true ease of myself,
As if another man appeared out of the depths of my being,
And I stood outside myself,
Beyond becoming and perishing,

A something wholly other,
As if I swayed out on the wildest wave alive,
And yet was still.
And I rejoiced in being what I was:
In the lilac change, the white reptilian calm,
In the bird beyond the bough, the single one
With all the air to greet him as he flies,
The dolphin rising from the darkening waves;

And in this rose, this rose in the sea-wind,
Rooted in stone, keeping the whole of light,
Gathering to itself sound and silence—
Mine and the sea-wind's.

ANNE SEXTON

1928–1974

Anne Sexton was born in Newton, Massachusetts. Her childhood was spent in Wellesley. She began writing poems in 1957, and studied with W. D. Snodgrass and Robert Lowell. Although she did not attend college, she held a professorship at Boston University, and taught the poetry class she used to drop in on, with Sylvia Plath, when it was taught by Robert Lowell. Sexton was the Robert Frost Fellow at the Breadloaf Writers' Conference in 1959, and she won the Pulitzer Prize in 1966 for *Live or Die.* She also wrote short stories and a play. Until her suicide in the fall of 1974 she lived in Weston, Massachusetts. Her books include *To Bedlam and Part Way Back* (1960), *All My Pretty Ones* (1962), *The Death Notebooks* (1974), and *The Awful Rowing Toward God* (1975).

The poems of Anne Sexton cruise through us like dreadnaughts, gun bones aimed at the chest: death lyrics, lamentations of passion, asylum messages, contemporary Grimm. Effective in both formal and informal patterns, a direct speech brightens her unexpected rhymes, and a precise voice orders the stark edges of her open forms. Anne Sexton is a poet of dark loveliness and bowel fury. Her poems go in and out like our shadows, and she brings us back from her Bedlam.

THE FURY OF BEAUTIFUL BONES

Sing me a thrush, bone.
Sing me a nest of cup and pestle.
Sing me a sweet bread for an old grandfather.
Sing me a foot and a doorknob, for you are my love.

Oh sing, bone bag man, sing.
Your head is what I remember that August,
you were in love with another woman but
that didn't matter. I was the fury of your
bones, your fingers long and nubby, your
forehead a beacon, bare as marble and I worried
you like an odor because you had not quite forgotten,
bone bag man, garlic in the North End,
the book you dedicated, naked as a fish,
naked as someone drowning into his own mouth.
I wonder, Mr. Bone man, what you're thinking
of your fury now, gone sour as a sinking whale,
crawling up the alphabet on her own bones.
Am I in your ear still singing songs in the rain,
me of the death rattle, me of the magnolias,
me of the sawdust tavern at the city's edge.
Women have lovely bones, arms, neck, thigh
and I admire them also, but your bones
supersede loveliness. They are the tough
ones that get broken and reset. I just can't
answer for you, only for your bones,
round rulers, round nudgers, round poles,
numb nubkins, the sword of sugar.
I feel the skull, Mr. Skeleton, living its
own life in its own skin.

THE FURY OF SUNRISES

Darkness
as black as your eyelid,
poketricks of stars,
the yellow mouth,
the smell of a stranger,
dawn coming up,
dark blue,
no stars,
the smell of a lover,
warmer now

THE FURY OF BEAUTIFUL BONES
North End: a section of Boston.

as authentic as soap,
wave after wave
of lightness
and the birds in their chains
going mad with throat noises,
the birds in their tracks
yelling into their cheeks like clowns,
lighter, lighter,
the stars gone,
the trees appearing in their green hoods,
the house appearing across the way,
the road and its sad macadam,
the rock walls losing their cotton,
lighter, lighter,
letting the dog out and seeing
fog lift by her legs,
a gauze dance,
lighter, lighter,
yellow, blue at the tops of trees,
more God, more God everywhere,
lighter, lighter,
more world everywhere,
sheets bent back for people,
the strange heads of love
and breakfast,
that sacrament,
lighter, yellower,
like the yoke of eggs,
the flies gathering at the windowpane,
the dog inside whining for food
and the day commencing,
not to die, not to die,
as in the last day breaking,
a final day digesting itself,
lighter, lighter,
the endless colors,
the same old trees stepping toward me,
the rock unpacking its crevices,
breakfast like a dream
and the whole day to live through,

stedfast, deep, interior.
After the death,
after the black of black,
this lightness—
not to die, not to die—
that God begot.

THE FURY OF HATING EYES

I would like to bury
all the hating eyes
under the sand somewhere off
the North Atlantic and suffocate
them with the awful sand
and put all their colors to sleep
in that soft smother.
Take the brown eyes of my father,
those gun shots, those mean muds.
Bury them.
Take the blue eyes of my mother,
naked as the sea,
waiting to pull you down
where there is no air, no God.
Bury them.
Take the black eyes of my lover,
coal eyes like a cruel hog,
wanting to whip you and laugh.
Bury them.
Take the hating eyes of martyrs,
presidents, bus collectors,
bank managers, soldiers.
Bury them.
Take my eyes, half blind
and falling into the air.
Bury them.
Take your eyes.
I come to the center,
where a shark looks up at death
and thinks of my death.
They'd like to take my heart

and squeeze it like a doughnut.
They'd like to take my eyes
and poke a hatpin through
their pupils. Not just to bury
but to stab. As for your eyes,
I fold up in front of them
in a baby ball and you send
them to the State Asylum.
Look! Look! Both those
mice are watching you
from behind the kind bars.

from HURRY UP PLEASE IT'S TIME

What is death, I ask.
What is life, you ask.

I give them both my buttocks,
my two wheels rolling off toward Nirvana.
They are as neat as a wallet,
opening and closing on their coins,
the quarters, the nickels,
straight into the crapper.
Why shouldn't I pull down my pants
and moon at the executioner
as well as paste raisins on my breast?
Why shouldn't I pull down my pants
and show my little cunny to Tom
and Albert? They wee-wee funny.
I wee-wee like a squaw.
I have ink but no pen, still
I dream that I can piss in God's eye.

I dream I'm a boy with a zipper.
It's so practical, la de dah.
The trouble with being a woman, Skeezix,

HURRY UP PLEASE IT'S TIME

Nirvana: in Hinduism and Buddhism, the attainment of rest, truth, and unchanging being, in which desire, passion, illusion, and the individual "self" are extinguished; loosely, any apparently unattainable place or state of complete rest, harmony, or pleasure.

is being a little girl in the first place.
Not all the books of the world will change that.
I have swallowed an orange, being woman.
You have swallowed a ruler, being man.
Yet waiting to die we are the same thing.
Jehovah pleasures himself with his axe
before we are both overthrown.
Skeezix, you are me. La de dah.
You grow a beard but our drool is identical.

Forgive us, Father, for we know not.

Today is November 14th, 1972.
I live in Weston, Mass., Middlesex County,
U.S.A., and it rains steadily
in the pond like white puppy eyes.
The pond is waiting for its skin.
The pond is watching for its leather.
The pond is waiting for December and its novacain.

It begins

Interrogator:
What can you say of your last seven days?

Anne:
They were tired.

Interrogator:
One day is enough to perfect a man.

Anne:
I watered and fed the plant.

My undertaker waits for me.
He is probably twenty-three now,
learning his trade.
He'll stitch up the green,
he'll fasten the bones down
lest they fly away.
I am flying today.
I am not tired today.
I am a motor.
I am cramming in the sugar.

I am running up the hallways.
I am squeezing out the milk.
I am dissecting the dictionary.
I am God, la de dah.
Peanut butter is the American food.
We all eat it, being patriotic.

Ms. Dog is out fighting the dollars,
rolling in a field of bucks.
You've got it made if
you take the wafer,
take some wine,
take some bucks,
the green papery song of the office.
What a jello she could make with it,
the fives, the tens, the twenties,
all in a goo to feed to baby.
Andrew Jackson as an hors d'oeuvres,
la de dah.
I wish I were the U.S. Mint,
turning it all out,
turtle green
and monk black.
Who's that at the podium
in black and white,
blurting into the mike?
Ms. Dog.
Is she spilling her guts?
You bet.
Otherwise they cough. . . .

The day is slipping away, why am I
out here, what do they want?
I am sorrowful in November . . .
(no they don't want that,
they want bee stings).
Toot, toot, tootsy don't cry.
Toot, toot, tootsy goodbye.
If you don't get a letter then
you'll know I'm in jail. . . .
Remember that, Skeezix, . . . ?

RICHARD WILBUR

1921–

Richard Wilbur was born in New York City. He graduated from Amherst College and Harvard, and served in the 36th Infantry Division in World War II. Formerly an editor and a professor at Wellesley College, Wilbur now teaches at Wesleyan University and is a skilled translator of such writers as Molière, Voznesensky, Brodsky, and Jorge Guillén. He has won the Oscar Blumenthal Prize for Poetry, the Edna St. Vincent Millay Memorial Award, the Pulitzer Prize, and the National Book Award. Wilbur lives in Cummington, Massachusetts. His books include *The Beautiful Changes* (1947), *Ceremony* (1950), *Advice to a Prophet* (1961), and *Waking to Sleep* (1969).

The poems of Richard Wilbur are elegant, mono-filamentine, cerebral, clarinette. His themes range from the natural to the social, and his predominantly formal structures are quickened by the quiet strength of his language and the exact focus of his eye. Wilbur knows the right use of rhetoric and he keeps his wits. The poems are informed by centuries of verse, but they speak in their own voice: poems, to use Wilbur's own phrase, of "the live tongue."

ADVICE TO A PROPHET

When you come, as you soon must, to the streets of our city,
Mad-eyed from stating the obvious,
Not proclaiming our fall but begging us
In God's name to have self-pity,

Spare us all word of the weapons, their force and range,
The long numbers that rocket the mind;
Our slow, unreckoning hearts will be left behind,
Unable to fear what is too strange.

Nor shall you scare us with talk of the death of the race.
How should we dream of this place without us?—
The sun mere fire, the leaves untroubled about us,
A stone look on the stone's face?

Speak of the world's own change. Though we cannot conceive
Of an undreamt thing, we know to our cost
How the dreamt cloud crumbles, the vines are blackened by frost,
How the view alters. We could believe,

If you told us so, that the white-tailed deer will slip
Into perfect shade, grown perfectly shy,

The lark avoid the reaches of our eye,
The jack-pine lose its knuckled grip

On the cold ledge, and every torrent burn
As Xanthus once, its gliding trout
Stunned in a twinkling. What should we be without
The dolphin's arc, the dove's return,

These things in which we have seen ourselves and spoken?
Ask us, prophet, how we shall call
Our natures forth when that live tongue is all
Dispelled, that glass obscured or broken

In which we have said the rose of our love and the clean
Horse of our courage, in which beheld
The singing locust of the soul unshelled,
And all we mean or wish to mean.

Ask us, ask us whether with the worldless rose
Our hearts shall fail us; come demanding
Whether there shall be lofty or long standing
When the bronze annals of the oak-tree close.

SPEECH FOR THE REPEAL OF THE McCARRAN ACT

As Wulfstan said on another occasion,
The strong net bellies in the wind and the spider rides it out;
But history, that sure blunderer,
Ruins the unkempt web, however silver.

ADVICE TO A PROPHET

Xanthus: an ancient Lycian city on the Xanthus River, rich in temples, tombs, and monuments; set afire by its citizens under siege by the Persians in 546 B.C., and burned by the Romans in 42 B.C., all the inhabitants perishing. The city was never restored. Some of its remains are in the British Museum.

SPEECH FOR THE REPEAL OF THE MCCARRAN ACT

McCarran Act: U.S. Act of Congress, 1952, also known as the McCarran-Walter Immigration and Nationality Act, one of whose provisions limited immigration into the U.S. from eastern and southeastern Europe.

Wulfstan: (A.D. 1008–1095), Bishop of Worcester who ended the capture and sale of slaves at Bristol; rebuilt the Worcester cathedral; and helped compile the Domesday Book, the record of William I the Conqueror's survey of England.

I am not speaking of rose windows
Shattered by bomb-shock; the leads touselled; the glass-grains
    broadcast;
If the rose be living at all
A gay gravel shall be pollen of churches.

Nor do I mean railway networks.
Torn-up tracks are no great trouble. As Wulfstan said,
It is oathbreach, faithbreach, lovebreach
Bring the invaders into the estuaries.

Shall one man drive before him ten
Unstrung from sea to sea? Let thought be free. I speak
Of the spirit's weaving, the neural
Web, the self-true mind, the trusty reflex.

A BAROQUE WALL-FOUNTAIN IN THE VILLA SCIARRA

for Dore and Adja

    Under the bronze crown
Too big for the head of the stone cherub whose feet
  A serpent has begun to eat,
Sweet water brims a cockle and braids down

    Past spattered mosses, breaks
On the tipped edge of a second shell, and fills
  The massive third below. It spills
In threads then from the scalloped rim, and makes

    A scrim or summery tent
For a faun-ménage and their familiar goose.
  Happy in all that ragged, loose
Collapse of water, its effortless descent

    And flatteries of spray,
The stocky god upholds the shell with ease,

A BAROQUE WALL-FOUNTAIN IN THE VILLA SCIARRA

scrim: a sheer, loosely-woven cotton or linen fabric; a semitransparent curtain (originally made from this fabric) used in theatrical productions.

faun-ménage: A faun is an Italic deity of the fields and herds, commonly represented as half goat and half man. *Ménage* means "household."

Watching, about his shaggy knees,
The goatish innocence of his babes at play;

His fauness all the while
Leans forward, slightly, into a clambering mesh
Of water-lights, her sparkling flesh
In a saecular ecstasy, her blinded smile

Bent on the sand floor
Of the trefoil pool, where ripple-shadows come
And go in swift reticulum,
More addling to the eye than wine, and more

Interminable to thought
Than pleasure's calculus. Yet since this all
Is pleasure, flash, and waterfall,
Must it not be too simple? Are we not

More intricately expressed
In the plain fountains that Maderna set
Before St. Peter's—the main jet
Struggling aloft until it seems at rest

In the act of rising, until
The very wish of water is reversed,
That heaviness borne up to burst
In a clear, high, cavorting head, to fill

With blaze, and then in gauze
Delays, in a gnatlike shimmering, in a fine
Illumined version of itself, decline,
And patter on the stones its own applause?

If that is what men are
Or should be, if those water-saints display
The pattern of our areté,
What of these showered fauns in their bizarre,

reticulum: a netlike structure; a network.

Maderna: Carlo Maderno, or Maderna (1556–1629), leading Roman architect of the 17th century, who determined the style of early Baroque architecture; chief architect of St. Peter's from 1603 until his death (he designed the existing nave as well as the facade of the basilica).

areté: Greek, meaning "virtue"; pronounced to rhyme with "Cape Cod Bay."

Spangled, and plunging house?
They are at rest in fulness of desire
For what is given, they do not tire
Of the smart of the sun, the pleasant water-douse

And riddled pool below,
Reproving our disgust and our ennui
With humble insatiety.
Francis, perhaps, who lay in sister snow

Before the wealthy gate
Freezing and praising, might have seen in this
No trifle, but a shade of bliss—
That land of tolerable flowers, that state

As near and far as grass
Where eyes become the sunlight, and the hand
Is worthy of water: the dreamt land
Toward which all hungers leap, all pleasures pass.

A LATE AUBADE

You could be sitting now in a carrel
Turning some liver-spotted page,
Or rising in an elevator-cage
Toward Ladies' Apparel.

You could be planting a raucous bed
Of salvia, in rubber gloves,
Or lunching through a screed of someone's loves
With pitying head,

Or making some unhappy setter
Heel, or listening to a bleak

A LATE AUBADE
aubade: a morning love song; a parting song of lovers at daybreak.
salvia: a garden plant with long spikes of brilliant red flowers; also known as "scarlet sage."
screed: a long, tiresome speech (or piece of writing).

Lecture on Schoenberg's serial technique.
Isn't this better?

Think of all the time you are not
Wasting, and would not care to waste,
Such things, thank God, not being to your taste.
Think what a lot

Of time, by woman's reckoning,
You've saved, and so may spend on this,
You who had rather lie in bed and kiss
Than anything.

It's almost noon, you say? If so,
Time flies, and I need not rehearse
The rosebuds-theme of centuries of verse.
If you *must* go,

Wait for a while, then slip downstairs
And bring us up some chilled white wine,
And some blue cheese, and crackers, and some fine
Ruddy-skinned pears.

Schoenberg: Arnold (1894–1951), a leading 20th-century composer and musical theorist; invented the 12-tone method of composition, also called the *serial technique.*

YUGOSLAVIA

VASCO POPA

1922–

Vasco Popa was born in Grebenac, Banat. He attended the universities of Vienna, Bucharest, and Belgrade. In 1949 Popa was awarded his degree in French and Yugoslav literature at the University of Belgrade. His first book of poems, *Crust,* was published in 1952. He is now an editor at the Nolit publishing house in Belgrade. Popa has won the Branko Radičević Prize, the Smaj Prize, the Lenau Prize, and the National Austrian Prize for European Literature. Other books include *Unrest-Field* (1956), *Poems* (1965), and *Secondary Heaven* (1968).

The poems of Vasco Popa are anti-rational parables, secret messages in which the code changes, puzzles in which the last piece is hidden in the reader's pocket. Popa is at once postulative, enigmatic, and probing. A strange and elusive outside world reflects our inner lives. His subject is humankind, his affirmation is the mysteriousness of life, his persona is a wry dwarf who sits by the fire telling stories with strange endings. Nearby an outsider muses over a deck of cards and whispers of quirks in man's condition.

THE LITTLE BOX

The little box gets her first teeth
And her little length
Little width little emptiness
And all the rest she has

The little box continues growing
The cupboard that she was inside
Is now inside her

And she grows bigger bigger bigger
Now the room is inside her
And the house and the city and the earth
And the world she was in before

The little box remembers her childhood
And by a great great longing
She becomes a little box again

Now in the little box
You have the whole world in miniature
You can easily put it in a pocket
Easily steal it easily lose it

Take care of the little box

BEFORE THE GAME

Shut one eye then the other
Peek into every corner of yourself
See that there are no nails no thieves
See that there are no cuckoo's eggs

Shut then the other eye
Squat and jump
Jump high high high
On top of yourself

Fall then with all your weight
Fall for days on end deep deep deep
To the bottom of your abyss

Who doesn't break into pieces
Who remains whole who gets up whole
Plays

FLOORNAIL

One is the nail another is pliers
The rest are carpenters

The pliers grab the nail by the head
With their teeth their arms they grab it
And keep pulling and pulling
Pulling it out of the floor
Usually they just wring its head off
It's hard pulling a nail out of the floor

The carpenters then say
These pliers are lousy
They crush its jaws break its arms
And throw them out of the window

Then someone else is a floornail
Another is pliers
The rest are carpenters

HIDE-AND-SEEK

Someone hides from someone else
Hides under his tongue
The other looks for him under the earth

He hides on his forehead
The other looks for him in the sky

He hides inside his forgetfulness
The other looks for him in the grass

Looks for him looks
There's no place he doesn't look
And looking he loses himself

HEART OF THE PEBBLE

They played with the pebble
Pebble like any pebble
Played with them as though it had no heart

They got mad at the pebble
Broke it in the grass
Startled they saw its heart

They opened the heart of the pebble
In the heart a snake
Sleeping spool without dreams

They roused the snake
The snake gushed upward
They ran far away

They looked from the distance
The snake coiled itself round the horizon
Like an egg it ate it

They came back to the place of the game
No trace of snake grass or pieces of pebble
No trace of anything in the circle

They looked at each other and grinned
They winked at each other

AFTER THE GAME

Finally the hands grab the belly
So the belly won't burst with laughter
Only there's no belly

One hand barely lifts itself
To wipe the cold sweat from its forehead
There's no forehead either

The other hand reaches for the heart
So the heart won't leap out of the chest
But there's no heart either

Both hands fall
They fall idly into the lap
There's no lap either

In the palm of one hand
Now the rain falls
From the other the grass grows
What can I tell you

TWO PEBBLES

They look stupidly
Two pebbles looking

Two sweets yesterday
On the tongue of eternity

Two stone tears today
On the eyelid of unknown

Two flies of sand tomorrow
In the ear of deafness
Two happy dimples tomorrow
In the cheek of daylight

Two victims two little jokes
Silly jokes without a joker

They look stupidly
With their cold asses they look
Speaking out of their bellies
Into the wind

Translations by **Charles Simic**

COPYRIGHTS AND ACKNOWLEDGMENTS

GERRIT ACHTERBERG "Eben Haëzer," "Accountability," and "Statue" (tr. Adrienne Rich) are reprinted from *Necessities of Life*, Poems, 1962–1965, by Adrienne Rich. Copyright © 1966 by W. W. Norton & Company, Inc. "City" and "Dwingelo" (tr. Adrienne Rich) are reprinted from *Leaflets*, Poems, 1965–1968, by Adrienne Rich. Copyright © 1969 by W. W. Norton & Company, Inc. All are reprinted by permission of W. W. Norton & Company, Inc.

AI CHING "Snow Falls on China" and "The Highway" (tr. Robert Payne) are reprinted from *The White Pony: An Anthology of Chinese Poetry*, edited by Robert Payne. By permission of Robert Payne.

BELLA AKHMADULINA "Verses About Georgia" and "The Waitress" are reprinted from *Fever and Other New Poems* by Bella Akhmadulina, translated by Geoffrey Dutton and Igor Mezhakoff-Koriakin. Copyright © 1969 by Geoffrey Dutton. Reprinted by permission of William Morrow & Co., Inc. "I Swear" is reprinted from *Poetry from the Russian Underground*, translated and edited by Joseph Langland, Tamas Aczel, and Laszlo Tikos. Copyright © 1973 by Joseph Langland, Tamas Aczel, and Laszlo Tikos. By permission of Harper & Row, Publishers, Inc.

RAFAEL ALBERTI "The Angel of Numbers," "Song of the Luckless Angel," "The Angel of Sand," "The Bad Moment," and "Two Children" are from *The Owl's Insomnia* by Rafael Alberti. Selected and Translated by Mark Strand. Translation copyright © 1972, 1973 by Mark Strand. Reprinted by permission of Atheneum Publishers. "Song of the Luckless Angel" appeared originally in *Pebble*; "The Angel of Sand" appeared originally in *Riverrun*; "The Bad Moment" appeared originally in *Kayak*; and "Two Children" appeared originally in *The Iowa Review*. "Red" is reprinted from *Selected Poems* by Rafael Alberti, edited and translated by Ben Belitt. Originally published by the University of California Press; reprinted by permission of The Regents of the University of California.

YEHUDA AMICHAI "Jews in the Land of Israel" is reprinted from *Songs of Jerusalem and Myself* by Yehuda Amichai, translated by Harold Schimmel. Copyright © 1973 by Yehuda Amichai. English translation copyright © 1973 by Harold Schimmel. By permission of Harper & Row, Publishers, Inc. "My Mother Once Told Me" and "King Saul and I" are reprinted from *Poems* by Yehuda Amichai, translated by Assia Gutmann. Copyright © 1968 by Yehuda Amichai. English translation copyright © 1968, 1969 by Assia Gutmann. By permission of Harper & Row, Publishers, Inc. "King Saul and I" is also reprinted from *Selected Poems* by Yehuda Amichai, translated by Assia Gutmann, and published by Cape Goliard Press.

CHAIRIL ANWAR "For Mrs. N.," "Twilight at a Little Harbor," and "On Top of the Mountain" are reprinted from *The Complete Poetry & Prose of Chairil Anwar*, edited and translated by Burton Raffel, by permission of Burton Raffel and the State University of New York Press. © 1962, 1963, 1964, 1968, 1970 by The Research Foundation of the State University of New York. All rights reserved.

INGEBORG BACHMANN "Wood and Shavings," "My Bird," "Fog Land," and "Songs in Flight" (tr. Daniel Huws) are reprinted from *Modern Poetry in Translation, #3*, and are translated from *Die Gestundete Zeit* by Ingeborg Bachmann—Copyright © R. Piper & Co. Verlag, 1957—and from *Anrufung des Grossen Baren* by Ingeborg Bachmann—Copyright © R. Piper & Co. Verlag, 1956. Reprinted by permission of Joan Daves and Daniel Huws.

AMIRI BARAKA [LEROI JONES] "Are Their Blues Singers in Russia," "Lerve," "Cops," and "Indians" are from *Black Magic Poetry 1961–1967*, by LeRoi Jones, copyright © 1969 by LeRoi Jones. Reprinted by permission of the publisher, The Bobbs-Merrill Company, Inc.

JOHN BERRYMAN The selections from "Homage to Mistress Bradstreet" are from *Homage to Mistress Bradstreet* by John Berryman, © 1956 by John Berryman. Reprinted with the permission of Farrar, Straus & Giroux, Inc.

English translation copyright © 1973 by The Third Press–Joseph Okpaku Publishing Company, Inc. Reprinted with permission. "Sundragon" ("Soleil Serpent," © Editions Gallimard 1946) and "Ruination" ("Perdition," © Editions Gallimard 1970) are translated by Robert Bagg from *Les Armes Miraculeuses* by Aimé Césaire, by permission of Editions Gallimard and The Third Press–Joseph Okpaku Publishing Company, Inc. English translation rights owned by The Third Press-Joseph Okpaku Publishing Company, Inc.

RENÉ CHAR "The Discoverers" by René Char (tr. Kenneth Rexroth) is © 1972 by Kenneth Rexroth, and appears in *One Hundred Poems from the French.* Reprinted by permission of the author and Pym-Randall Press. "Four Poems on the Cave Paintings at Lascaux" (tr. Robert Bly) is reprinted from *The Sixties,* #5, (Fall 1961). Copyright 1961 by Sixties Press. By permission of Robert Bly. "Alberto Giacometti" (tr. Charles Guenther) is taken from *Recherche de la Base du Sommet* by René Char, © Editions Gallimard 1955. By permission of Editions Gallimard and Charles Guenther. The excerpt from "Four Fascinators" (tr. Richard Stern) is reprinted from *Contemporary French Poetry,* edited by Alexander Aspel and Donald Justice. Copyright © University of Michigan 1965. All rights reserved. By permission of The University of Michigan Press.

CHONG CHI-YONG "Spring Snow," "Nostalgia," and "Lake" are from *Contemporary Korean Poetry,* translated and edited by Ko Won. Reprinted by permission of University of Iowa Press. "Measles" and "Windowpane" (tr. S. E. Solberg) are reprinted by permission of the University of Washington Press.

FAZIL HÜSNÜ DAĞLARCA "Dragged Along," "The Idiot," "Unity," "Fire," "Thought," and "Hollow Echo" (tr. Talât Sait Halman) are reprinted from *Modern Poetry in Translation,* #10 (Spring 1971). By permission of Talât Sait Halman. "It is the Sea" and "Night of the Amnesty" are reprinted from *Selected Poems of Fazıl Hüsnü Dağlarca,* translated by Talât Sait Halman, by permission of the University of Pittsburgh Press. © 1969 by the University of Pittsburgh Press.

LÉON DAMAS "In Single File" is reprinted from *Negritude: Black Poetry from Africa and the Caribbean,* Edited and Translated from the French by Norman R. Shapiro. Copyright © 1970 by Norman R. Shapiro. Reprinted by permission of October House, Inc. "Social Graces" (tr. Michael Harper) and "Position Paper" (tr. Robert Bagg) are translated from "Savoir Vivre" and "Position" in Léon G. Damas' *Pigments,* published by *Présence Africaine,* Paris (1962). By permission of Michael Harper and Robert Bagg.

JIBANANANDA DAS "Grass" and "Twenty Years Later" (tr. Mary M. Lago and Tarun Gupta) are reprinted from *Beloit Poetry Journal* (Fall 1965), by permission of Mary M. Lago and Asokananda Das. "The Corpse" and "Immemorial Foxes" (tr. Chidananda Das Gupta) are from *An Anthology of Bengali Writing,* edited by Buddahadeva Bose. Reprinted by permission of The International Association for Cultural Freedom and The Macmillan Company of India Limited.

RENÉ DÉPESTRE "Violence" and "Mouth of Lights" (tr. James Scully and, Susanna Lang) and "Black Ore" (tr. James Scully) are reprinted from *The Massachusetts Review,* © 1974 The Massachusetts Review, Inc. By permission of *The Massachusetts Review.* "Bouche des Clartes" (Mouth of Lights) appears in a special edition of the review *Présence Africaine,* entitled *Haiti: Poètes Noirs* No. 12 (1959) published by *Présence Africaine,* Paris (1959). "Minéral Noir" (Black Ore) appears in René Dépestre's *Minéral Noir,* published by *Présence Africaine,* Paris (1956).

MOHAMMED DIB "Meridian," "Element #2," "Element #4," "Mad Hour," and "Contre-Jour" (tr. Eric Sellin) are reprinted from *Contemporary Literature in Translation,* No. 13 (Summer 1972). By permission of Eric Sellin. The poems first appeared in *Ombre Gardienne* by Mohammed Dib, © Editions Gallimard 1961.

DAVID DIOP "Africa" (tr. Lucille Clifton) and "Rama Kam" (tr. Henry Braun) are printed here by permission of the translators. "Afrique" (Africa) and "Rama Kam" appear in David Diop's *Coups de Pilon,* published by *Présence Africaine,* Paris (1962).

GUNNAR EKELOF "Even Absentmindedness Is a Magnificent Landscape" and "Tomba dei Tori, Tarquinia" (tr. Muriel Rukeyser and Leif Sjoberg) are reprinted from *Selected Poems* by Gunnar Ekelof, copyright 1967 by Twayne Publishers, Inc. Reprinted with the permission of Twayne Publishers, A Division of G. K. Hall & Co. "Monologue with Its Wife," "The Swan," and "When One Has Come As Far As I in Pointlessness" are from *I Do Best Alone at Night*, Poems by Gunnar Ekelof, translated by Robert Bly with Christina Paulston. Copyright © 1968 by Robert Bly. Reprinted by permission of Robert Bly and Paul Lawson, Publisher, The Charioteer Press.

ODYSSEUS ELYTIS The excerpt from "Axion Esti" (tr. Edmund Keeley and George Savidis) and "Seven Days to the Neverness" (tr. Stuart Montgomery) are reprinted from *Agenda*, Vol. III, No. 1 (Winter 1968–1969), by permission of *Agenda* and Stuart Montgomery. The excerpts from "Heroic and Elegiac Song for the Lost Second Lieutenant of Albania" (tr. Paul Merchant) are reprinted from *Modern Poetry in Translation*, No. 4 (1968), by permission of Paul Merchant.

ALLEN GINSBERG The excerpt from "Wichita Vortex Sutra" is from *Planet News* by Allen Ginsberg. Copyright © 1968 by Allen Ginsberg. Reprinted by permission of City Lights Books.

JORGE GUILLÉN "The Horses" (tr. Richard Wilbur), copyright © 1959 by Richard Wilbur, and "Death, from a Distance" (tr. Richard Wilbur), copyright © 1961 by Richard Wilbur, are reprinted from his volume *Advice to a Prophet and Other Poems*, by permission of Harcourt Brace Jovanovich, Inc. "Nature Alive" (tr. James Wright), "The Thirster" (tr. W. S. Merwin), "The Cemetery" (tr. Norman Thomas di Giovanni), and "The Devoted Lovers" (tr. Mark Strand) are reprinted from *Cantico: A Selection* by Jorge Guillén. Edited by Norman Thomas di Giovanni. Copyright © 1954, 1957, 1959, 1960, 1961, 1965 by Jorge Guillén and Norman Thomas di Giovanni. By permission of Little, Brown and Co., in association with The Atlantic Monthly Press.

NICOLÁS GUILLÉN "My Little Woman," "Oven-Stone," and "Small Ode to a Black Cuban Boxer" are reprinted by permission of the University of Massachusetts Press from *Man-Making Words: Selected Poems of Nicolás Guillén*, translated by Robert Márquez and David Arthur McMurray. Copyright © 1972. "Can You" and "Problems of Underdevelopment" are from *Patria O Muerte: The Great Zoo & Other Poems* by Nicholás Guillén, edited and translated by Robert Márquez. Copyright © 1972 by Robert Márquez. Reprinted by permission of Monthly Review Press.

PAAVO HAAVIKKO "The Second Poem" from "The Winter Palace," "The Wood of the Pine-Tree" from "Birthplace," and "In the Dream" from "The Bowmen" are from *Selected Poems* by Paavo Haavikko, translated by Anselm Hollo. (Cape Goliard Press, 1968; distributed in the United States by Grossman Publishers). Reprinted by permission of Jonathan Cape Ltd., Olwyn Hughes, and Anselm Hollo.

ANNE HÉBERT "The Thin Girl" and "Our Hands in the Garden" (tr. A. Poulin, Jr.) are printed here by permission of A. Poulin, Jr. and Georges Borchardt, Inc. for Editions du Seuil. "Alchemy of Day" (tr. A. Poulin, Jr.) and "Bread is Born" (tr. Maxine Kumin) are translated from "Alchimie du Jour" and "Naissance du Pain" in *Poèmes* by Anne Hébert. Used by permission of Musson Book Company, Don Mills, Ontario, Canada.

ZBIGNIEW HERBERT "Elephant" (tr. Peter Dale Scott) and "Apollo and Marsyas" (tr. Czeslaw Milosz) are reprinted from *Selected Poems of Zbigniew Herbert*, translated by Czeslaw Milosz and Peter Dale Scott (Penguin Modern European Poets, 1968). Translations © Czeslaw Milosz and Peter Dale Scott, 1968. By permission of Penguin Books Ltd. "Five Men" (tr. Jan Darowski) is reprinted from *Polish Writing Today*, edited by Celina Wienewska, Translation by Jan Darowski copyright © Penguin Books Ltd., 1967. By permission of Penguin Books Ltd. "She Dressed Her Hair" (tr. Frederic Will and Leszek Elektorowicz) is reprinted from *Micromegas*, Vol. II, No. 3, by permission of Frederic Will.

MIGUEL HERNANDEZ "The Soldier and the Snow" (tr. Timothy Baland), "Lullaby of the Onion" (tr. Robert Bly), and "I Have Plenty of Heart" (tr. Robert Bly) are reprinted from *Miguel Hernandez and Blas de Otero: Selected Poems*, edited by Timothy Baland

and Hardie St. Martin. By permission of Robert Bly.

MIROSLAV HOLUB "Death in the Evening," "Silence," "The Village Green," and "A Dog in the Quarry" (tr. George Theiner and Jan Milner) are reprinted from *Selected Poems of Miroslav Holub* (Penguin Modern European Poets, 1967). © Miroslav Holub, 1967. Translations © Penguin Books Ltd., 1967. By permission of Penguin Books, Ltd.

TED HUGHES "Song," copyright © 1957 by Ted Hughes, and "The Thought-Fox," copyright © 1957 by Ted Hughes, are reprinted from *The Hawk in the Rain* by Ted Hughes, by permission of Harper & Row, Publishers, Inc. "The Thought-Fox" appeared originally in *The New Yorker.* "To Paint a Water Lily," copyright © 1959 by Ted Hughes, "The Bull Moses," copyright © 1959 by Ted Hughes, and "Witches," copyright © 1958 by Ted Hughes, are reprinted from *Lupercal* by Ted Hughes, by permission of Harper & Row, Publishers, Inc., and Faber and Faber Ltd. "A Vegetarian" is reprinted from *Wodwo* by Ted Hughes. Copyright © 1962 by Ted Hughes. By permission of Harper & Row Publishers, Inc., and Faber and Faber Ltd. "Crow's Undersong," copyright © 1970 by Ted Hughes, is reprinted from *Crow* by Ted Hughes, by permission of Harper & Row, Publishers, Inc., and Faber and Faber Ltd.

GYULA ILLYÉS "Successful Effort" (tr. Frederic Will and Julia Kada) is reprinted from *Micromegas*, Vol. IV, No. 2, by permission of Frederic Will. "Brazilian Rain Forest," "Do You Rembmer?" and "Work" (tr. William Jay Smith) are printed here by permission of William Jay Smith.

ROLF JACOBSEN "Old Age," "The Morning Paper," "The Glass Shop," "S-s-sh," "The Old Woman," and "May Moon" (tr. Robert Bly), copyright 1973 by Robert Bly, are printed here by permission of Robert Bly.

JUAN RAMÓN JIMÉNEZ "Full Moon," "Oceans," "Dawn Outside the City Walls," "I Am Not I," "At First She Came to Me Pure," and "Being Awake" (tr. Robert Bly) are reprinted from *Lorca and Jiménez: Selected Poems,* edited and translated from Spanish by Robert Bly (Beacon Press, 1973). Copyright 1973 by Robert Bly and reprinted with his permission.

FERENC JUHÁSZ "Violet-Eyed Little Sister," the excerpt from "Power of the Flowers," and the excerpt from "Crown of Hatred and Love" are reprinted from *The Boy Changed Into a Stag* by Ferenc Juhász, translated by Kenneth McRobbie and Ilona Duczynska. By permission of Oxford University Press, Canadian Branch. "Silver," "Gold," and "Then There Are Fish" are reprinted from *Selected Poems of Sandor Weores and Ferenc Juhász* translated by David Wevill (Penguin Modern European Poets, 1970). Copyright © Ferenc Juhász, 1970. Translations © David Wevill. By permission of Penguin Books Ltd.

PATRICK KAVANAGH "Epic," "The Goat of Slieve Donard," "A Wreath for Tom Moore's Statue," "Kerr's Ass," "Come Dance with Kitty Stobling," "To a Late Poplar," and "Inniskeen Road: July Evening" are reprinted from *The Collected Poems of Patrick Kavanagh.* Copyright 1964 by Patrick Kavanagh. By permission of The Devin-Adair Company, Publishers.

ABBA KOVNER "And below us It Flows. Slowly," "From Another Homeland," "I Hear Wings Flapping on the Sand," "Sixth Gate: A Sandstorm Hits a New Moon's Face," "The Evening Before," and "Getting Late" are reprinted from *A Canopy in the Desert: Selected Poems* by Abba Kovner by permission of The University of Pittsburgh Press. © 1973 by The University of Pittsburgh Press.

PHILLIP LARKIN "Next Please" by Philip Larkin is reprinted from *The Less Deceived* by permission of The Marvell Press, England. "Afternoons" is reprinted from *The Whitsun Weddings* by Philip Larkin by permission of Faber and Faber Ltd. "High Windows," "Cut Grass," and "The Explosion" are from *High Windows* by Philip Larkin. Copyright © 1974 by Philip Larkin. Reprinted with the permission of Farrar, Straus & Giroux, Inc., and Faber and Faber Ltd.

FEDERICO GARCÍA LORCA "The Guitar," "The Quarrel," "Little Infinite Poem," "Ghazal of the Terrifying Presence," and "Ghazal of the Dark Death" (tr. Robert Bly) are reprinted from *Lorca and Jiménez: Selected Poems,* edited and translated from Spanish

Division of Holmes & Meier Publishers, Inc., and by permission of Heinemann Educational Books Ltd.

NICANOR PARRA "The Borders of Chile," "I, Sinner," "Everything Seemed Fine Before," "How Many Times Do I Have to Tell You," "As I Was Saying," "Seven," and "Warnings" are from Nicanor Parra, *Emergency Poems,* translated by Miller Williams. Copyright © 1972 by Nicanor Parra and Miller Williams. Reprinted by permission of New Directions Publishing Corporation.

CESARE PAVESE "Instinct," "Grappa in September," "Simplicity," "Fatherhood," and "Atavism" (tr. William Arrowsmith) are reprinted by permission of Joan Daves. Copyright © 1973 by William Arrowsmith. The translations appeared originally in *American Poetry Review.*

OCTAVIO PAZ "Salamander" is from Octavio Paz, *Configurations,* translated by Denise Levertov. Copyright © 1965 by Octavio Paz and Denise Levertov Goodman. Reprinted by permission of New Directions Publishing Corporation.

SYLVIA PLATH "The Moon and the Yew Tree," "Daddy," and "The Bee Meeting" are from *Ariel* by Sylvia Plath. Copyright © 1963 by Ted Hughes. "Blackberrying" is from *Crossing the Water* by Sylvia Plath. Copyright © 1962 by Ted Hughes. Originally appeared in *The New Yorker.* All are reprinted by permission of Harper & Row, Publishers, Inc., and Olwyn Hughes.

FRANCIS PONGE "The Frog" (tr. Cid Corman) is reprinted from *Things* by Francis Ponge (Grossman Publishers, 1971) and is translated from "La Grenouille" in *Le Grand Recueil* by Francis Ponge. © Editions Gallimard (1961). By permission of Cid Corman, Eric Sackheim, and Editions Gallimard. "The Oyster" (tr. Tod Perry) and "Rule" (tr. Donald Justice) are reprinted from *Contemporary French Poetry,* edited by Alexander Aspel and Donald Justice. Copyright © University of Michigan 1965. All rights reserved. By permission of the University of Michigan Press. "The Nuptial Habits of Dogs" is from *Poems & Texts: An Anthology of French Poems, Translations, and Interviews with Ponge, Pollain, Guillevic, Frenaud, Bonnefoy, Du Bouchet, Roche, and Pieynet,* Selected and Translated, with Interviews and an Introduction by Serge Gavronsky. Copyright © 1969 by Serge Gavronsky. Reprinted by permission of October House Inc.

VASCO POPA "The Little Box," "Before the Game," "Floornail," "Hide and Seek," "Heart of the Pebble," "After the Game," and "Two Pebbles" are reprinted from *The Little Box* by Vasco Popa, translated by Charles Simic, by permission of Charles Simic and The Charioteer Press.

HENRIKAS RADAUSKAS "The Winter's Tale" (tr. Randall Jarrell) is from *The Woman at the Washington Zoo* by Randall Jarrell. Reprinted by permission of Atheneum Publishers. "The Fire at the Waxworks" (tr. Randall Jarrell) is from *The Complete Poems* by Randall Jarrell. Copyright © 1965, 1966, 1967, 1968, 1969 by Mrs. Randall Jarrell. Reprinted with the permission of Farrar, Straus & Giroux, Inc.

MIKLOS RADNOTI "Red Shore"–Copyright © 1970 by Steven Polgar, Stephen Berg and S. J. Marks, "Goats"–Copyright © 1968 by Stephen Polgar, Stephen Berg, and S. J. Marks, "I Don't Know" and "The Seventh Ecloque"–Copyright © 1972 by Mrs. Miklos Radnoti, Steven Polgar, Stephen Berg, and S. J. Marks, "Postcard 1"–Copyright © 1969 by Steven Polgar, Stephen Berg and S. J. Marks, and "Postcards 2,3,4"–Copyright © 1967 by Steven Polgar, Stephen Berg and S. J. Marks, are reprinted from *Clouded Sky: Poems* by Miklos Radnoti, Translated by Steven Polgar, Stephen Berg and S. J. Marks. By permission of Harper & Row, Publishers, Inc.

YANNIS RITSOS "And Relating Them," "The Decline of Argo," "A Plough by Itself," "Midnight," "Unacceptable," and "Reversal" (tr. Nikos Stangos) are reprinted from *Gestures* by Yannis Ritsos, by permission of Cape Goliard Press and Jonathan Cape Ltd. "Evening" (tr. Paul Merchant) is reprinted by permission of Paul Merchant. "Evening" appeared originally in *Modern Poetry in Translation.*

THEODORE ROETHKE "The Shape of the Fire," copyright 1947 by Theodore Roethke, and "The Rose," copyright © 1963 by Beatrice Roethke as Administratrix of The Estate of Theodore Roethke, are from *The Collected Poems of Theodore Roethke*. Reprinted by permission of Doubleday & Company, Inc.

GEORGE SEFERIS "Mathios Paschalis Among the Roses," "The Last Day," the excerpt from "Mythistorema," and the excerpt from "Stratis the Sailor Describes a Man" are reprinted from *Poems* by George Seferis, translated from the Greek by Rex Warner. English Translation © Rex Warner 1960. By permission of Little, Brown and Co. in association with The Atlantic Monthly Press, and The Bodley Head. The excerpt from "On State" and the excerpts from "Summer Solstice" are reprinted by permission of the publishers from *Three Secret Poems* by George Seferis, translated by Walter Kaiser, Cambridge, Mass.: Copyright, 1969, by the President and Fellows of Harvard College. "Against Woodwaxen . . ." (tr. John Chioles), copyright © 1972, by The Atlantic Monthly Company, Boston, Mass., is reprinted with the permission of Maro Seferis and *The Atlantic Monthly*.

LÉOPOLD SÉDAR SENGHOR "All Day Long," "Spring Song I," and "For Organ Flutes" are from *Selected Poems* by Léopold Sédar Senghor. Translated and Introduced by John Reed and Clive Wake. Copyright © Oxford University Press 1964. Reprinted by permission of Atheneum Publishers, U.S.A., and Oxford University Press, England. "Black Woman" (tr. Lucille Clifton) and "Congo" (tr. George Keithley) are printed here through the courtesy and special permission of Atheneum Publishers (publishers of the John Reed and Clive Wake translations of "Black Woman" and "Congo" in *Selected Poems* by Léopold Sédar Senghor). CAUTION: The Clifton and Keithley translations are not available for reprinting. "For Two Horns and a Balafong" (tr. John Reed and Clive Wake) is reprinted from *Nocturnes* by Léopold Sédar Senghor. Copyright 1971. Used with the permission of The Third Press–Joseph Okpaku Publishing Co., Inc., and Georges Borchardt, Inc. for Editions du Seuil. "Joal" (tr. Sylvia Washington Bâ) is from *The Concept of Negritude in the Poetry of Léopold Sédar Senghor* by Sylvia Washington Bâ (copyright © 1973 by Princeton University Press), p. 189. Reprinted by permission of Princeton University Press.

ANNE SEXTON "The Fury of Beautiful Bones," "The Fury of Sunrises," "Hating Eyes," and "Hurry Up Please It's Time" are from *The Death Notebooks* by Anne Sexton. Copyright © 1974 by Anne Sexton. Reprinted by permission of Houghton Mifflin Company.

NICHITA STANESCU "March Rain" (tr. Roy MacGregor Hastie) is from *Anthology of Contemporary Romanian Poetry*, edited by Roy MacGregor Hastie, published by Peter Owen Ltd., London, and reprinted with their permission. "Song" and "Second Elegy" (tr. Robert Bly and Alexander Ivasinc), copyright 1973 by Robert Bly, are printed here by permission of Robert Bly. "The Sleep Containing Saws" (tr. Petru Popescu and Peter Jay) is from *London Magazine*, March 1973, and is reprinted by permission. "Eighth Elegy: Hyperborean" (tr. Roy MacGregor Hastie) is reprinted from *Modern Poetry in Translation* #9, January 1971, by permission of Roy MacGregor Hastie.

ALFONSINA STORNI "You Would Have Me White," "Men in the City," "The White Talon," "Sierra," "One," and "I Am Going to Sleep" are reprinted from *Nine Latin American Poets*, translated by Rachel Benson, by permission of Anaya–Las Americas.

SHINKICHI TAKAHASHI "Fish," "Stitches," "Rat on Mount Ishizuchi," and "Afterimages" are reprinted from *Afterimages: Zen Poems of Shinkichi Takahashi*, translated by Lucien Stryk and Takahashi Ikemoto, © 1970 by Lucien Stryk and Takahashi Ikemoto, with permission of The Swallow Press.

TOMAS TRANSTRÖMER "The Open Window" and "Upright" (tr. May Swenson with Leif Sjoberg) are reprinted from *Windows and Stones: Selected Poems* by Tomas Tranströmer by permission of the University of Pittsburgh Press. © 1972 by The University of Pittsburgh Press. "After a Death" and "Out in the Open" are reprinted from *Night Vision* by Tomas Tranströmer, translated by Robert Bly, by permission of London Magazine

Editions. "Strophe and Antistrophe" and "Allegro" (tr. Eric Sellin) are reprinted from *New Directions in Prose and Poetry, #9* (1966), by permission of Eric Sellin and Tomas Tranströmer.

TCHICAYA U TAM'SI "The Flight of the Vampires" (tr. Norman R. Shapiro) is from *Negritude: Black Poetry from Africa and the Caribbean.* Edited and Translated from the French by Norman R. Shapiro. Copyright © 1970 by Norman R. Shapiro. Reprinted by permission of October House, Inc. "The Belly Remains" and the excerpt from "The Dead" are reprinted from *Selected Poems* by Tchicaya U Tam'si, translated by Gerald Moore, by permission of Heinemann Educational Books Ltd.

GIUSEPPE UNGARETTI "Bitter Chiming" is reprinted from *Selected Poems* by Giuseppe Ungaretti, translated by Patrick Creagh (Penguin Modern European Poets, 1971). © Arnoldo Mondadori Editore, 1969. Translation © Patrick Creagh, 1971. By permission of Penguin Books Ltd. "Senseless My Steps" (tr. Robert Lowell) is reprinted from *Translations of American Poets,* edited by Jean Garrigue (Ohio University Press, 1970) by permission of The Academy of American Poets. "Flight" (tr. D. M. Pettinella) and "A Dove" (tr. Andrew Wylie) are reprinted from *Books Abroad,* Autumn 1970, by permission of the University of Oklahoma Press.

CÉSAR VALLEJO "Here, Ramon Collar," "The Spanish Image of Death," and "Funeral Train Following the Taking of Bilbao" are reprinted from *Spain, Let This Cup Pass from Me* by César Vallejo, translated by Alvaro Cardona-Hine. Reprinted by permission of The Red Hill Press, Fairfax, California, publishers of the first full English translation of *Spain, Let This Cup Pass From Me* in 1972. "To My Brother Miguel" (tr. John Knoepfle and Robert Bly), "The Anger that Breaks a Man Down into Boys" (tr. Robert Bly), "Black Stone Lying on a White Stone" (tr. Robert Bly and John Knoepfle), and "Masses" (tr. Robert Bly) are reprinted from *Neruda and Vallejo: Selected Poems,* edited by Robert Bly (Beacon Press, 1971), by permission of Robert Bly.

XAVIER VILLAURRUTIA "Cemetery in the Snow" and "Nocturne of the Statue" (tr. Donald Justice) are from *New Poetry of Mexico,* selected, with notes, by Octavio Paz, Ali Chumacero, Jose Emilio Pacheco, and Homero Aridjis. Bilingual edition edited by Mark Strand. Copyright © 1966 by Siglo XXI Editores, S.A. English translation Copyright, © 1970 by E. P. Dutton & Co., Inc. Reprinted by permission of the publishers, E. P. Dutton & Co., Inc. "Eternal Nocturne" is reprinted from *Nine Latin American Poets,* translated by Rachel Benson, by permission of Anaya–Las Americas.

ANDREI VOZNESENSKY "Autumn" (tr. Stanley Kunitz), "The Last Train to Malákhovka" (tr. Jean Garrigue), and "Ballad of 1941" (tr. Stanley Moss) are reprinted from *Antiworlds and the Fifth Ace* by Andrei Voznesensky. Edited by Patricia Blake and Max Hayward. © 1966, 1967 by Basic Books, Inc., Publishers, New York. "Foggy Street" (tr. Richard Wilbur) is reprinted from *Antiworlds and the Fifth Ace* by Andrei Voznesensky. Edited by Patricia Blake and Max Hayward. © 1963 by Encounter, Ltd., © 1966, 1967 by Basic Books, Inc., Publishers, New York.

DEREK WALCOTT "Junta" is reprinted with the permission of Farrar, Straus & Giroux, Inc., from *The Gulf* by Derek Walcott. Copyright © 1963, 1964, 1965, 1969, 1970 by Derek Walcott. The excerpts from *Another Life* by Derek Walcott are reprinted with the permission of Farrar, Straus & Giroux, Inc. Copyright © 1972, 1973 by Derek Walcott.

RICHARD WILBUR "Advice to a Prophet," copyright, 1959, by Richard Wilbur, was first published in *The New Yorker.* It is reprinted from his volume *Advice to a Prophet and Other Poems.* "Speech for the Repeal of the McCarran Act" and "A Baroque Wall Fountain at the Villa Sciarra," © 1956 by Richard Wilbur, are reprinted from his volume *Things of this World.* "A Late Aubade," copyright © 1968 by Richard Wilbur, is reprinted from his volume *Walking to Sleep.* All are reprinted by permission of Harcourt Brace Jovanovich, Inc.

INDEX OF AUTHORS, TITLES, AND TRANSLATORS

A
B 6
C 7
D 8
E 9
F 0
G 1
H 2
I 3
J 4

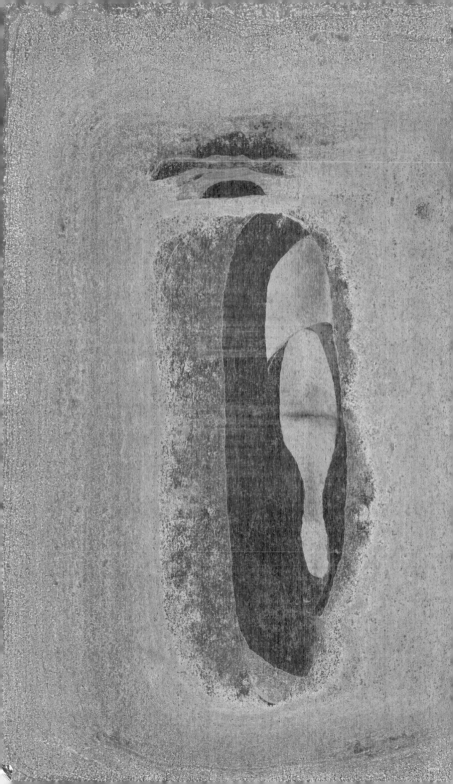